IT DOESN'T HAVE TO BE THIS WAY

A Spirit Alliance

Marty Rawson

It Doesn't Have To Be This Way
A Spirit Alliance

CONTENTS

PROLOGUE

"Why do I care so much, when I am only visiting?"

– Marty Rawson

I have started writing this book, or variations of it too many times to count. My sense of urgency is renewed as I write this prologue due to the fact that I am currently hospitalized in the Intensive Care Unit with Covid-19.

To start off with, if you are closed minded or religiously dogmatic at all, this book is probably not for you – there's your fair warning.

I have found that people believe what they want to believe, and nothing so trivial as facts, proof or evidence will ever change their minds. I make no effort to change anyone's mind, so, if the information in this book resonates with you – great, and if not, that's okay too. While it is my intent to uplift and empower you, the reader, this is not your typical, warm and fuzzy, feel-good, rose-colored glasses, everything-is-perfect kind of spiritual book. Those books are wonderful, and they serve a purpose, but some people prefer a more hands-on, pragmatic approach to spirituality, and life. This book is for them. It will actually teach you how to work with energy and Spirit.

My entire life I have experienced those things that, apparently, most people are still wondering about – whether or not they are "real". I didn't understand why other people thought the way they did, and they obviously didn't understand me. The paranormal and spiritual experiences I had from an early age truly opened my mind up, but made it hard to relate to what most would call "normal" people! There will be a substantial portion of this book devoted to these experiences so people can relate to some of the various ways spirit can interact with those of us in the physical. There are many experiences that have been left out, as well. Understand this though, Spirit will work with you and communicate with you in the way that is right and appropriate for _you,_ not necessarily how they did with me.

Even as a young child, I had memories of before I came into this lifetime. I can literally remember some of the conversations and planning that went into the development of my "soul contract" for this lifetime. This is done with incredibly wise, divine beings who have great wisdom and insight that is unfathomable to our human minds.

I had been asked to come here, and I remember telling them that I did not feel ready to come into another lifetime yet, as I felt I needed to recover from the previous incarnation. They seemed to think I was ready, and they had a purpose for asking me to do this. Obviously, they won that argument! I had been working on healing from my last incarnation with the beloved and wonderfully magnificent Archangel Raphael. I recall a leisurely stroll we took together, as he comforted me with his divine wisdom once again, prior to coming into this lifetime.

At the Council where we were planning my life contract, I remember trying to pack as many karmic life lessons into this lifetime as I could, in order to make this lifetime "worth" the effort. My Higher Self has yet another goal set for me, and I needed to wrap up these things here first. So, with the confidence of someone who has no idea what they are actually doing, I packed all the life lessons I could into one more lifetime. I can tell you now, I feel like I have lived at least 5 different and distinct lifetimes in this incarnation alone.

At one point towards the end of the "Life-Contract" gathering, a very wise and particularly distinguished "Gentleman" made the comment: "This is too much. You won't make it, and if you do make it through this, you will just barely make it!"

I hate to say it, but my "self" had too much arrogance (disguised as confidence), for my own good, and I insisted I could and would make it! – I have regretted my arrogance in that situation many times throughout this life, and have sincerely apologized several times to this wise gentleman who tried to warn me. I will do it again when my time to go home comes, and I shall, forever-more, heed his advice! His words were more accurate than I can say, and I have indeed "just barely made it".

I was given the choice of three different sets of parents to choose from, each of which would provide the prerequisite DNA necessary for the life lessons that had been set up. I again chose the most difficult set up in order to attain the most soul growth and "burn off" the maximum amount of karma possible, during this incarnation. I already knew this incarnation was to be on Earth, but I was informed I would be born a male, in the United States. I was quite glad to hear both of those things, because to be honest, it is easier to be born a male on Earth right now and I have had plenty of lifetimes being born into classical, abject poverty.

There are more memories of this time, but at the end they showed me Earth – as it was at that time, and what I would look like towards the end of my life, if I did indeed "make it". Finally, they showed me what my "Home" looked like from "where I was going", which instilled in me a lifelong affinity for Orion's Belt.

After that I made final preparations for the actual journey into this incarnation, and then…a long, blinding slide through a tube of clear, white Light!

Perhaps it was because of these memories, that I can distinctly remember the first time I stood up to, and got into an argument with an adult figure, not in my family. I was no more than 7 or 8 years old and it was in Sunday school. The teacher repeatedly used the phrase "the fear of God" in the course of her lesson. I was instantly annoyed and quite offended! I raised my hand and informed her that there was absolutely no reason to fear God! God was Love, and that my own stupidity and my own actions were the only thing I needed to fear! Needless to say, I was immediately told to be quiet and sit down, but her unconvincing arguments afterwards totally failed to explain away her use of such an inappropriate phrase.

I, of course did not realize it at the time, but this was the beginning of the end of my formal relationship with organized religion! I knew if this was what they were teaching, they did not know, nor did they understand God at all! I rarely attended organized religious services after that, but I attended enough to understand that what they seemed to be offering, didn't do a thing for me. I always felt emptier after their services than before I went in.

I did however, go on to study many religions when I got older, so I could personally learn for myself what they were teaching, as opposed to what other people say they teach. I have found that you can ask many members of any given religion what they teach and believe, and you will get just as many different answers! I have also learned it is absolutely absurd to ask people of one religion what people of any other religion believe and teach!

When you get past the various dogmas of religions, they all teach the same thing, in slightly different ways and to some extent, different depths. The vast majority of what they teach is the same. That's because the original teachings came from the same place. Since then, different people in different areas put their own spin on things and developed their "religions". They then immediately commenced to kill each other over the small number of differences they themselves concocted! But, I digress, we will get into that later.

I have also studied many forms of Spirituality, indigenous and otherwise. (Again, I did not ask others what they taught and believed.) The beauty of the indigenous forms of Spirituality is that it was so thoroughly interwoven within their everyday lives. They firmly understand the concept of the Creator existing within All That Is and All That Is existing within the Creator. They never embraced separation from God, they embraced their unity with all Life and "the Great Spirit"!

My intent for this book is to relate enough personal spiritual/paranormal experiences to let you get a feeling for why I believe as I do. To let you know who I am, and to show you that Spirit still loves all of us unconditionally! In fact, Spirit wants you to know one thing in the *Eternal Now*:

You are Loved more than you can ever, possibly imagine!

I also want to give enough straight-forward instruction for how to actually do many of the spiritual things people hear about. Reading about someone else doing something is nice, but after a while, people need to have their own experiences to prove to themselves that this is not only very real, but that they can do it themselves! If you are truly interested in Spirituality...you **can** do Spiritual "magic", which is nothing more than consciously working with the Higher Realms, and realizing who you are.

When "Spirit" started teaching me in a more direct manner, I realized quickly that they were empowering me, personally. They were helping me to stand up, with my chin up, and walk in my own truth. They did not want me to rely on them for everything, they were not there for me to lean on constantly, they were there to help me stand on my own so I could work **_with_** them. This is my goal for others as well. I want to help you empower yourself. I hope you find enough information and inspiration in this book to empower you to begin or continue your own journey, and your own adventure, with the wonderful Beings of Light assisting you!

I also wanted to explain how we, and Earth, got to where we are. What is the Galactic History and why is everything, the way it is – right here, right now? How do we make sense of our current situation and what is the best course for us to take?

I wanted to share ideas, and at least initiate a dialogue, on how to change and heal our civilization so we can develop a society that actually works for the highest good of all concerned, including Earth itself.

I do not claim to have all the answers to anything, or even any of the answers, for that matter. But, if I can stimulate constructive dialogue and provoke people into actual – critical, independent thought, I will feel like I have accomplished my goal.

I would also like to add a few words on the "New Age" movement and Spirituality. Recently, an individual told me they were really getting tired of "all the spiritual stuff out there." I told them to remember that their Spirituality is their relationship to the Divine and not in what any other people are saying or doing.

Please remember at all times that Spirituality is your relationship with "God" and the Divine Beings of Light who work within the Divine Plan. It is in working with them that you will remember who you really are and you will then be able to stand in your own Light and work with them – as family!

The new age movement is made up of a wide variety of humans with as wide a variety of motives. These people put out a lot of things, saying an incredible variety of things that can conflict with one another. Some are very good, but obviously, not all of it is coming from the highest source.

Not all of it is truth. It is increasingly noticeable that many of these are trying to use fear as a weapon to generate income during stressful times.

Be very careful of what you take in and choose to believe. If it is based in Love and empowers you, it is of the Divine. If it is based in fear and disempowers you, it is of man. The "New Age", the Age of Aquarius is about cooperation, not competition!

Pay attention to your body and how you feel when you read or hear their messages, and whether or not they are continually asking for money. Money is not bad, it simply represents your time and energy, but using fear to manipulate you into paying endless fees to someone is the tactic of deceitful people. Also remember, never fight the Dark side! That is simply bringing them lunch. Anyone "fighting" the Dark side is still working within the old 3D human consciousness and mindset of organized religion.

Work on your relationship with the Divine that is all around you, especially in nature and in meditation, and connect with it – in your heart. It is a very personal thing.

That is what will feed your soul. That is Spirituality, and no one can take that from you.

For those of you that can feel something isn't "right", but don't understand why or what it is, please consider that this feeling is your soul nudging you towards remembering who you really are, so you can do what you came here to do! The world's energy is chaotic as can be, while we go through the "Shift". The only place to turn is inward and upward. The physical world is very misleading right now and not very fulfilling. You're part of the ground crew sent to fix that.

It is my hope that you find this book informative, thought-provoking, and helpful. If you find some of this content to be unfamiliar or hard to understand, please continue reading on and look up those topics to became more familiar with them. Entire new fields of interesting topics just might open up for you. There is nothing more invigorating for the mind and spirit than the excitement of learning some brand new, really amazing things!

I truly hope you will choose to join those of us already involved in intentionally creating a world where our systems and institutions actually work for the highest good of all concerned, and where we live in an enlightened society that honors the Unity of All life and the Earth! That is the Divine way, and after all,

– Divinity is your birthright!

CHAPTER 1

TRAIN WRECK WAITIN' TO HAPPEN

*"It's not supposed to be like this…
and it doesn't have to be this way!"*

– Spirit

A major purpose for writing this is to show people that no matter how screwed up you are, and no matter how big of a mess you make of your life, Spirit loves you more than you can possibly imagine, and you can turn your life around anytime you choose.

They have proven this to me, and will prove it to you as well, if you only give them a chance.

"God" and all of "Spirit" is, and is about – Love. Not fear.

By showing you my journey of grand imperfection, I hope you are inspired to choose the journey home, into the Love and Light where Spirit awaits with open arms!

I am including enough personal information in this book for you to become somewhat familiar with who I am, and with some of the circumstances that made me this way.

The first major "metaphysical" event that I recall was a "missing time" experience when I must have been 7 years old. We had recently moved to a new city and state and both my mother and stepfather had to work. There was a church that offered full day "school" for children during the summer months, and my mother thought that was the safest place for us to spend our days. I now assume it was a Catholic church due to the fact that it was run by nuns. At the time, I didn't know one religion from another, it just seemed like the nuns were angry and the classes were boring!

On one particularly nice, sunny day we received a reprieve from the usual classroom lectures and were marched down the street in 2 by 2 formation, to a local park a few blocks away. There must have been a hundred of us!

The park was surrounded by tall Douglas fir trees that shaded the entire interior of the park and the playground equipment. As we arrived at the entrance to the park, I was mesmerized by the brilliant shafts of sunlight breaking through the trees to brighten the otherwise darkened interior. It was a stunning play of light with a beautiful green background, at least to me.

Apparently, none of the other children found it to be as captivating as I did, and they all took off running for the swings, teeter totters and other playground equipment. By the time I got to them, they were all taken and I had no choice but to wait my turn.

The teeter totters were the largest I had ever seen, so I decided to lean up against a tree next to them and wait for the next available opportunity. I distinctly recall looking at the closest set of teeter-totters and thinking that the bigger kid on the right was going to have to kick off the ground or the littler kid on the left would be stranded in the air! I then looked down at the ground by my feet.

The very next thing I knew, I was at the far end of the park from the entrance, looking at the ground and walking slowly. I was slightly disoriented and as I looked up, I realized the park was almost totally empty of people! The playground equipment was up ahead to my right and the entrance to the park was straight ahead, at the far end of the Park. Just as I started to get upset, I was "informed" (for lack of better words) that "they" had taken me in order to do something for me that I needed to have done, and that "they" were my friends. "They" did not and would not harm me." With this "information" came the actual feeling of love and friendship which instantly erased all fear and concern. I didn't have a clue who "they" were, but "they" felt like friends and family, and I knew I liked them! "They" were definitely nicer than most of the people I knew!

I started to walk towards the entrance to the park when I heard, faintly at first, but with increasing volume, a woman's voice yelling my name. It didn't take long for an incredibly irate "sister" to appear at the entrance to the park and for the screaming to reach a whole new level. I quickly found out that I had been gone for a couple hours, and that I was definitely going to learn my lesson and not repeat that disappearing act again! Even though she asked several of the expected questions, she of course had no interest in anything I had to say, and proceeded to screech like a proverbial pterodactyl, the entire way back to the church. (I considered myself to be quite an expert on dinosaurs at the time.)

It quickly became clear that no one else was interested in hearing what I had to say either, so I quit trying to tell them. I learned at a young age not to talk about anything unusual that happened to me, to anyone!

The second major incident occurred in the same city. It was two or three years after the above incident that the next memorable event took place. I was walking across an empty bank parking lot next to our house one nice summer morning. There were a few fluffy clouds in an otherwise blue sky.

Suddenly, my vision began to shift into sort of a "fish-eye" lens type of focus, but the colors of everything became more vibrant and pronounced.

I stopped in my tracks and a male voice stated very clearly: "It's not supposed to be like this, and it doesn't have to be this way!"

With this statement came a huge amount of information pertaining to exactly what this statement meant. I saw images of the world as it was (this was during the late '60s). I knew that it was in fact an indictment of practically everything within our civilization or society as we know it. The very foundation of our society was built on proverbial quicksand and it was inevitably destined to either collapse or destroy itself. This was during the race riots of the late '60s and I actually thought the end of society was much closer than it ended up being.

This event caused me to start watching the news and start learning about things most kids were not interested in. It did not take long to notice the corruption that pervaded our society, nor did it take long to recognize that most people not only expected it, but seemed to actually like it. Oh, most wouldn't actually say they liked it, but they would support it, endorse it, and most definitely vote for it! As time went on, I began to learn many of the specifics the "voice" had been referring to, first-hand.

To top things off, I continued to have experiences with the darker side of reality. Everything from discarnate beings, to poltergeists and even demonic entities. It seemed that this world was nothing but corrupt people lying, cheating and stealing from one another, unless they were killing them! This was at least my perception at this point, and it hasn't changed drastically since. I have just learned over time who to let into my life, and more importantly, who not to.

As I got older, the corruption that pervades our society became so evident, I saw it in every aspect of life. I found humans to be liars and manipulators, with no conscience. I came to simply treat other people the way they treat me. I have found that rude, arrogant people can't stand that.

Needless to say, I did not grow up perceiving the world in the same way others apparently did. I thought differently than other people did. I felt differently than other people did, about a lot of things. I questioned everything and have always been a critical, independent thinker who tended to look at the big picture. The cost of this was an uncomfortable feeling in many social situations and a feeling of not fitting in. As I got older I looked around and saw what passed for normal on this planet and decided that not fitting in with "normal" probably wasn't such a bad thing. I will say that I did seem to have a gift that others didn't seem to have. I would often get a feeling or a knowing of something or to do something. If I followed it, things went well for me. If I didn't, well let's just say that didn't happen more than once. I remember ignoring it that *one* time and I ended up getting beaten up by my older brother. With motivation like that, I learned quickly to follow this inner guidance. I also realized that I could "feel people". In other words, I could often tell what a person was like just by being in their presence. It wasn't until I became an adult that I learned that these gifts are referred to as Clair-cognizance and Clair-sentience. I have also experienced many brief instances of clairaudience and clairvoyance. These do not occur anywhere near the frequency that I would prefer, but it does seem that I get the information I truly need, when I need it.

The house we lived in when I was in grade school, had its own share of strange happenings. I never knew it at the time, but I was not the only one who avoided the landing on the stairs, especially at night. There was a slender window in the wall there, that was especially to be avoided. I found out years later that everyone in the family felt uneasy on that landing and with that window. I used to get in trouble for hopping the railing and landing on the floor just to avoid even stepping on the landing.

All I knew was that I felt an evil presence on that landing, especially at night. I just knew that if I ever even glanced into that window, I would see something I didn't want to – staring back at me. There was always a cold, malevolent feeling there.

The other strange thing that happened there quite often was the disappearance of random objects for up to a week or so at a time. No matter what it is was, and no matter how long we looked, we could never find the missing objects. A few days to a week later, the missing object would be found sitting by itself on the kitchen table or a countertop. This happened time, after time, after time. After a while we *almost* got used to it.

We eventually moved from the city to a small town in the mountains. When I was 14, I was standing in front of our house talking to a couple of neighbor kids. I saw a sudden streak of red light come from the east between a couple of mountains. My startled reaction caused the other two to turn around and we all witnessed a glowing red sphere hovering stationary over the lake to the north of us. It hovered there for only a couple of seconds and then disappeared in another streak of red light going straight upwards. The original movement from between the mountains to in front of us, took no more than one second for it to cover a good 5 miles. We did find out later that people in 2 towns to the east of us reported seeing this as well.

This was prior to the release of the movie Close Encounters of the 3rd kind. When that movie did come out, the thing that freaked me out was the red sphere that followed the alien spacecraft in the movie. It looked exactly like what I had witnessed. I had never heard of anyone seeing or speaking of flying red spheres – before then or since. Little did I know that this was the beginning of a life-long string of events that would occur. Only some of which are shared here.

The problem with knowing the world isn't the way it's supposed to be, experiencing things most people don't and having memories from before coming into your own lifetime is the frustration with humanity that they seem to want this world to be the way it is. When you know how it could be and the people seem to embrace corruption and self-destruction, you eventually lose hope, get angry and give up. Just because something was good enough for your parents or your grandparents, does not mean you shouldn't make the improvements that are possible in your own lifetime. We all have the duty to leave our children with a better world than we were born into. Boy, have we have failed miserably at that one!

My family life was as dysfunctional as could be and I finally left home at the age of 15. I had already started to develop ulcers by this time. I went into a foster home that was no better than the mess I had just fled. The foster mother had a truly sadistic streak and was soon caught fooling around with a guy she worked with. My mother had an affair also that she didn't even try to hide, and I came to believe that females were incapable of actually, and truly, loving anyone for real, especially without cheating. At least most of them anyway. This had disastrous effects on my future relationships, obviously. (Be careful what you believe, because you create your reality, absolutely!)

This was all in the early to mid-70's and I found that the only escape available was getting high, which stopped the dreams, or should I say, the nightmares. One year later, I went to another state to live with my real, biological father.

My mother had previously tried to tell me that my father was a horrible man, and that if I thought living with her was bad, I would really think life was hell if I lived with him! She never said anything specific, just vague, derogatory statements. I came to find out, if I had known what my father was really like, I would have done everything I could to go live with him as soon as I could have! He was truly a good man. In the darkness I had already come to know – as this world, he was truly a breath of fresh air. He was straight-up and honest. The only problem, was me. I had grown to be too independent for my age, and by the time I did go to live with him, I was looking for a roommate, and my father was looking forward to the father-son relationship that he of course, wanted.

Although I was one of the youngest people in my grade at school, I started working as soon as I moved in with my father. He did not make much money and if I wanted anything, this was the only way to get it.

Between my junior and senior years in high school, I got a job setting up a department store in town. The manager told us that the ones who worked the hardest and did the best job would get hired on permanently, to work in the store. About one month into my senior year, I earned the Automotive and Sporting Goods Departments. This meant I had a job I could rely on and I moved out of my father's home and got my own apartment. My relationship with my father improved even more and we became very close, we just didn't live together anymore. I was the only student in high school who was working full time, had my own apartment, took total care of myself and could write my own notes when I stayed home "sick"!

I must say, I took particular pleasure in how much of a fit the "office ladies" worked themselves into when I would bring a note in after taking a sick day, which said: "I stayed home yesterday because I was sick."... which was also signed by myself. I can still see them muttering and sputtering and stamping their feet, whispering remarks of disapproval to each other as I strolled out of the office. It is one of the few fond memories I have from this time and it still gives me an occasional chuckle! I did finish high school though, and graduated with my class.

I must also say, I had moved into an area of the country that was totally dominated by one particular religion. I had not experienced religious control of this nature and did not exactly fit in. I was, of course, immediately ostracized by the majority of the local population. This caused me to retaliate by making sure no one would mistake me for one of them by not conforming to their rigid dress code and grooming style. I had come from a melting pot of every nationality and religious background, where no one asked you about your religion, to a place that looked like Mayberry RFD and the first question out of everyone's mouth was if you belonged to their religion!

This particular religion had and still has to some extent, a reputation for being clean cut, honest and forthright. While I do know some members that live up to this, the majority are just like everybody else in this dark little world, they just – as a culture – keep all of their dirty little secrets to themselves and even attempt to have their "clergy" settle criminal matters amongst their members, so nothing gets "out". This is not conjecture, this is personal observation and experience. I have even been told point blank by one of their leading "Members in Good Standing" that: "It is not reality that counts, it is perception! Everything is perception!" As for myself, I find this to be a philosophy of unconscious and immoral people. This combined with their habitual and blatant judgement of others, by means of "scuzzing" non-members in public, has, shall we say, failed to endear them to my heart. The females are particularly bad about doing this to other females they deem to be "less than" themselves.

The more I saw, the more disgusted I was with this world. The more disgusted I became, the angrier I got and the more I turned to substances as a crutch. I knew it didn't have to be like this, but the entire world seemed to revel in its corruption and dishonesty, at least from my point of view, based on what I was seeing! Although I eventually became addicted to several substances throughout the course of my earlier years, I can honestly say that I maintained a much higher level of morality and integrity than the pompous hypocrites conducting business and politics in our society, day after day. At least I can say truthfully, that the only one I was harming was myself.

I eventually quit every substance I was addicted to – cold-turkey, as they say. This includes both alcohol and tobacco, although I had a few relapses with alcohol. After all, it is SO available and accepted as America's drug of choice! It always amazed me that the drug that has the most detrimental effect on the brain, the consciousness and the body, and which causes more bloodshed and broken families – is the one that is preferred and accepted as legal by the majority of people on this planet! Kind of says something about our level of consciousness all by itself, doesn't it? I have always found it hilarious when some drunk starts lecturing people about not smoking pot, or "doing drugs". All the while they are falling down drunk on the worst drug of all! Now I am not advocating the use of cannabis, but there is truth to the saying that "Five guys drinking will start a fight, but 5 guys getting high will start a band."

With all this negativity and my personal issues, it did not take long at all in my life to invite equally negative and screwed up people into my life to join in the fun. After all, like energies attract, but I was not aware of this concept until much later! The biggest life lesson I have had in my life was this: "Be careful what you ask for." And by ask for, I mean who and what you invite into your life!

Eventually, this train wreck hit rock bottom and I found myself sitting on my living room couch literally asking God to take my life. This was before I quit drinking. I was, in fact – at the time, hell bent on drinking myself to death, and I was much closer to it than even I realized.

On several occasions in my life, whenever a drastic change was inevitable, I would get an extremely uneasy, nervous feeling unlike anything else, that would cause me to pace back and forth incessantly. It had to happen to me several times before I recognized it for the omen that it was. Well, here it came again, and it would not let up! I eventually told a co-worker of mine about it, and that something big was about to happen and change my life, but I had no way of knowing what it was.

The very next night, I had a headache that would not quit and was unable to go to work. This was very unusual for me, because I have rarely gotten headaches in my life.

Sometime, in the wee hours of the morning, I was rudely awakened by the thunderous crash of what sounded like someone hitting a very large oriental gong with a sledge hammer, right next to my head! I had been sleeping on my back. By the time I opened my eyes, I swear, I was about a foot off the bed, and my heart in my throat! Talk about a rude awakening! I landed on the bed still in a dazed stupor, wondering what just happened. My logical mind knew there was no gong in the house, but I was still trying to figure out what that sound was. The only thing I could do was get up and look around, so I did. From the far end of the hallway, I could see both the front and back doors. There was no one at either door. The only one around was my cat, who followed me back to the bedroom after a cursory look around. I got back into bed and tried to chalk it up to just one more unexplainable thing in my life. I lay down and I remember being unusually aware of the back of my head touching the pillow.

Instantly, an extremely rapid series of images flashed in front of my eyes. I was suddenly sitting on top of a train, speeding around a gentle curve in the mountains. Suddenly up ahead, I saw the tracks ran straight into the solid rock wall of the mountain. The train did not slow down, in fact it seemed to pick up speed. It crashed full speed into the solid granite wall of the mountainside and exploded into thousands of flying pieces. I was thrown into the air, and "knew" that this had killed me.

Then again, instantly, the same train ride started over. I was on top of the train again, and going around the same gentle curve. This time, I noticed a spur of the tracks that cut off to the right and went up the side of the mountain. This time, the train took this spur and it started to climb up the mountain. I remember seeing many wildflowers scattered through the brush at the edge of the Quaking Aspens on the hillside. The train would climb and then level off and then climb some more and level off again. This happened a few times, and the feeling was very nice and very peaceful. – Then everything stopped –

Suddenly, my consciousness was back in my bedroom, and now I was sitting up in bed. There were two very large "men" standing by my bed. One, at the foot of the bed and one beside it. When I say large, I don't mean just bigger than usual. The one at the foot of the bed was barely under 8 feet tall, with shoulders at least 4 feet wide and a huge, thick, barrel chest. The one to my right on the side of the bed, was maybe a couple inches shorter, but had even broader shoulders and a thicker chest! They were dressed in solid black and they were _**not**_ happy!

I looked around quickly to get my bearings and just about the time I should have started to panic, I felt it. – Love – Not just any love. A love so palpable, so pervasive, so-utterly-thick – that fear could not exist in its presence. There was a small part of me, deep inside, that seemed to vaguely remember this. There was an odd familiarity to this, like a lost memory. Then it suddenly came to me! This was what *home* felt like! We don't *ever* get to feel this here! Yet I was feeling it... I was actually feeling the palpable thickness of Divine Love that was the reality back home in the higher dimensions. The memory came rushing back.I looked up at the Being at the foot of my bed, whom I now somehow knew, without a shadow of doubt, was an Angel, despite his choice of apparel. (I later found out that black clothing is worn by them when they are mourning the impending the loss of life of the person they are "Guardians" for.) Although his mouth didn't move, I heard him loud and clear! He said, (quite firmly, I might add) "This is your last warning, quit or die!"

I knew exactly what he was talking about. I had had several odd occurrences take place in the previous weeks that should have gotten my attention. I had been, as I said, knowingly drinking myself to death for quite some time. Between that and the weird stuff that happened rather routinely in my life, I had simply brushed off what were actually life and death warnings.

I replied "What do I do? If it's in the house, I'll drink it! I know me!"

He responded "You've already been told what to do!"

I instantly remembered about 2 weeks before, when I had been talked into going to a lady who had a very impressive reputation locally, as a card reader. I had never been to one, nor had I met her before, and yes, I was sober when I went. She used regular playing cards, and as soon as she laid the cards out in front of herself, she got a puzzled look on her face, hummed and hawed and mumbled something to herself, then looked me right in the eyes and asked me if I drank a lot. This did take me off-guard a bit, but I replied simply "yes". She said, "No, I mean a lot. Like you can't live without it." I again replied with a simple yes. She said "Well, they are screaming at you to stop! I could see this if you were 80 years old and had nothing to live for, but they are showing me that you have a lot of beautiful stuff ahead of you." I wasn't really sure I wanted to stop at this point, but I asked her "How do you just stop?" Her response was simply "Go see a hypnotherapist!" I don't really remember much else of that reading. Nothing else really seemed important. I did listen to it, and even heeded the warning, at least for about 3 days, until I got mad about something. Then I dove right back into the bottle.

I had no sooner recalled all of this when my Angels showed me, or should I say, they caused me to *experience* – what I would feel like if I did kill myself by drinking. I would not be judged by God or anyone else. (None of us are, ever.) *I* would judge me! The disappointment and remorse I experienced in myself was even worse than what I was currently going through in my physical life! They then helped me to experience and remember how utterly sacred these lives are and how they are regarded in the higher realms… How I was SO CLOSE to throwing something truly and utterly sacred away, like it was garbage! The feelings were far worse than everything I was going through here in this lifetime put together. The full impact of my decisions were being revealed to me at that very moment.I don't actually recall getting out of bed, but the next thing I knew, I found myself on one knee with my head down in front of the one who was talking, at the foot of the bed. I was so incredibly ashamed of myself. I was apologizing over and over saying "I'm sorry, I'm so sorry." He responded "You should be. Now get up. This is beneath who you are."

I got up and sat on the bed and looked at both of them. That last comment shook me. "Beneath who I am?" What did that mean? I was sitting there on my bed with 2 huge beings who were not in good humor to say the least, but still in the thickness of love that was beyond this world. They were starting to seem familiar. I knew these two. I realized; they have been with me forever. I was starting to remember. They were… my guardian angels.

The tall one at the foot of the bed then said "Now lie down and go to sleep." I did as I was told without even thinking about it. As soon as my head touched the pillow this time, I was out. Instantly.

When I first opened my eyes the next morning, I began to have a thought. That thought was "Boy! That was one wild dream!" The exact instant my mind hit the "d" in dream, my brain instantly felt like it was going to explode! It was so sudden and so excruciatingly painful, there was no doubt that it was in response to me relegating this experience to a dream. I literally yelled out loud "Ouch! Okay! Okay! It wasn't a dream!"

And instantly, the pain vanished! With that I exclaimed, "Damn! I didn't know you guys could do that! That hurt!"

Then I laid back down and thought about things. Shit just got real! Now I *knew* the truth, there was no need for faith. Faith, in the usual sense, was for those who don't *know*.

Eventually, I got up, went into the kitchen and got a piece of cantaloupe and a piece of honey dew on a small plate and then went into the living room to sit down.

This was the same spot where about a month before this, I had sat and literally prayed to God and asked him/her to take my life. I remembered saying "If the rest of my life is going to be like this, like it has been... I'm done. I want out." Now I sat there and very calmly debated internally what I wanted to do. On the one hand, the thickness of Love that was so utterly pervasive at "Home", was practically irresistible. Then I remembered how utterly horrible I felt the night before, when I had experienced the remorse I would feel if I killed myself. I actually went back and forth a couple of times. Then I thought, *well, this isn't a game where you get to roll the dice again in a "do-over". Death is permanent, at least as far as this lifetime in this body goes, and they did imply there could be some good stuff ahead of me. What the hell, I guess I'll give it a shot.* With that I got up, and went to the look up a hypnotherapist.

A couple weeks after this happened, a friend of mine started telling me about how he felt his wife was wasting money. She had been going to some "Angel Reader". He thought the entire concept was totally absurd, but his use of this phrase hit me like a thunder bolt! I had never heard of this, but I knew his wife as well, and immediately went to talk to her for the contact information for this person. It took a month for me to get an appointment. During that time, I cleaned myself up, went to my hypnotherapist and meditated as best as I knew how. When the day finally came, I had a whole page full of questions I wanted to ask about. I will never forget meeting this wonderful lady! She was a short, fiery red head who emanated so much Love and Light I couldn't believe it... She literally radiated her beautiful energy like no-one I had ever seen! We adjourned into a small room for our session and she quickly went into a very brief grounding routine to settle herself in. Almost instantly – I was having a real-time conversation with my Angels! They were much happier now! They applauded my efforts to heal my life and then started talking. By the time they were done, they had answered every single question I had written down on my paper. Every single one – without me ever giving voice to a single one. They knew exactly how to word things so that it resonated with me personally, which added to my assurance that this was indeed legitimate! At the end of this reading, they gave me a few books to read and suggested I take up Kriya Yoga. Wouldn't you know it, this wonderful Angel Reader knew an individual who practiced Kriya Yoga right here in town. It didn't take long for me to search him out and get initiated.

I never saw my wonderful Guardian Angels in the physical like I did during their intervention, again. I have felt their presence and they have spoken to me when needed, but they have not appeared to me physically since then. They do have a great sense of humor though, and they, and many others have guided me ever since.

I have been stumbling down this road ever since! Spirit has guided me and even used a few harsher methods for my lessons, when I left them no choice due to my own stubbornness. I am no saint by any means, but I know they love me anyway! They have guided me to teachings and experiences that are not even within the concept of most people's reality on this planet. I will be sharing some of those with you later on. Some of the later chapters will be devoted to explanations of spiritual topics as Spirit has shown me, and as my own "knowings" recall. Some will be concerning the current issues facing humanity, and some will be concerned with the process of healing our Selves so we can heal our world.

There are many experiences I have had that I am not including in this book. I do not want this to be all about me, with an "I did this and I did that" type of format. As I said before, I will include enough personal information, to give you an idea of who I am and *some* of my experiences with Spirit that formed my understanding of working with them.

CHAPTER 2

ADVENTURES IN HEALING

*"The Spiritual Journey is a process of accepting your Darkness
and Loving it into the Light!
It is learning to be "At One" with your Duality"*

- Marty Rawson

For the next year and a half after the Intervention spoken of in the first chapter, I went to work, went home, read all the books that called to me, and meditated. I discovered the works of Dr. Joshua David Stone during this time. There was something about the core message of his work that appealed to me, and he gave you tools to use. I didn't want to just read about other people's experience, I wanted to learn how to accomplish things -and he gave specific instructions on how to accomplish spiritual goals, such as raising your light quotient/vibrational frequency.

The thing about truly embarking on the spiritual path is that it will force you to be devastatingly honest with yourself. Dr. Stone's work heavily emphasized dealing with what he termed the Positive ego and the Negative ego. I still like this view and description in spite of the new age un-popularity of the terms positive and negative. (Hate to say it but these are valid aspects of life in the 3rd dimension and denial of negativity doesn't actually void its existence.)

One aspect I had a really hard time internalizing was the concept that "You create your reality absolutely". I had a hard time with this for quite some time because my logical 3rd dimensional human mind knew that there were many, many things that had happened to me that were "done to me – by others". I could fill court rooms with witnesses who could honestly testify to this. I struggled with this for months. I also understood that if this caused me this much anguish, it was something I would eventually have to come to terms with, so I kept at it. One afternoon, as I walked through the living room, I had an epiphany that stopped me in my tracks. I had not even been thinking about this at that particular moment. It just happened. Suddenly, I saw it all – I saw how it was my thoughts, my emotions and my actions that had drawn all these incidents to me! I had truly created all of it myself! Just not in the way I had been looking at it. I saw that as incidences had occurred in my youth, I had in that moment, decided that "that" was the way things worked. With these decisions about how things worked in this world, I had created beliefs. The Universe then literally had no choice but to continue to bring me what I believed! As the Universe brought me more circumstances that conformed to my beliefs, my beliefs became etched in stone.

Immediately following this epiphany, I had this vision in my mind's eye of me standing in front of a huge Mt. Everest sized pile of 'crap' that was my life, and all I had was a teaspoon to try to shovel it! I don't really know if it was my own thought or if it was Spirit talking to me, but I thought, *Man! It took a lot of effort and energy to create a pile of 'crap' **that** big!* That was a very humbling and demoralizing thought, but immediately after that, I had one of the most empowering thoughts I've ever had, *If I have enough power and energy to create this… what would happen, what could I do, if I turned it all around and put that much energy into going in the opposite direction?*

So, I dug in and re-committed myself. I worked on building my Light Quotient. This is the concept that by meditating on and practicing "Being Love" you are bringing this energy into yourself instead of any negative thought forms you may be used to having. I'm still working on this. I always will be. Especially in this life, on this world! And even more, especially at work!

One of the Universal Laws states that Higher vibrational frequencies will always transmute lower vibrational frequencies. This is how you "Love" your dark side into the Light! You will not succeed by denying your dark side or by hating it. You must be devastatingly honest with yourself and take each thing that is shown to you one at a time. Deal with them and learn to love these aspects of your past into the light. They were there to teach you lessons. If they still affect you strongly, chances are you didn't learn the lesson! We will cover Healing the Past later on.

Please understand that the Earth is the Emotional University of our galaxy, if not the universe! It was never meant to go this low in vibrational frequency, but Spirit knows how to make the very best of every situation. Since the frequency did drop as low as it did, they simply used the situation as the ultimate opportunity for soul growth through the emotional body. We come here to learn the deepest lessons that life has to offer anywhere in all the dimensions! We can accomplish as much or more in one lifetime here, as we could in at least a million years of comparable time in the higher realms. That's why souls keep coming back! It's a tough school; the school colors might be black and blue, but who cares? It's the fast track! Because of this, do not be surprised when issues you have dealt with resurface. It is very much like the layers of an onion. You may have to look at your issues several times before they truly, no longer bother you. Rest assured it is time well spent and will be well worth it in the long run.

It was during the 1st year and a half after the Divine Intervention that I discovered some of my favorite authors through their books. While there are many of them, one who always comes to mind first is "The Light Shall Set You Free" by Norma Milanovich. It seemed as if this book was speaking directly to my soul – I devoured it and treasure it to this day. This led me to another of her books, "We the Arcturians", and "Connecting with the Arcturians" by David K. Miller. I had already experienced many things that were not of this earth, and now I was finding out that many of the star nations are in fact divine beings and are here to help! It also showed that you can communicate with them, and they will work with you. Talk about a spiritual smorgasbord! Needless to say, I was excited. I set about meditating on them and started including them in all of my spiritual work as matter-of-factly as I did with the Angels.

It took some time, but I did eventually begin to feel their presence. One day, I went into meditation, when suddenly I found myself standing in a room. In front of me about 20 feet away, was a short, cream-colored wall rising only a couple of feet, with the windows above it extending to, and curving into the ceiling. Outside of this room, I was staring into space! I could see all the stars in the distance. Very slowly, a "being" began to materialize right in front of me, between myself and the window. When it finished, he was still translucent, meaning I could still see through his body. He was truly a being of light! He had a quite rounded head, he had no hair, but he had the kindest eyes and the most beautiful smile I have ever seen. I could literally feel the love emanating from this beautiful being. To be honest, I stood there speechless, smiling like an idiot, totally dumbfounded! Then the full realization of what was taking place dawned on me, and I got so excited that I instantly brought myself out of the meditation. Talk about mixed emotions! I was so angry at myself for not controlling my emotions and bringing myself back to this reality, and at the same time, I was so excited about actually having experienced standing on their ship, in their presence, and amidst such love. This experience created an entirely new definition of the word "beautiful" for me!

I began to meditate on them even more. I would ask them on a nightly basis to allow me to come aboard and sit in their Ascension seats and their healing chambers while I slept. I have been aboard their ship since then, and experienced a variety of things, but nothing compares to the first visit and seeing that beautiful being of light, that beautiful Arcturian soul staring back at me! I will always cherish that.It was about this time that I received an invitation to be a guest speaker at the Festival of the Christ in Crestone, Colorado. The host of the event had gotten my contact information from Dr. Joshua David Stone. This was very intimidating to me, as I had never done any public speaking. To add further intimidation, I found out that some of my favorite authors were going to be speaking at this event as well. This included Dr. Norma Milanovich, Patricia Cota Robles, and David K. Miller. I could not believe that I was being asked to speak on the same stage as these incredible people whom I literally considered to be my mentors and my heroes! I spent a great deal of time writing up what I thought was a truly magnificent speech. I also had my 1st experiences of channeling at this time. The first thing I knowingly channeled was a short meditation for the planet and all that reside on it, involving calling in the Cosmic Rays to fill the entire world. This was actually my introduction to the Cosmic Rays, and I would have to go on studying to learn more about them.

(I highly recommend the teachings of Djwal Khul, the Tibetan, as he is the original source and teacher of this vast Science of the Rays. Over the years there have been so many different, conflicting versions of the Cosmic Rays come out, that I highly recommend you stick with the teachings of Master Djwal Khul. He is awesome.)

When I got to Crestone, I had the pleasure of meeting the aforementioned authors, and many other wonderful people. I was one of the last speakers. By the time it was my turn to speak, all of the material that I had written down had already been covered due to the fact that most of it was based on the works of the authors that had already spoken! I was not exactly feeling very intelligent at this point, and had to throw my entire speech away. Now I had to get up in front of this group, full of people I idolized and try to give a speech with no preparation. When I first got up to the podium, I had a brief vision of myself turning around and crashing through the wall behind me, much like the old Kool-Aid commercials! Instead, I told everyone that I paid very close attention to all of the talks that had been given and that I wish to address the one main topic that no one had addressed specifically. That topic was Divine Love. I was so nervous that I found an elderly lady in the crowd who had a very kind smile and basically just talked to her. Behind her about 2 rows, was seated the author David Miller. I could not tell what he was thinking, but the look on his face had me very intimidated, so I tried not to look at him! I believe at this point, somebody must've taken over because I don't remember hardly anything I said. I do remember speaking about the Divine Invitation of the Rainbow Warriors to come to Earth, and then doing the meditation that I had channeled. It must have gone well, because the reaction of the crowd was overwhelming. To this day I have gratitude for whomever helped me through that.

After my speech, I found out that David Miller was offering channelings from the Arcturians! In spite of the look that I had interpreted as intimidation (due to my own issues), I forced myself to approach him and request a reading. To my delight, he was a very nice and personable man, and he scheduled an appointment for his first available timeslot.

When I got to the reading, he was again so nice I couldn't believe I could have possibly thought otherwise. To my surprise, when he started the reading, it was Sanat Kumara that came through first. I only knew enough about Sanat Kumara at the time to know that I was in the presence of one of the greatest beings of light in the spiritual hierarchy of this universe. Sanat Kumara is an Elder of the highest standing in the Arcturian civilization. He is the one referred to as the "Ancient of Days". To top that off, after his initial discussion, *his* Higher Self – Vywamus came through! They had a lot of good advice for me, and congratulated me on how far I had to come in the last 18 months. It wasn't until they said this that I calculated back and realized that it had indeed been 18 months since the divine intervention!

The Arcturian civilization never actually descended into the 3rd Dimension like Earth did. They stayed in the higher dimensions and are the "Shepherds" of this galaxy. They are always willing and more than able to assist anyone working in the light and are particularly adept at healing emotional issues. They are a higher dimensional civilization that exists in the 5th dimension and above. Their ship, the Athena, was specially "made" for their mission to Earth and is commanded by the extraordinary Commander Juliano. They have special navigators who train to link up with the ship mentally for complex maneuvers, but the ship itself is literally alive, and can act to protect itself and the crew as needed. Oh yeah! Now that's some cool stuff! I swear... To know an Arcturian is to Love the Arcturians!

Anyway, back to Crestone. There is no way I can relate all there is to tell about the events that took place in Crestone. The Arcturian presence was constant, as was that of the Angelic Realm. There was a special un-scheduled event that took place though, that I will never forget, and I must share.

Towards the end of the event (If I remember correctly), as the day was just getting started, the host announced that the schedule had changed and we would be doing something else. The tone was quite serious and the crowd went silent.

He introduced a man from New Zealand who had been trained by the Maori people. He had been a part of the group of people hosting the event. He informed us that the night before, while in meditation, he had been approached by Spirit and had been asked to present something to the group. He explained that in the extra-biblical texts, there was a story of an Angel by the name of Azrael who was credited or blamed (as the case may be) for teaching humanity the "sciences of the heavens". In other words, he had taught humans how to do things like astrology, cloud reading and other mystical arts. He taught women how to use make-up and men how to make swords and other things that he thought would help advance us. The only problem was, apparently, he didn't think to ask the permission of the spiritual hierarchy before doing so! This got him in more trouble than could be imagined and soon, according to the story, Archangel Michael and Rafael were sent to "bind him, and cast him into a pit of darkness!" In other words, his penance was that he had to go play for the *other* "Team", because he screwed up. He immediately became one of Lucifer's top "generals" (for lack of a better term) and had been in that role ever since. The thing was that everything in this universe is raising in its vibrational frequency and whether anyone knew it or not... that included the "dark side"! He had decided enough was enough and was leading the charge of the Dark side, back into the Light! He was hoping that we would allow him to come in through this gentleman from New Zealand who was a very gifted trance channel, and talk with us to share a bit more of the story, than any of us knew.

The group was willing, but I must admit, I was a little apprehensive. This amazing man went into a brief ceremonial dance that was definitely Maori in origin in order to prepare himself for this channeling, then he slowly came to a stop with his back to the crowd and was slightly bent over. He slowly turned around and his face was contorted into a truly malevolent grin and he let out a laugh that was as evil as I've ever heard! It was as if you could see the "demon" over-laid onto the man. Most everyone reacted simultaneously and it took all I had to stay in my seat. In an instant, his whole demeanor changed.

His laugh transformed into a normal, light-hearted laugh and the expression on his face changed to one with a genuine smile. He stood up straight and apologized, saying he couldn't help but have a little fun! He then introduced himself. He said he was once known as the Archangel Azrael. He re-iterated the story of his transgressions in ancient times and his subsequent banishment to the dark side. He informed us that on the dark side he went by the name "Azazel", and he wished to share a few things with us.

He said the entire Universe is ascending and that included the dark side! He said he had decided to lead the charge of the dark side back into the Light, as stated before, and that this discussion was the final part of the service work he needed to do in order to truly be accepted back into the Light.

He then stated that humanity hadn't yet comprehended the seriousness of what was taking place in the "shift" and his primary statement for humanity as a whole was simple: "GROW UP!"

He said throughout all the ages, humans have committed atrocities against other humans that the ones on the dark side would never have even imagined initially. Not only crimes against each other but against the planet itself. He said he has watched as we do these things, which of course, cause reactions and/or consequences which come back on humanity. Then, inevitably, we blame either God or "the Devil" for whatever happens, just like little children who cannot fathom that their actions have consequences! He re-stated that it was past time for humanity to grow-up. We made this mess and it is our responsibility to clean it up!

He went on to say that we had not been given the true story as to what had happened in the original plan for this planet after the fall of consciousness, and that he would like to share it with us. He said that the Divine plan for the Universe was based on duality as a powerful means of soul growth and experimentation – because nothing had been done exactly like this before.

After Earth's fall in consciousness, this theme was extended for use in the lower 3rd dimensional realm that Earth resided in.

It was apparent that Love would naturally be associated with the Light and that therefore Fear would be associated with the dark. There were obviously those who would represent the Light, but there was no-one willing to represent the dark. They asked for volunteers. With the clarity that exists in the higher realms, there was no-one who immediately stepped forward to do this. Eventually, Lucifer stepped forward and said he would agree to do this thing, on one condition! That condition was – that this "experiment" had to have a fixed end time, it could not go on for-ever.

He stated that he would do this out of his love for the Creator and his belief in the divine plan. He knew that by representing the "Dark" that he would be blamed for and associated with all the atrocities and negative actions committed by humans throughout this ordeal. They then concocted a cover story to conceal the true plan so no-one would know it was a set up. That cover story was the biblical account of a "revolution in Heaven" and God banishing Lucifer and his associates for a simple disagreement. He then stated that the "End Time" for this whole experiment was now! This shift in vibrational frequency that the entire Universe is going through was determined to be the most logical time for the end of this whole façade! He also stated that only the "very top" of the Dark-side have ever known the whole story. The truth was kept from everyone else to keep it "real".

So, yes there are demons and entities that humanity has essentially created and/or empowered through our thoughts, words and deeds. All the negative energy humanity has ever created is still here. It cannot go anywhere. It is what we are wading through every day. This planet has been quarantined ever since and our "mess" is confined to our own planet. We trashed it and we now have to filter and transmute all this negative energy through our own selves. The only way to get rid of it is to transmute it into the Light by using the higher frequencies of Love. This is essentially what Lightworkers do. So buckle up, buttercup – this is gonna be quite the ride!

The following day, we were asked if we would once again allow Azazel/Azrael to come in again. This time there was really no hesitation in our mutual agreement. As soon as he came in, he thanked every one of us for allowing him to give his message the day before. He stated that it had been the last bit of service work that he needed to accomplish in order to be accepted back home, into the Light. He then informed us that his personal ascension back into the Light was to take place right then, and we were all invited to attend! All we had to do was relax and go into a meditative state. I remember fervently and passionately praying that I not be left out and I did my best to do as he said.

Suddenly, I found myself in what seemed to be a truly humongous semi-circular stadium type setting. There seemed to be countless beings in attendance. I could not make out the features of anyone in the stadium, they were just bodies…alive, but seemingly featureless to my eyes. If we were to compare this to a clock for purposes of relating this vision, the "stadium seating" took up a half circle from the 3 o'clock to 9 o'clock positions. I was viewing this from about the 4 o'clock position fairly high up. Down in the center of the flat "ground" area, approximately even with the center of this half circle, there was a shallow, concave bowl that emitted a soft light from underneath. At the 12:00 position of this lighted circle of Light stood Azazel/Azrael. All alone, dressed in a dirty white robe. In front of him was an assembly of individuals standing only about ten to fifteen feet in front of him.

As I watched the scene below, the small group of men in front of Azazel/Azrael, and he himself were the only ones I could see with any clarity. As I watched, I noticed two individuals move a couple steps closer to Azazel/Azrael while apparently in private conversation. As soon as I focused on them, I realized or should I say I "Knew" that "Jesus", or Sananda as I have come to know him, was the closest one and the one behind him was Emmanuel. This really surprised me! I had heard only the tiniest amount of information about Emmanuel, but not enough for him to ever just pop into my head. But I got very strongly that this is who it was. Cool! They finished talking and Jesus approached Azazel/Azrael and seemed to communicate something to him. Very shortly he reached his right hand up above Azazel's/Azrael's head.

In that instant, my position instantly changed from 4 o'clock, up high in the bleachers to about the 7:30 position and right down (seemingly) on the floor and only about 50 feet away from him. As soon as Jesus's hand touched Azazel's/Azrael's head, I could see a beam of Light go straight down through him. The dirt and grime on his robes literally slid off to the floor as if they were liquid and his robe was suddenly bright white and shining. It began to shuffle and flutter and suddenly I realized that what looked like robes was transforming into wings right before my eyes! He then lifted them both and extended them as far up and back as possible, stretching them after so long! It was the most stunningly beautiful sight I have ever seen – I was mesmerized! He held them stretched wide open for a few ecstatic moments, shook them one last time, and let them slowly settle back down.

The next thing I knew, I was sitting back in my seat in Crestone and everyone else was coming back into their bodies as well. Not a word was spoken by anyone in the crowd. I do not recall the host speaking, but we all knew it was time to go to lunch. There was only one local restaurant available and we all drove there in our vehicles. To this day I wonder what the staff thought about that day. We had approximately 100 people who had come in for lunch at the same time and not one person spoke. Not one word. We all just pointed to what we wanted on the menu. It was the oddest sensation; it was like we were all struck "dumb" and by that, I mean literally speechless! I think if I had to, I could have forced myself to talk, but there was no desire whatsoever to do that. It took about four hours for any of us to start talking again. That's a little over 100 people simultaneously struck speechless for four hours! When we did finally compare experiences, it was immediately apparent that every single one of us had the exact same experience.

I believe it was the following morning that Azrael asked to address our group one final time. He was enthusiastically welcomed. Believe it or not, he thanked us! He thanked us for allowing him to talk to us as he had the day before, and for this allowing him to come "Home". He told us that if any of us ever needed him, especially if we had trouble with the "dark" side, we could call on him! He said he was once again Azrael and no longer Azazel but those on the dark side still knew who he was. He said "Yes, you can call in Michael and he will come in swinging his Sword! But you can call on me too!" Everyone laughed at the image of Michael appearing, swinging his sword. It did seem funny at the time! He assured us that if we need help, we only had to call on him. I have since taken him up on that promise and although I will save that for later, I can assure you, he keeps his word!

CHAPTER 3

DEEPER LEVELS OF HEALING!

"Facilis descensus Averno;
Noctes atque dies patet atri ianua Ditis;
Sed revocare gradum superasque evadere ad auras,
Hoc opus, hic labor est."

– Virgil

"Easy is the descent into Hell;
Night and Day the door to the black gods is open;
But, to reverse your steps and climb back up
and escape into the open air…
This is work. Here is where the Labor is."

– Virgil

When I got home from Crestone I was lit up with Love and Light and feeling incredible! For about one day. Then, everything went to hell! I had the strongest desire to start drinking again. I had impulses and sudden desires to do everything that a person working in the Light – shouldn't do! I could not shake it! Almost a week after I got home, I was just beginning to wake up one morning when I realized something really bizarre was going on. My insides were churning like something was alive inside of me. It felt like it was two "things" inside me fighting. Before I knew it, I was literally being thrown around on the bed like a rag doll! It was like a scene from a horror movie and I was totally helpless to what was going on. When it eventually subsided, I got up and just sat there, wondering what in the hell was happening to me! I knew that I was actually possessed by something that was really, really seriously bad!

That same afternoon I received a phone call. It was the gentleman from New Zealand who had channeled Azrael in Crestone the week before. (I am refraining from using his name, as I do not have his contact information and therefore do not have his permission to reveal his identity. I will not violate his right to privacy.) He immediately informed me that he had gotten my phone number from the host of the event at Crestone after having been told by Spirit that I needed his help and that he should come visit me! He then asked so very calmly "Does that sound right to you?" I was absolutely stunned. I told him Yes! Yes a thousand times! "Are you sure? I was told to spend a week with you!" Oh yes! Please, please do! You are more than welcome!!" A day or two later he arrived. I spent those two days thanking Spirit for having my back and helping me. They are so awesome I do not have the words to express my Love and admiration for them all!

I learned more from this man in one week than everyone else combined that I have ever met. There is no way I can go into all we did but there are definitely some major things that I will share and a few that will remain un-shared for the time being. On one of the evenings, he spent with me, he calmly but matter-of-factly informed me it was time. We sat on the floor of my living room and he went into a brief meditative state and then appeared to look right through me or maybe deep into my being. He suddenly jerked his head back and said in a rather urgent tone "We're gonna need help with this one. I've never seen anything quite like this!" He then called in Archangel Michael and his Legions of Light and I remembered to call in Azrael – Seemed like a good idea to me. The entire area literally became congested with the presence of Angels! I could actually feel them around us. He then went back into his trance-like state. He had a brief conversation with Michael and turned the whole thing over to him.

I closed my eyes and simply tried to remain as calm as possible. I "saw" a vortex in my mind's eye. I soon realized it wasn't a vortex, it was something spinning ultra-fast such that it soon reached such an extreme velocity that individual parts of it began to break loose and fly off, only to be caught by Michael's Legions of Angels surrounding us. It kept going and going, there were hundreds of them! When it was done, there was a lone being standing there. Not demonic or anything from the dark side, but a being of Light. There was a pause, then this walking master said to me: "Wow. That was interesting! I've never seen anything like this and I've never seen Spirit deal with an entity like this! Let me check into this and see what the deal is."

I sat patiently while he checked out what was going on. It was obvious that he was listening to someone (presumably Michael) telling him about it. He soon came out of that "conversation" and said "Wow! OK. Well this is interesting! This all started thousands of years ago, on what is now the steppes of Russia." As soon as he said this sentence, I got a clear vision in my mind's eye of a camp on the semi-barren steppes under the moonlight. As he spoke, I saw the entire scene unfold. There was a very barbaric tribe of what I would have to call raiders or marauders who lived on this portion of the steppes. This rather small but extremely nasty group of individuals made their way by raiding others and killing, kidnapping and stealing what they wanted from those around them. They were particularly dark and most all of them had attracted demonic entities that had possessed them. They were basically a pack of possessed, homicidal maniacs on the rampage. Their main camp had a pit close by that they kept a pack of wolves in that they had captured. When they raided others, they would kidnap certain people, especially females, both young and adult. They would decide who they wanted to keep as slaves and then rape and torture the rest. When they were done with them, they would literally throw them into the pit with the wild wolves. It didn't take long, and the wolf pack itself became possessed by demonic entities that fed off the energy of the fear and terror experienced by the victims.

A being of Light somehow became aware of this situation and rushed to try to help in some way. This being of Light was an aspect of my own higher self! When it went into the pit to try to help or comfort the victims on this particular night, it was attacked in what is commonly referred to as a "dog-pile" (pardon the pun!), by the demonic entities in the pit. They wrapped themselves around it, and more joined in until they literally had this Being of Light trapped in the center of their demonic mass. As time went on, more and more dark entities joined in until it became quite strong and took on an individualized awareness of its own. This had an extremely negative demonic, wolf energy. It has roamed this planet ever since, wreaking havoc to feed upon the fear and hatred it generated by causing the people it possessed to commit unthinkable atrocities. I saw in my mind the aftermath of some of these horrible scenes and realized the being at the center, was forced to watch every single thing this "demon" consortium had ever done. This had gone on for approximately the last 7,000 years!

I now had a choice. I could take this aspect of "my" soul into myself as I am in this lifetime, or I could send it home, then and there. He re-iterated that this being had done nothing wrong. It had been forced to witness what had happened. I suddenly had great compassion for this brave aspect of my higher self that was right before me. I felt the last thing that I wanted to do was to make 'him' feel unwanted or un-loved by any judgement on my part! I immediately stated that I would be honored to have 'him' join me, if that was 'his' desire as well (after all, he had already been a part of me when he was trapped inside this demon that possessed me since I was a child!) My friend said okay, and told me to sit up straight and relax. I did so, and immediately had the most bizarre physical sensation you can imagine! I very clearly felt a tangible force of energy entering me through my crown chakra. It got wider and wider as it entered my body through my Crown chakra. I realized it felt like a triangular shape, and it stopped descending into my body when the wide part of the "triangle shape" reached my shoulders. There was a brief but very odd sense of dual perception as this was happening. It settled in with a small, involuntary shudder of my physical body and the sense of dual perception suddenly vanished.

Looking back on it, I am amazed that I didn't become a psychopathic murderer or something of the sort. When this was going on, I had a brief memory of setting up this scenario in my soul contract. It was something that had carried on for far too long, and there was a good chance for this to work in this lifetime. So, you see, even abuse and demonic possession can have a positive outcome. You just never know how things are going to work out!

My friend then informed me that we weren't done. He said, there is another one! This one is not anything like the other one. "In fact," he said, "I'm going to let you do this one!" "What exactly do you mean by that?" I said. He replied, "I am going to let this next entity enter me and you are going to have the chance to talk to him and get him to ascend on his own."

"Whoa, whoa, whoa!" I protested! "You're going to let him enter you! And you want me to talk him into ascending? I don't know how to do that!" He chuckled a bit, as if it were nothing, and said, "Relax, I will help you." He then went into another meditative state and when he opened his eyes again, I was definitely talking to someone else. His features seemed to change as did his mannerisms and expressions. His voice even changed! He had that classic smirk on his face that every person in the world has wanted to slap off of someone's face at some point in their life. He started to laugh tauntingly and looked up at me finally with his head tilted down a bit. "Hahahahaha," he laughed. "Boy, have I had fun with you! Do you know we've had several lifetimes together? Oh yeah! I come back to you every chance I get! Boy, have I had fun making you drink so much and watching you make an ass out of yourself!"

Instead of getting angry at this point, I found myself just staring at him and having a profound sense of pity for him. I realized he was something or someone with the juvenile mentality of a spoiled and extremely deviant teenager. I just looked at him and my gaze softened as I started to have more pity and even compassion for this poor, misguided, screwed up being I had in front of me! My friend came out of the trance state and talked to me himself at this point. He told me that I needed to talk to him and try to get him to want to ascend back into the Light and go home. "Just try," he said. He then went back into trance and my deviant little tormentor was back. I just stared at him with as much Love as I could muster. He did not like this at all. He told me to quit looking at him like that. I told him "Thank you!" "For what!?!" he said, "For literally tormenting you and making you do all the stupid shit I made you do?!" I said "Yes. All of it. Do you realize how much soul growth you helped me accomplish during these lifetimes you have been with me? You helped me learn lessons to a depth that means I will never have to repeat those lessons again! It was painful, but it is over now! Thank you for the lessons!" He scoffed and said "That's crap. You didn't learn anything. I played you like a puppet and I'll do it again!" I told him "No, this is over and you are going to have the opportunity to go home! Back into the Light, into the higher dimensions!" He openly laughed at this concept and said "There is no way they would ever let me go back!" I told him, "It's about unconditional Love!" He laughed even louder, then said: "That's bullshit! That's not real! Do you have any idea what I have done?" I replied, "I may not know what all you have done, but you know absolutely everything that we have done together and therefore everything I have done! You know for a fact that Spirit has proven beyond a shadow of doubt that they still Love me! They know EVERYTHING I have done, and *you know* they still Love me! If that's true for me, then you know it's true for you too!" I could tell that statement actually made him start thinking! I began to re-iterate some of the main talking points and told him over and over that it was possible and all he had to do was be willing to go with the Angels still surrounding us. I don't know exactly what it was that tipped him towards accepting the offer, but suddenly without any forewarning, he departed with an Angel!

My friend slowly re-opened his eyes after centering himself and said "Good job! That's how it's done! Spirit never infringes on anyone's free will, even discarnate beings or demons! But if we can team up with Spirit and are willing to act as intermediaries to talk them into wanting to go home, well...that's perfectly okay!" He congratulated me on helping my first being from the dark side ascend and made the comment that every time we help dark entities of any kind ascend, we help elevate the vibrational frequency of the planet. I hadn't looked at it like that before and suddenly felt very good about the whole evening!

There is an important point I would like to make concerning the dark side. While it is true that the Light never intended for this planet to descend as low as it has in vibrational frequency, they always make the best of every situation. They are the consummate "Lemon-aide" makers!

Once they saw how low the vibrational frequency of this planet had gotten, they basically stepped back for a moment and said "Hmmm, how can we use this to our long-term advantage?" It took not long at all (probably nano-seconds) for them to realize the enormous potential for soul growth, if a soul incarnated with amnesia on a planet created with such highly charged emotional foundation! They realized that these incarnated souls would be starting out in a dense world with a consciousness that was actually closer to the dark side than they were to the "Light". This would make the journey and the subsequent accomplishment staggering in scope!

They knew that these beings would, in their juvenile mindset phase, believe that only the "physical" world was "real". They knew that, being closer in vibrational frequency to the dark side, these beings would actually have more contact and become aware of the dark side first. They also knew that over time, even the densest of these beings would realize that if there was a dark side...there must be a "Light side!" This is how the Dark serves the Light. They wake up the dense, materialistic-minded people to the fact that the non-physical dimensions exist, and that is, in fact, the very first step in a soul's growth, and journey back into the Light. It is inevitable that this journey home will take place, because the lack of Love and Light is painful to a soul, and will eventually create enough stimulus for even the darkest soul to decide to play the part of the prodigal son, *and go Home.*

This is why they created the entire façade concerning Lucifer and his rebellion and then allowed humans to run with it, over the millennia. They knew humans would need someone to assign blame to, as, in our juvenile state of consciousness we would not, as a species, be mature enough to take responsibility for our own actions. In this...they were absolutely spot on. We have "Acts of God" that we literally blame on God and try to say they are punishments for "our wickedness" and while we are committing those acts of wickedness against one another, we say "the Devil made me do it!" Anything to avoid taking responsibility for our own actions!

We are just now getting to the point where our scientists understand that consciousness affects matter. When are we going to take the next logical step and realize that it is our own backwards, unconscious energy that is causing these "Acts of God" and *devil*ish actions against one another? But, we would have to grow up to actually take responsibility for our own actions – That doesn't appear to be likely any time soon, even though it *must happen NOW* in order for humanity to save itself. At least the majority of its population, anyway.

Anyway, back to what we were talking about...

While he was with me that week, we did many things. We explored several of my past lives and I got to literally step into them for a brief moment, actually feeling my emotions from those lives. We re-activated an etheric head-piece I had used as a Priest of Osiris during a lifetime when I lived at the ancient Osirian Temple at Abidos, Egypt. I could feel it light up and was quite intrigued that I knew naturally how to re-activate it! I was introduced to an aspect of my Higher Self, or perhaps, an aspect of my Higher Self's Higher Self! I got to feel a small taste of his power and authority. It was quite intimidating and I suddenly felt very small and humble. He "reminded" me of an ability I possess due to my "relationship" with this being. This was the ability to create and send "Mini-Merkabahs" of Light to others. He explained that a great deal of Lightwork and healing assistance to others can be accomplished in this manner. If, at any time, I was to see someone who needed help, physically, mentally, emotionally or Spiritually, I could simply create a Merkabah of Light and send it to them, without them needing to know anything about it. He said their soul would have the choice to accept these or not, so I would not be violating anyone's free will. As if on cue, as he was explaining this, we heard sounds from outside the house and looked out to see a small child riding his skateboard down the street. He was only 5 or 6. Just a cute little feller having fun, learning to ride his skateboard. That is until he hit a rock directly in front of the house across the street and took a header onto the pavement! I started to jump up to run outside but my friend stopped me. He said, "This is a perfect time to practice this!" By this time the little guy had gotten up and had started to cry and scream from the pain and shock of it all. My friend looked at me and smiling, said "On three... One, two, three...!" At that, we both created mini-Merkabah's in our minds' eye and shot them at this poor little boy across the street. It was amazing how fast the response was! In about two seconds he immediately stopped crying and looked at his scraped-up hands with quite a puzzled look on his face! We could tell his hands didn't hurt anymore and he was bewildered by the sudden loss of pain! I was equally stunned by this impromptu opportunity to demonstrate Spirit's power when we humans are willing to simply cooperate with them and just be willing to try! We both were smiling as we watched the little guy pick up his skateboard and walk on down the street.

On another afternoon, he extracted some etheric implants the Greys had put in me to transmit feelings and emotions to them. They would often trigger these implants to cause certain reactions in me so they could retrieve the data or info they wanted. (They have a very interesting story and are not all bad or negative, but I will stress that the renegades, are not considered trustworthy!) I found out that this planting of etheric implants for this purpose was quite common. No wonder I thought humanity was nuts! A great many of us are being manipulated to over-react to various situations – that explained a lot to me.

He affirmed the Lineage of my Soul. (Not all of us have the same lineage. In fact, there is quite a bit of variety as far as soul lineage goes on this planet!) I had the opportunity to have several talks with Beings from the Spiritual Hierarchy of this Universe who once again had me feeling very small and humble, but so very grateful!

It was the most incredible week of my life as far as spiritual work goes! There were many things that happened that I am not at liberty to divulge at this point. Perhaps never, as what has passed is past and the truth of some things can only ignite negativity in many. Let's just say that there are some who have pretended to walk in the Light, who have given themselves names that sound like they are of the Light, who have had some very, very dark practices done under their oversight. I can also say that during this week, many innocent souls were freed to go home into the Light and some other very dark souls/entities were taken to their right and appropriate places.

At one point, one morning, I received a phone call from one of my sisters. She informed me that one of my aunts had passed away the night before. She said Aunt June had come to her the night before and apologized to her for not listening and finding out the truth about some of the family's dirty laundry. I hung up and told my friend what had been said. He nodded his head and said, "I know!" She's been here all morning bugging me and she won't stop!! Was she a short fiery red head?" "Laughing, I said, "Yes, She was!" "Well," he replied, "That's definitely her!"

He told me, "She wants our help. She came to you because she somehow knew you could help, and when she got here, she could tell I could see and hear her. But she will not stop! Good Lord! For some reason she doesn't know how to go home! She needs help!"

I explained to him that she was unable to have children and had literally been "madder than hell" at God for this reason, for her entire adult life. She sometimes said she didn't even believe in God. He responded by saying "That's the danger of forming beliefs based on faulty thinking. We do create our realities, absolutely. That includes what happens to us after we cross over! Her anger towards God and yet telling herself she didn't believe in God is quite a combination that had her basically in her own form of limbo. She is afraid and very upset about it all and now really wants help!" "So, what do we do?" I asked. "We will go into meditation, go find her and help her find her way up into the Light," he said as if he were stating the most obvious thing in the world! "Oh!" I thought to myself. "How silly of me! Why didn't I think of that?"

With his guidance, we did exactly that. We went into meditation again and soon found her huddled up in a corner in a dimly lit, non-descript corner in what seemed like an odd building with no rooms, just disjointed hallways. It was very plain and bland-looking with a very lonely feeling. I wondered how she could be here like this and also have been with us in the living room at the same time? It didn't make sense to me. I would have to ask about that. We greeted her and she was very grateful to see us. She was more than willing to stand up for us as we took her hands, and we escorted her out of that dreary place and eventually up and out into an open field on a mildly rolling landscape. It appeared to be a lovely afternoon! Right off the bat, up came Uncle Joe, her husband who had crossed over years before, riding on his favorite horse "Sugar". (A picture of him and Sugar is on his tombstone! He was the last of the true, old-time cowboys who died in the saddle at 84 years old, leading a round-up as honorary head of that round-up.) He quickly rode right up, reached down to help June onto the back of Sugar and without any hesitation rode off with her as quickly as he had come!

I was asked to speak at her funeral, and although I did not relate any of this there, I definitely felt her presence and I can guarantee you she was happier than I had ever seen her!

I will be forever grateful to this wonderful gentleman, this walking Master who was so in tune with Spirit that he would follow their guidance and help people all over the world. He is truly one of the greatest souls I have had the honor to meet on this journey of life! He soon took his leave and continued on his lighted path. I think of him often, with sincere gratitude.

CHAPTER 4

INITIATION, REUNION AND EGYPT

*"Spiritual Growth takes precedence over technology.
It is the raising of Consciousness that allows us
to perceive and comprehend the more advanced concepts
available in the higher dimensional frequencies!"*

Marty Rawson

I had started doing energy work at a local resort town and was thoroughly enjoying the opportunity to meet and work on a variety of people. As I was talking to one of the employees one day, she gave me another woman's name and phone number, and suggested I call this lady for a "reading". I asked her what kind of reading, and she was vague in her response. She just insisted this lady was very good!

A few days later I got the feeling I should call, so I did. A lady answered in a pleasant voice, and I introduced myself and explained why I was calling. She replied, "Well, let me check you out. Please uncross your legs." I was quite surprised by this, because I did indeed have my legs crossed! I uncrossed them and set up a little straighter. She hummed and made other seemingly involuntary sounds indicating she was deep in inspection and contemplation, then finally said "Yes. Yes, I will see you"! She then gave me her address and told me when to come to her house. I had the distinct feeling that I had just been laid wide open and scrutinized more so than ever before!

Her house was a quaint red brick house in a nice, normal residential neighborhood. I knocked on the door and it was soon opened by a short, sweet looking lady a bit older than I was. She smiled, but her gaze went straight through me. First, she looked at my face, then shifted her gaze above my head. She then dropped her gaze to my feet and slowly ran her eyes up my body to above my head a second time! Talk about being scrutinized! I was just starting to get uncomfortable when she apologized and invited me in. She told me to have a seat on her couch and said before we got started, she wanted to give me a little test. She started asking me questions about certain things in her house. Like which color was agitating me, and so on. I answered as spontaneously as I could and when she stopped asking questions, she said that I had about an 80% accuracy in my intuitive capacity. I asked her if that was considered good and she said "Oh yes, quite good".

I asked her about her intense scrutiny when she answered the door. She stated that when she first opened the door, she saw two bats circling above my head, and they were representative of Maya Bat Medicine. She said this was the highest form of "medicine" of the Mayan culture because it had to do with death and the afterlife. She said this energy would likely cause reactions from people, possibly negative, without them knowing why. She also said My higher self was one of the few who actively worked with the "Black" ray. When I told her I had never even heard of the Black ray, she replied that it was one of the advanced and lesser-known Cosmic Rays. It is the Ray of Unmanifested, Potential Energy. – (I have, since then, had a quite dramatic "visit" by a very unique and special Bat! Like many other people, I have had several visits by other Animal Totems as well.)

She invited me back to the room in her house where she did her "work". It was a smaller rectangular room just wide enough for a massage table to sit cross ways at one end.

She truly was a delightful lady. She started the session out by calling in the Angels and Masters for assistance. She then went into a rather humorous confession of her loving 'crush' and adoration for St. Germain in particular. The joy she exuded was infectious and the feeling lightened significantly.

She had me lay on the massage table and spent some time doing her own unique form of energy work. It was truly unlike anything I had ever experienced before or since, but it was very effective! She seemed to be able to find that perfect balance between playing and working with serious intent. At one point she told me to "do your Yogic breathing". I didn't even really know what that was at the time, but my body just started doing it. Soon, she called in Archangel Michael and informed me that I was to receive his "Sword and his Armor"! Michael wields the "Flaming Blue Sword of Truth". This helps one discern the truth. (A very handy thing to have in a world full of deceit and corruption!) The armor, well, it protects you! I was delighted to hear this, but I had never heard of anyone receiving the Armor of Michael before! I "saw" myself being presented with the Sword, and it was amazing, but the really amazing thing was the armor! She told me to just lye very still. Almost immediately I felt the entire back half of my body feel as if it had turned into large effervescent bubbles! I do not have any other way to describe it! I could not feel the table I was laying on, all I could feel was the sensation of the back half of my body, feeling like it was made up of bubbles! I was not expecting this by any means! It lasted for several minutes and then slowly began to subside. She seemed to take particular enjoyment from the look of amazement on my face!

Within mere moments, she then informed me that I had another visitor. It was Lord Buddha! I did not know she was a trance channel until his voice came through her! I could literally feel his presence to my left, but his voice was coming through her as she stood by my feet! I guess I expected a soft and gentle personality. His voice was booming and full of authority! Talk about a commanding presence! He spoke only briefly and got right to the point.

He said "We do not call ourselves Christians, or Buddhists or Muslims or by any of the names of the religions of this planet. These only serve to create separation among one another!

We are the Great White Brotherhood and we are here to serve the highest good of everyone on this planet and throughout this universe! Remember this and share it with those who will hear!"

(For those unfamiliar with the Great White Brotherhood, the "White" refers to the Clear-White Light of the Creator, which is a fusion of all colors and represents Divine Love and Light. It has nothing what-so-ever to do with the petty differences in skin color used to manipulate and divide people on this planet! Spirit could care less if we had stripes or polka dots or glitter on our butts! I also refuse to change the name of the Great White Brotherhood to something some might consider more "politically correct" for gender purposes. The Great White Brotherhood is made up of the greatest Beings of Love and Light in our Universe, both female and male and regardless of their souls, star-origin. Since this name is what *they use*, it is good enough for me and I will continue to use it.)

She then went into a deep meditative state for a few minutes. When she came out of it, she informed me of some specific information concerning my higher self. She said this was a large part of why I had had the experiences I had all my life. She told me that I had agreed to this before I came in to this life.

She informed me then, that we had even more visitors! She said these were special visitors from some of the Star Nations that I have had a long, long relationship with. I could almost see them physically! There were five of them. I closed my eyes and got a clearer image in my minds eye of them! She introduced the first one on the far left as being a representative of Lyra! He took a half step forward, smiling and gave a small but dignified "nod" of his head! It was like seeing an old friend! I knew that I knew him! I just couldn't recall his name! I wanted to jump up and hug him, but I didn't move a muscle! She channeled the word "Greetings! Nice to see you again!" She then moved on to the next individual who was a Pleiadean. The third was from Sirius, the fourth was from Vega! It was the same routine for each of them! This felt like a reunion of long, lost dear old friends! I couldn't believe this was actually happening! Finally, she got to the last one. She said, "And finally, we have the representative from Orion!

When she said this, I literally saw a very familiar face seemingly leap out towards me and shout a particular phrase. Instantaneously, my entire being, and especially my mind was slammed over, incredibly hard and fast, and then back upright! It felt like I had been physically knocked over and instantly brought back upright, and a tremendous amount of information and memories had been downloaded in that fraction of a second! I instantly remembered exactly who this was! This was my best friend in the entire Universe! We have spent lifetimes together and I remembered one special, very significant one. I had memories of this lifetime as a child, and even had dreams of this place, and him! It was in the Orion system, on a beautiful planet that was already ascended. It had architecture that we would say was reminiscent of the Greeks with the white columns and stately appearance. I remembered playing with my friend when we were both children! We developed such a close friendship we became inseparable. Whenever we got the better of the other one, we would taunt the other playfully with a particular expression. As we matured, we remained very close friends. We developed our own buddy system if you will. When one of us incarnated onto any planet, the other one would stay in the higher realms and serve as one of their guides. When we needed to assist the incarnated one in remembering who they really were, we had set up this trigger from our childhood in that life, to basically shock the other one into remembering, while downloading a huge light-packet of information to them! It was actually a little painful but for the most part, stunningly shocking! I remembered so much!

Neither this wonderful lady nor myself had been consciously expecting anything like this! When the initial shock subsided in what must have been a few seconds, we looked at each other and started laughing hysterically! I explained to her shortly after, what had happened. She was as surprised as I was and said she hadn't experienced anything like this before! Obviously, I hadn't either!

It took me a couple of weeks for my energy to settle. Anyone who has had serious energy work done, knows that there is a strong emotional release afterwards. It is in fact the purpose for the work, but it does not always feel good! To be honest, sometimes it sucks, but it is always worth it in the long run!

After the initial release of a ton of emotional baggage following this event, I really started taking a closer look at myself and who I am. It was obvious that the typical storyline humans tell themselves on this world isn't even close to the truth. I started to remember things more clearly from before I came into this life. Not everything mind you, just specific bits and pieces that were relevant to me. I also started to have more memories of certain lives I've lived. As this process continued, I noticed I needed to be grounded, more and more. It really helped me in so many ways. This is as good a place as any to share a very handy method of grounding with you.

There are many ways to ground yourself, but I would like to share a very good one with you so more people can receive the benefits of being grounded when they need it. (If you have ever had that airy-fairy "space cadet" feeling where you felt couldn't buy a thought – you needed grounding! It doesn't have to get to that point to be helpful, but you probably know what I mean!) Anyway, here's what you do:

Note: This only works in houses that have metal (Steel or Copper) pipes/ plumbing in them.

Walk up to your kitchen sink. Stand there for a few moments and clear your mind and your senses. Set your awareness on your body. Pay very close attention to just feeling your body. When you are calm and relaxed, slowly and gently reach your hand out and wrap it around the faucet. Just hold it and feel. You will feel a very gentle and pleasing wave of energy ripple through your body from your head all the way to your feet.

This, like most meta-physics is simple 8th grade physical science in action. You are a bio-electromagnetic being - animating a meat wrapped skeleton. If your energy gets scattered or disrupted, it can get out of phase or incoherent, and then energy does not flow properly and you have trouble thinking, talking,…

We are made to live within the electro-magnetic field of this planet and its magnetic field can help us balance ourselves when we need it. The plumbing in your house is grounded directly into the Earth. When you wrap your hand around the faucet, you too are then grounded directly to the Earth. It's like pushing a reset button! Very quick, very easy and best of all, it's free!

I started feeling very close to Gaia around this time in particular. I have always had a deep love for this planet and have appreciated her beauty every day of my life!

It was Gaia herself that confirmed Spirit's instructions to me on the wisdom and heartfelt service we can provide to both her and discarnate beings, by offering them the opportunity to go home into the higher realms, or to where-ever is right and appropriate for them. We are not forcing them, we are offering them a great gift. Every time a Being of lesser light goes into the Light, the vibrational frequency of the planet itself rises, and they get to experience the joy of living in the Love and Light of Source, or wherever they feel is right for them!

I also started to be really drawn to the Druidic path as I continued my work with Gaia. I found myself needing to make certain ceremonial items and was immediately drawn to Runes. It all felt so utterly natural. I even recalled a lifetime as a Druid. Now, in contrast to this, I had also taken the training for the Melchizedek Method Levels 1 and 2 from the lady who certified me in EMF Balancing© Technique earlier. I had also taken Level 3 from the head of the Melchizedek Method , Alton Kamadon in L.A. and Level 4 from him as well in Boulder Colorado.

Alton Kamadon had announced a special Melchizedek Method Event in Egypt! It was set for the Spring of 2003! Only those of Level 4 would be invited for this special 17-day adventure! Now, I should tell you, there are no words to describe how deeply I wanted to go to Egypt for this event! I have always had a deep interest and desire to go to Egypt! My ultimate dream vacation was coming true!

Now all I had to do, was prepare myself spiritually and energetically for my trip to Egypt. This was a task in itself. The United States was preparing to invade Iraq under the pretense of weapons of mass destruction that our own inspectors had already stated didn't exist. Despite the contrived motivations given publicly, we were definitely going to invade Iraq for the oil, and the country itself was still reacting to 9-11. This was not a comfortable environment to build up ones Light Quotient and develop inner peace and tranquility! It took a lot of work to keep myself centered!

For those of you who are not familiar with the Melchizedek Method, let me fill you in on it briefly. It was founded by Alton Kamadon who was a former student of Drunvalo Melchizedek. As I have been told (That's my "Hear-say" disclaimer, by the way!) Drunvalo, the author of the Flower of Life Books, Volumes 1 and 2 and the founder of the Flower of Life School, had taken a leave from teaching for personal reasons. He had channeled a very complex method for activating the Merkabah. The literal "Light Body" referred to in ancient writings. His system was a complex, multi-step process that had very specific breaths and other techniques involved at every step of the way. It was effective, but in actuality, was far too much for the average Earth human to memorize.

During Drunvalos' hiatus, Thoth came to Alton Kamadon and gave him a system of Merkabah activation that was easier for we simple minded humans to grasp! Please understand that I love Drunvalo's books and teachings. He is one of the giants whose shoulders we stand on as we go forward! I devoured his Flower of Life Books long before going to Egypt. I desperately wanted to see if I could verify the information in his books! As far as I was concerned, I was a student of both he and Alton in spite of rumors of a falling-out between them! I can honestly say that Alton Kamadon always spoke very highly of Drunvalo Melchizedek whenever his name came up. I loved what they both were doing and just wanted to learn all I could!

The Melchizedek Method was a "Light-body Activation and Multi-Dimensional Healing Technique" that was taught to Alton through the Spiritual Hierarchy, particularly Thoth. Rather than a complex multi-step step process, it broke the whole thing down into levels of Lightbody activation that would be permanently activated, one after the other. Each building on the previous level(s) of light-body activation. This way, people simply had to take the activation training for each level and it was done.

The thing that really drew me to the Melchizedek Method, was that it was experience based. The Melchizedek Method did not go deeply into talking about or even teaching different types of spiritual activities. You would spend a very short time being introduced to a certain type of spiritual concept or activity, then you would go into a guided meditation and receive the necessary activations to your light body! While in meditation, you, along with the entire group in the class, would then experience this "activity". Right from the beginning, you were "Doing", not just reading about it! This is priceless. As I will say repeatedly, once you have had your own experiences with the Divine, no one can ever take them from you! People can say or believe whatever they want, but from that moment on, *you know*!

(After Egypt, I would go on to take level 5 from Alton Kamadon in Dallas Texas, his final seminar prior to his moving on from this world!)

For now though, I was preparing for Egypt!

It had been a lifelong dream of mine to go to Egypt and see the pyramids. I had no idea how fantastic this trip would be! It ended up being far beyond my wildest expectations. As I was preparing to go to Egypt, I "stumbled" upon an ancient Druidic "spell of binding". I had never been into spells, but I could not get this one out of my head. Spirit absolutely would not leave me alone until I had it memorized. This was no small feat, because it was a rather long spell in an unusual "dead" language. I even talked to my wife, (my fiancé at the time) wondering why they were insisting I study and learn some ancient Druidic spell before going to Egypt?! It was a "Spell of Binding" for crying out loud, which meant it didn't do anything by itself except "seal" or "bind" whatever had gone before it. Although I could not make sense of it, I simply complied with Spirit's demands and learned the spell by heart. Once I had it thoroughly memorized, the sense of urgency dissipated and all was fine once again.

I landed in Cairo in the evening, two days before the invasion of Iraq in March of 2003. The rest of the world's tourists were not exactly beating down the doors to get into Egypt at this time, as we were only about 500 miles from the border of Iraq, and Egypt itself is 90% Muslim. The media in the west was doing their best to depict all of Islam in an extremely negative light and brand all Muslims as fanatical terrorists. My personal experience was quite remarkably different!

The meeting place for the Melchizedek Method was the Mena House Hotel just across the street from the Giza Plateau and the Great Pyramid itself. The original structure was built as a "Hunting Lodge" for the King of Egypt, I believe back in the 1800s. It is fabulous! The original structure has been greatly expanded and is now a beautiful resort. I will never forget my first sight of the Great Pyramid, bathed in spotlights from the ground and the moonlight above, as we came up the street towards the Mena House Hotel – it was magnificent! My soul simply rejoiced and the feeling of familiarity was incredible. I could feel the energy; the energy of the vortex was palpable, almost throbbing and pulsating in its power! That first night as I closed my eyes to try to get to sleep, I saw the "Amrit" nectar spoken of in Hindu texts, in my mind's eye. It was like a liquid light that appeared to have the consistency of honey that wanted to slowly drip down from above my third eye! I played with it for some time before falling asleep. If you are not familiar with this concept, I suggest you look it up. It is a very real phenomenon and is not only enjoyable, it lets you know you are on the right track, so to speak!

Our first meeting as a group was in the morning after breakfast. I definitely needed coffee! I was finding out what the term "jetlag" really meant, on a very personal level! Several cups of coffee and a couple of "Turkish

Coffees" as well, and I actually started to wake up. By the time we got to the convention hall in the hotel, I was wide awake and feeling on top of the world. The main building was like something out of a movie – white marble walls, red velvet carpets and gold accented decor, it was truly luxurious! I never realized how many people were there until that morning. Alton Kamadon soon took the stage and welcomed everyone. He announced that we had around 130 people from 29 counties around the world! He then started making a few general announcements. As he was talking, I noticed a few Egyptian men standing against the walls of the convention center. Alton soon introduced them as our guides for the duration of our trip. They had been chosen specially for our group due to their familiarity with all of the ancient Temples in Egypt and their experience with giving Spiritual tours throughout Egypt.

After the general announcements, Alton had everyone in the group go into meditation and simultaneously activate our Merkabahs. The actual moment of activation is accomplished with a very forceful out-breath familiar to many on the spiritual path. The instant we all activated our Merkabahs, we blew the power out in the entire hotel! The wiring could not handle the intense electromagnetic pulse of our combined energy and we all laughed at this, but our new guides were looking at each other in a very puzzled manner! They had never seen anyone "activating their Merkabah" before and certainly did not expect the power to be blown out. It took quite some time, but eventually the power came back on. We spent that first day going over the itinerary and other information the group needed to know.

The second day, we met in the Convention Center again. We activated our Merkabahs again and we blew out the power again! Our guides actually laughed with us this time. I could tell they still didn't quite know what to think, but they knew they were witnessing something they had never seen before! We had greater things to do on this day. We had been granted sole access to the Great Pyramid on that day and the following day. Our guides told us they had never seen any group granted sole access before – ever!

The Giza Plateau is operated by the Egyptian Military. It may be officially under the jurisdiction of the Council of Antiquities, but the military personnel are who you see actually guarding the plateau and conducting operations. The guards at the Pyramids were extremely nice fellows; very professional, but very personable as well. As we assembled outside the entrance, I was praying to be in the front of the group because that portion would be going into the so-called King's Chamber on the first day. I really don't recall how it happened, because I thought I was too far back in the crowd to make it, but by the time we went through the initial tunnel you have to crawl through to get to the Grand Gallery, I was at the front. As we climbed up the Grand Gallery itself, I was right behind Alton Kamadon and his fiancé, and the third person to enter the King's Chamber.

I took a few moments to examine the interior of the chamber. The walls were extremely smooth granite stone; it felt as smooth as glass! The so-called "Sarcophagus" was equally as smooth. "Carved" out of solid granite I believe. It appeared to be part of the same rock slab that made up the floor. This too was perfectly smooth and flat – this alone was an engineering marvel! We cannot cut out or should I say "machine" out a solid granite box like this – to this very day! The most skilled and advanced stone cutters in the world have testified to this. The so-called "Sarcophagus" is also way too small to be an actual sarcophagus, unless it was for an infant or a small child. More on this later. Our group got inside the King's Chamber and went into meditation again. We all activated our Merkabahs simultaneously, and again – we instantly blew out the power on the entire Giza Plateau! The great Pyramid is lit inside with a string of light bulbs strung throughout. Our guides later told us that they watched from their positions guarding the entrance, as the military personnel panicked over the sudden power outage. They had to yell down to them to tell them not to worry about trying to fix it, that the power would come back on by itself and that we would be just fine inside in the dark. We were inside meditating, so the darkness didn't matter to us at all. At one point in our meditation that was actually an activation for the Great Pyramid itself, Alton called on Lord Melchizedek and Metatron to assist us all in our efforts. I had the sudden feeling of being lifted up, almost as if being lifted by a huge fan from below us. I heard from inside my own solar plexus "Now you have it, Own it." With that I knew I had been re-initiated inside the Great Pyramid! Oh yes, I had been here, in this very room, in ancient times…I knew it and I could feel it!

As we left the Great Pyramid, the power was just coming back on. Again. From inside my own being, I heard a voice, very clearly say, "When you step out from the entrance, turn around and look up!" I did as I was told and cast my gaze up the slope of the Great Pyramid to see a ring of hawks circling the apex of the Pyramid in a perfect circle; there must have been 15 to 20 of them, it was stunning! I immediately thought of the Egyptian God Horus and ancient Egypt's spiritual relationship with the hawk. I now needed to know exactly what the hawk signified, specifically to the ancient Egyptians. Later that afternoon I had the opportunity to look it up on the internet at the Mena House. The hawk represented the concept of bringing the Divine into the physical! That was exactly our intent for this activation of the Great Pyramid and for our entire trip! We were literally there to activate all the ancient temples along the Nile, including (of course) the Pyramids, thus, helping the Earth and Humanity to bring the Divine into this physical world.In the ancient times, the Egyptian Mystery Schools were renowned throughout the known world. Great mystics from as far away as India had come to study there. (Now that's saying something considering everything India had going on at the time!) There were two "halves" of their teachings. The Feminine and the Masculine. The feminine was signified by the Left Eye of Horus, and the Masculine was signified or represented by the right Eye of Horus. The initiate, once accepted as a student, would start their training at the Temple of Isis in Philae, far up the Nile from Giza. They would go through extremely extensive training to develop their intuitive abilities, which are feminine in nature. Only after mastering the Feminine aspects of themselves, were they taught the Masculine aspects. This ensured they had a compassionate connection with the divine and their intuition fully developed prior to applying the Masculine teachings to our physical world. *(This is a concept I believe we could learn a lot from and truly feel it should be implemented into our societies worldwide!)*

The Great Pyramid served as the Final Initiation Chamber that the "Adept" would enter only after going through 20 years of training through all the successive Temples up the Nile. The Great Pyramid itself is built according to Sacred Geometry and perfectly aligned to true North. It is also placed in what has been called "The navel of the Earth" due to its location at the center of the Earth's land mass. Its alignment and geometry, combined with its exact structural design, makes the location of the so-called King's Chamber with its "sarcophagus" the exact sweet spot for the energy generated by the Pyramid. It is designed as a true vortex to take an individual etherically to one of two places. Either the famed Halls of Amenti, within the Time-Space folds of Earth, or the Great White Lodge of the Great White Brotherhood, located on Sirius!. Both of these are, of course, in the higher, 5th dimension.

The entire Egyptian Mystery School was created to allow individuals who were ready, to ascend while in the physical body and have the opportunity to actually meet with the Spiritual Hierarchy in one of these two locations to determine what their service work would be as they carried on as a living Master in their lifetime. This was before someone started calling different peoples – different religions as we know them today. Back then, it was understood that everyone was simply forming their own connection to that which is Divine.

The so-called "King's Chamber"   *The so-called "Sarcophagus"*

The Pyramids serve a second purpose as well. This is by no means a less important purpose. It has been theorized that the Great Pyramid was built for generating energy. This is true, but in a very specific manner. It draws in energy and feeds it into the pyramidal grid that exists throughout and across the planet. Being in the center of the world's land mass, it is uniquely situated and oriented for this purpose. Anyone who has done any in-depth research on this subject knows that there are pyramids all over this planet, some of them even larger than the ones at Giza! The pyramid shape is integral to the Light/Energy structure of this universe and is fundamental to the transmission of energy through the grid system. This grid was originally set up by the Atlantean Masters when they realized their world was doomed and that the next "wave" of consciousness coming behind them was "of a lesser Star" as they say, and would be subjected to intense, lower forms of fear, control, and domination. This pyramidal grid has been the primary reason we have not sunk into pure darkness as a civilization! So, yes, the pyramid does harness and generate power. It channels this energy into an artificial grid that extends across the entire planet, and helps stop humanity's consciousness levels from dropping even further.

The "Queen's Chamber niche   *Entrance and Niche*

On the next day, we again entered the Great Pyramid and had it to ourselves. I entered the so-called Queen's Chamber this time. Again, we activated our Merkabahs and yes, again we knocked out the power on the Giza Plateau! This made 4 consecutive activations and just as many consecutive power outages, all in exact synchrony! This time we heard helicopters circling overhead though, shortly after our activations! We found out later that our Merkabah activations were registering on the Egyptian Militaries radar and electronic monitoring equipment and they were quite perplexed by these successive EM readings! Now that's impressive!

As you crawl into the so-called Queen's Chamber, you will notice a large, cut-out niche in the wall to your left. Set back in, within this cut-out is a shelf or bench area. It looks as though it was made to hold a substantial statue in ancient times. If it wasn't, it should have been! Behind this "bench" was a rather small steel gate at the front of a tunnel going back into the Pyramid itself. This tunnel was just large enough for an adult to crawl through on their hands and knees. I decided this bench was a perfect place to sit for our ceremony for this day, so I planted myself there.

After our ceremony on this day, I asked if anyone had a flashlight. I borrowed one and used it to look back into the tunnel behind the gate. The gate was unlocked and easily swung open. I must admit, I could not resist a look! Another gentleman from Ohio followed me in. The tunnel went back a short distance then curved to the left and then back to the right before opening into a small open "room". There were a couple of stones that had partially collapsed from the ceiling but were holding each other up in a "v" formation. I had to duck under them to reach the far wall where a small shelf was. We had heard that a couple of Japanese Archeologists had gotten permission to dig this tunnel after using sound penetrating equipment to discover this room. Rumor also had it that they found a gold statue and both they and the statue immediately disappeared. I cannot vouch for any truth to that story, but I figured if it was true, this shelf was the only place a statue could have been. I can vouch for the tunnel and the room! The most impressive thing about it was the feeling. It felt like sacred ground and I knew I was being watched. So could my friend from Ohio. He soon decided he didn't like the way he was feeling and headed back out. There was an intense, almost apprehensive aspect to how this room felt. I knelt and gave thanks to those who were guarding this place and thanked them for allowing me to be in this sacred space where very few humans have ever been. I thanked them for serving the Light and protecting the Pyramid. The feeling did indeed become lighter and I simply stayed kneeling and meditated for a short while. I could feel at least two beings watching me intently from just a few feet away. They were beings of Light, but they were also guardians who took their job very seriously. I thanked them again and with a slight bow, slowly left.

(Upon returning home, I told my wonderful Angel Reader friend about this. She confirmed that I was correct in who and what they were and that since I had shown respect, I had been welcome. She said two others went in after I left and had not shown the proper respect. She said they were not welcome and had left just in time to avoid, shall we say, "difficulties". The cool thing about this is that I had heard a man and a woman had went in after I did, but had not told her about them.)

Our trip through Egypt was phenomenal. They opened the Cairo Museum of Antiquities to us privately, after regular business hours, so we could have the place to ourselves. The thing that drew me in the most was Akhenaten's and Nefertiti's display. The next day we were off to the Step Pyramid of Saqqara. Before leaving the Pyramids for the rest of our journey, we had a pre-dawn gathering and meditation between the paws of the Sphinx. Normally, tourists cannot even get close to the Sphinx. It is walled off to protect it. I made sure to get several pictures up close!

Soon, the day came for us to fly to Aswan and the Temple of Isis at Philae. We got to the Cairo airport nice and early but were held in the terminal. Before too long, it was announced that there was a sand storm sweeping across the Sahara and no one was allowed to fly anywhere in the country! It wasn't too long after that – that I witnessed why. It was my first sand storm.

The host of our tour definitely had a lot of influence. He announced shortly that he had arranged for accommodations for all of us at a hotel about 2 blocks away. We quickly bussed over there and met in their very large dining area. Alton announced that he had been told by Spirit that there were dark forces that did not want us to succeed in our purpose for being in Egypt! He told us that we should meet in small groups of 4 to 6 people and activate our Merkabahs and meditate. He specifically warned everyone not to allow any energy of conflict to arise. Conflict would only strengthen the dark entities trying to stop us. *(This is always good advice. This is why most Catholic priests have a problem exorcising demonic beings... they go into it as a "fight". Trying to fight the dark side is doing nothing more than bringing them lunch!)*

We broke up into small groups very naturally, as if we all knew who we were supposed to be with. The group I was with asked me if I would lead the meditation and Merkabah activation, but I felt very strongly that I needed to focus and concentrate on every step of the process. I suggested one of the ladies in our group lead the session and everyone agreed. As soon as we had activated our Merkabahs the wonderful lady from British Columbia who led that portion asked Spirit to bless the entire country with Love and Light for the highest good of all concerned. We then went into silent meditation. It was at that moment that I knew why I had had to memorize the Spell of Binding! I did not feel comfortable at all saying it out loud and I was concerned no one would understand what it was, or why it needed to be done. After a little while she began speaking to Spirit again, asking that the Spirit help the sand storm subside, and we be allowed to continue our journey. I hesitated for what seemed like an eternity, but must have been a minute or two in reality. The sense of urgency was building to insurmountable proportions quickly! Finally, I asked if anyone minded if I recited a Spell of Binding. They immediately said "Sure, of course...!" I immediately felt a sense of will power well up inside of me and I heard myself speaking with a tone of authority that surprised me! I knew what the words meant and I meant them as I spoke them! As soon as I finished speaking the words of this ancient spell, there was a very physical sensation that took place. It felt like someone had dropped a twenty ton lid onto a equally massive stone box; I could feel the percussive wave reverberate as it spread out! There was such a sense of finality to it, combined with a physical jolting, that I asked everyone else if they felt it. Their eyes and their answers were in unison. A couple of them asked "What was that?!? That was amazing!" The lady from B.C., who had led the Merkabah activation asked if the spell was of Druidic origin, and I confirmed it was.

The storm had been going on for hours at this point, but within less than one hour, the storm had totally died down and we got the notice that we could catch our flight!

We very quickly left the hotel and went straight to the airport a couple short blocks away. When we walked out to the plane to board it, I was a little taken aback. I swear, it would not have surprised me to find out that this was the same plane they used to film the Indiana Jones movies! It looked like it should be in an Aircraft Museum! Nevertheless, we all boarded the plane and this old, flying tin can might have rattled quite loudly, but it flew perfectly – all the way to Aswan. When we landed there was no wind. By the time they rolled the steps up to the plane and started letting us off, the wind had started to pick back up. By the time we all got into the airport terminal, from the plane, the entire country was shut down again, due to the sand storm starting all over again! It had stopped exactly as long as it took us to make our flight and literally, not one minute longer! We went to our hotel and waited out the storm sleeping. The next morning we awoke to a beautiful clear sun-shiny day. Every morning I was in Egypt, I would wake up and ask "Okay Spirit! What do you have in store for me today?!" Every single day they gave me my own personal tour of each and every temple we went to. We cruised down the Nile in a very nice ship and excellent food.

I had previously studied Drunvalo Melchizedek's books, The Flower of Life – Volumes 1 and 2. I was determined to find every reference I could from his books, regarding the temples in Egypt. I had forgotten which temple some of these references were at, but Spirit led me to them without fail. Many times, I would just find myself apart from the group, quite unintentionally, and a local person would call me over and point out the more interesting things at that temple. These were invariably the very things I had desperately wanted to find! There were also many other surprises as well.

Kom Ombo was incredible. The walls with their huge bas relief carvings are magnificent and the mummified alligator is definitely something you don't see every day! There was a group of locals selling merchandise on the plaza in front of the temple entrance, and one lady standing outside the temple who had a basket full of saffron at least 4 feet in diameter that had to be worth hundreds of thousands of dollars over here in the U.S. – I couldn't help but wonder if she had any idea of the value of her herb basket, on the world market. Unfortunately I do not speak their language.

While we were at Luxor, one of our guides that had been with us the entire trip took about a half dozen of us to a very small building to the north and outside of the proper temple grounds. He asked us if we had heard of Sekhmet? Some had heard the name but none of us really knew much about her. We stood outside this small building that was the size of a shed, while he told us the legend of Sekhmet. He told us that she was one of the older goddesses of the Egyptian Pantheon and that she was represented as a lioness. She was originally a goddess of maternal, nurturing energy, but, as legend would have it, had, on one particular occasion, gotten very, very drunk. In a drunken rage, she had then massacred thousands of innocent people! The carnage went on and on until other "gods" intervened and stopped her. When she sobered up and saw what she had done, she was horrified and she begged forgiveness and devoted herself to becoming the goddess of Healing and Motherhood. He then informed us that inside this small, one-roomed building was an ancient statue of Sekhmet. He said that every time he came here, he would take a small group like ours into this shrine and meditate.

We went in and simply went into a standing meditation with no talking whatsoever. It took a couple of minutes, and then I felt it. There was definitely a presence in this room with us. It was very warm and loving, but it felt like I was being inspected at a soul level at first. Then it softened and soon it reminded me of the Love a mother has for her newborn baby. It was so beautiful I literally lost myself in it! I have no idea how long we were in there, but I did not want to leave. Eventually we had to, and as we walked away from this little, tiny shrine I could tell it impacted everyone else, just as it had me. Our guide was smiling from ear to ear knowing we all had indeed experienced what he had wanted to share with us! We all thanked him sincerely.

We went from temple to temple having many of them to ourselves for our meditations. The only two places where I felt anything negative was at Hatshepsut's Temple and at a small place devoted to caring for the dying. That ancient "Infirmary" did not feel really bad, but it did not have a good feeling either. Hatshepsut's Temple however, definitely had some serious negativity to it. It was the only temple on the entire trip that everyone felt uneasy and could not go into meditation at all. When we got to the Osirion Temple things got a little more interesting for me. I had recalled prior to this that I had had a lifetime in the truly ancient times of Egypt as a Priest of Osiris. When we first approached the temple, it just didn't feel right. Not bad, – just not right. As we continued into the temple we were informed that the temple we were in at that moment, was the "New" temple built several thousand years ago – basically and almost on top of – the older "Osirian Temple" of truly ancient times. When we got to the back of the "new" temple we found the remnants of the actual Osirion Temple. This portion had the right feeling to it! Not necessarily the right look, but definitely the right feeling. It had the feeling of home! At least for me.

We took a little time to do the tourist thing and investigate what we wanted to. I had a couple of my new friends hold me from falling into the murky water at the bottom of the Osirion while I got my coveted pictures of what is possibly the oldest Flowers of Life on the planet, which are burned into granite stone pillars of the Osirian Temple; there are two of them. After we got our interest satisfied, we got ready for our meditation. I found a nice spot at the edge of the Old Osirion complex where I could dangle my feet over the edge. We went into meditation.

I went out. I went completely out. I don't recall anything at all! I did come out of it at the same time as everyone else did, but I do not know how. I may as well have been in a deep sleep or a coma as far as I was concerned.

The Osirian, original temple at Abydos   *Flowers of Life burned into granite.*

We got up, grounded ourselves as much as possible and eventually started walking back through the temple. It was then that I noticed I had started humming. Six notes or tones. Then it repeated. And repeated, and repeated and repeated!

I could not stop myself; I literally could-not-stop-myself! It was starting to annoy those around me once we got on the bus! I didn't even notice when I would start – it was a truly unconscious act. Eventually I realized it was not going away, and I simply closed my eyes and hummed it silently to myself in my head. It took literally a full week to stop myself from just randomly starting to hum these tones. It has been almost 20 years now since this occurred and occasionally, I will realize that I am once again humming this sequence of tones!

In my own mind, when I start humming this, I get a picture of many of "us" priests sitting together in a large group outdoors. It is a summoning or a "calling". It was what was used in ancient, ancient times to call forth one of the higher star nations that worked with humans at that time. We would get together and sit in meditation, toning this "call" to our friends from the skies until they arrived. The only thing I can relate it to that most people would be familiar with is the set of five tones in the movie

"Close Encounters of the Third Kind". It is similar, but is much more harmonious and the end note flows right back into the beginning note, so it has a natural, endless flow to it. I have often wondered if the writers of that movie had unknowingly channeled that part of that movie and had simply gotten the tune off a little. I guess we'll never know! It does have a calming and soothing effect on my mind and nervous system as well.

I must say, the people of Egypt truly restored my faith in humanity. When I left the States, we had not really had our daily lives impacted. The price of gas had not even gone up like it would shortly! Yet, at least half the people of this country were screaming for the total annihilation of a country that had absolutely nothing to do with 9-11. Most of these people call themselves Christians. These same people continuously paint Muslims as radical extremists, hell bent on the destruction of everyone else. When I got to Egypt, I was treated better than I am treated by people in my own country. The people of Egypt, at this time, were suffering daily just from the threat of the impending war. It actually started two days after we landed in Cairo. I saw people so poor that they were willing to do any work whatsoever, just to try to feed their children any leafy vegetable greens they could get! Their economy is substantially supported by tourism, and most of the world was not willing to venture within 500 miles of the coming conflict. I met people from every walk of life in Egypt. I saw the extreme poverty that made me want to cry just knowing that it existed; I met wealthy and powerful people. From one end of the country to the other, and from one end of society's wealth to the other, these people all recited the same thing. All they said was, "We must pray! We must pray for peace. Saddam is crazy, Bush is crazy! We must pray for them, that there be peace!" It was like the whole country memorized this special mantra! All I can say is that when people are impacted to this extent and they have the strength of character and the faith to conduct themselves with this level of integrity, they are a people who are truly living their religion! I do not say this to knock people who claim to be Christian. I say this to simply show the world what living your religion looks like! May it serve as an inspiration to others. This reminds me of a question someone once asked HH the Dalai Lama. I do not have the exact quote, but it was to this effect: "What religion should I follow" His answer was "Pick one. Any one. But…Live it well!"

We concluded our trip with a 3-day stay at the Oberoi Beach Resort, Sahl Hasheesh, a luxury resort on the banks of the Red sea. It was as beautiful and as picturesque as any picture postcard I have ever seen. We got to snorkel in the Red Sea, swim with dolphins, and relax. It was amazing, peaceful, and stunningly beautiful.

On one afternoon, myself and two others decided to journey into the city of Hurghada. We were warned to stay away from certain areas of the city due to rioting over the war. Foreigners, especially Americans, were warned to be very careful. I checked-in with Spirit and got that it was safe for me to go, so I did. It was a quick but otherwise uneventful cab ride from the resort to Hughada. Egyptian Taxi drivers do not mess around in getting you to your destination!

I had been tasked by my lovely fiancé to bring back an authentic belly-dancer outfit. A request I was obviously quite happy to comply with. As the 3 of us went shopping, we all went our separate ways. After asking at several stores, I finally got directions to a large facility where they sold authentic belly dancing outfits and I walked there. After I walked in, I was met by an Egyptian man who spoke English. When I told him what I was looking for, he pointed to a doorway in the back of the store. I went through this doorway and found myself in what looked like a stock room. There were 3 guys in the room who greeted me and asked me how they could help. They started showing me various outfits. I eventually looked back towards the entrance I had come through and noticed there were about 20 Egyptian men standing in the doorway with their arms folded and staring at me. At first, I must admit, I felt a little apprehensive. I was a lone American, in the back of an Egyptian store and no one in the world knew exactly where I was. I was outnumbered over 20 to 1. I spoke to Spirit in my own head and told them: "You guys said it was safe for me to come here and I sure hope I can still trust you mean that!" With that I simply gave the men in the doorway a friendly nod of the head and continued my dialogue with the men I was talking to. The men in the doorway eventually started to break up and seemed to lose interest in me. I purchased a nice outfit for my fiancé and left without any problems. I did thank Spirit sincerely for helping to keep this whole situation peaceful! I am quite sure I was the politest American they have ever met to this day. We left the Red sea and went back to the Mena House Hotel for our final day in Egypt. Most people went shopping for various items to take home. I headed back to the Great Pyramid by myself.

I went inside and found a guard at the entrance to the "King's chamber". I asked him what it would take to have the room to myself for a bit, and he informed me that would not be possible. I pulled out a wad of Egyptian pounds from my pocket, and we soon had an agreement. After everyone else had left, I went in and got into the so-called sarcophagus. This was more difficult than I had imagined, because it is quite short in length. I had to bend my knees up drastically in order to fit inside.

Once inside, I immediately cleared my mind and went into a meditative state. I had already journeyed to the Halls of Amenti on a few occasions, so I set my intention to go to the Great White Lodge on Sirius. At first I felt nothing, and then... suddenly, there I was, standing on the steps of the magnificent, Great White Lodge itself! The sanctity of the place was truly humbling and nearly overwhelming. The architecture was absolutely stunning in its grandeur. I had just soaked-in the sacred energy and peaceful ambiance of the place, when I suddenly found myself lying in the "sarcophagus" inside the Great Pyramid again. It was a brief, but wonderful experience that is indelibly imprinted in my memory. This proved to me, at least, what the Pyramid was used for, and that it still works perfectly. As I left, I thanked the guard sincerely for allowing me this extraordinary experience! I'm pretty sure I floated back to the hotel, I sure felt like I did. My curiosity had been satisfied for the time being, and it was time to go home. As time went by and events unfolded, I had many more experiences with Spirit, from all types. My understanding grew, and my memories became stronger and soon I had to have answers to more questions and deeper issues.

How does this all work? How did we come to be where we are now? Who are we really?

What is the point of it all? What can we do? What should we do?

CHAPTER 5

CONNECTING WITH BEINGS OF LIGHT AND CLEARING THE REST

"Higher Vibrational frequencies will always transmute lower Vibrational Frequencies"

The Universal Laws

The answers to the previous questions are laced throughout the rest of this book. A couple of concepts I would like to share now, is how to connect with Spirit and what to do afterwards. This may seem like basic stuff to those who have been naturally working with Spirit, but to some people, it's a foreign concept and to others, it may even sound like an outlandish concept. Negative or low frequency beings are a part of this world and you may well find that out for yourself. Clearing them is a necessary duty of all light workers. Clearing negative beings however, is not as basic for most people. Even for many of those who do spiritual work.

There is an old saying that goes "You have to see it to believe it!" Well, when working with Spirit it is better to understand that "Sometimes you have to believe it, in order to see it!" Obviously, this is not always the case, but for the most part this seems to be true.

In order to bring Spirit into your life, you must do one very important and basic thing first. You have to invite them!

It sounds deceptively simple, because it is! Most people just don't take the time or put forth the effort to give Spirit a truly heartfelt invitation into their life! Spirit will not ever violate your free will, therefore they can only intervene to the extent that their actions do not do so. When you invite Spirit into your life in an active, everyday manner, you have granted them the authority to act on your behalf in a far greater fashion! After that, there are a few more things. I could go on and on with a list of suggestions, but the point I really want to make is to pay attention to what Spirit is saying, or showing to you! If you do not pay attention, *very closely* to the things Spirit is showing you throughout your day, you will miss what they are telling you! You must pay attention to all the little idiosyncrasies in your life, and you must trust them! If you do not trust them and follow them, Spirit will eventually quit showing you things! They really are your best friends and they love you unconditionally, but if you ignore them, their interaction with you will eventually be reduced. This is only logical and reasonable.

We need to remember that we too, are spirit. A large portion of connecting to Spirit is realizing you are never separate from Spirit in the 1st place. You must, however, invite them into your life, in a loving and gracious manner.

There are many types of spirits that you can make contact with. There are Angels, many types of angels. There are the Ascended Masters. There are deceased loved ones. There are many entire civilizations that have ascended into the light, both on Earth and off. And, there is what we call "the dark side".

I only work with the light and we will show you how to protect yourself from the dark side.

Remember this, the front door to the Spirit world is through your Heart, not the intellect.

The intellect is a nice companion to the heart, but, like a pet, it has to be trained, otherwise you will spend all your time running around cleaning up the messes it makes! As a friend of mine once so eloquently put it: "The mind thinks it knows everything. It doesn't know shit! – Wisdom comes through the Heart." Try this:

Take a deep breath in through the nose, hold it for a second and let it out through the mouth with the sound "Aah". When you relax and say "Aah", it opens up the heart. Try it.

Learn to trust your feelings instead of your mind! Learn to tell the difference.

The intellect judges, it causes you to be self-conscious, so you don't move freely. It scrutinizes everything. It is critical.

When you are in spirit, you lose yourself, and your heart opens. You begin to feel like you truly are part of life, not separate from it. Many times, their guidance comes into your head as a thought. You may – and probably have many times – mistaken it for your own thoughts!

Pay close attention to how things are phrased in your "thoughts". If it is phrased as if someone is speaking to you, someone probably is.

If you follow it, magic happens. If you ignore it – you may suffer the consequences. Not as punishment in any way, but when someone tells you to "duck" you might want to listen!

Einstein was once asked how he discovered the Theory of Relativity. He replied, "I didn't do anything. I was listening to music and it just dropped in!" That's how it happens. You create the receptacle and it just drops in! Everyone has done this. The challenge isn't to get the information, the challenge is to recognize it and do something with it!

You need to remember to feed your spirit! These are the things that make you feel happy to be alive! We feed the physical and mental bodies but we neglect the Spiritual...

What feeds your soul, a walk in nature – fresh flowers – cooking – art – music – meditation?

What are the things that make you feel good about being you and being alive?

Be in the moment! Do what you love doing! These are the things that will feed your soul.

It doesn't mean you have to do everything you think of. Just do the ones that you can, that feel right.

Then;

SEE SPIRIT IN ALL THAT IS!

Connecting with Spirit is through feelings! Not intellectual "knowing".

You have to learn to trust your feelings if you are going to work with Spirit!

Practice connecting with your Angels!

Guardian Angels – They are your personal guardians and are there to assist you in completing your life's goals and or mission! They help keep you on your path! They are the only ones who can manifest physically in human form!

Connect to your guardian angels as you go to bed. Try to feel where they are.

Archangels: The most powerful angels to interact with the physical realms directly. They are in essence the living manifestations of the various characteristics of Source/God.

Michael is the Living Embodiment of the Will of God.

Raphael is the Living Embodiment of the Healer within God...etc.

There are also Helper Angels, Ascended Masters and yes, your own Higher Self, all of whom are looking forward to renewing your acquaintance.

Practice trying to feel where your Guardian Angels are. Try to feel the subtle difference in energetic vibration of the different types of angels. PAY ATTENTION TO YOUR BODY!

Intuition is feeling.

Guidance also comes through everyday interactions. Your guides/angels will guide you and will guide others to interact with you. Try asking them about any given topic you are wondering about – and let them come through. Try writing what they have to say. (In a quiet, safe place, of course.)

HOW TO TELL GOOD GUIDANCE FROM BAD:

Good guidance will:

Empower you but will not make you "special" or flatter you.
Will never order you or "tell you" what to do.

> Be in the highest good of all concerned.
> Be consistent.

Bad guidance (usually from the ego or dark beings masquerading as a being of the Light):

> Will flatter you or make you "special".
> Will tell you what to do, and will even order you to do things.
> Will tell you to do things that are not in the highest good of all concerned.
> Be inconsistent

There are many ways they can work with you. The following is a perfect example of how they worked with me, long ago. This one event was the beginning that developed into decades of learning about the healing arts and working with Spirit.

During the first year and a half of my healing, I had the strange and sudden but insistent feeling that I needed to go to a small resort town about 100 miles away. I did not have the foggiest notion why; I just knew I needed to take a short road trip to that little town!

When I got there, I still didn't have a plan. I had only gone a couple blocks down the main street in this small town when I looked to the left and saw a small park at the end of a dead-end street. All I can say is, it felt right, so I turned left. I parked towards the end of the street and got out of my car. I looked towards the park and saw a small sign at the park entrance, again pointing to the left. It was pointing to a small book store/ gift shop that was nestled in amongst the trees in this quaint little park. Its appearance was practically out of a fairy tale. I was more than a little intrigued by now, so I had to check it out! It was mostly a book store, but had all of the other typical items like crystals, pendulums and such. It was absolutely packed with merchandise and people!

The aisles were very narrow, just wide enough for one person at a time! There was no waste of space here! I looked around and ended up walking straight to the opposite corner of the shop from where the door was. I looked at the shelf of books in front of me and one particular book caught my attention. I picked it up and found that it was "Pranic Healing" by Choa Kok Sui. It had a nice salmon-colored cover, but I had not heard of this before, so I put it back and kept looking. For about a minute! I felt the strongest urge to go back and pick up that book again. I went back, picked it up and looked at it again, reading the jacket cover and then put it back again. I tried to look at other books, but nothing appealed to me *at all*. I tried to just leave the store but only made it half way across the little shops area when I simply had to go back and get that damn salmon-colored book! I went straight back, grabbed it off the shelf and headed for the counter. When I got to the counter, I saw a chrome tear-drop pendulum that caught my eye all of a sudden! I didn't argue or hesitate this time and bought both the book and the pendulum. Now, I was finally ready and able to leave!

So, here I was in this little resort town that had a lot of things going on, on a beautiful summer afternoon. I decided to go get a motel room for the night. While I was in the room, I opened up the book to check it out. I had not even gotten through the first chapter when I heard myself saying "I do this." Not, "I am going to learn how to do this!" But "I do this!" I already knew this stuff! I devoured the book and the next thing I knew it was almost midnight! I had read almost the entire book that day! This was the beginning of my love affair with energy work. At least in this lifetime! Doing energy work led to studying other forms of healing as well. Soon I was trying to develop a well-rounded system that would address the wide array of issues humans deal with. I did not realize that I did not have to re-invent the wheel, but I'll get to that later!

Over time I bought all of Master Choa Kok Sui's books. His deeply spiritual approach appealed to me. Due to the fact that I had trained in the martial arts for quite a few years, I already understood the concept of "Chi", which is Prana, the living life force. I had already learned how to "push" my energy or Chi to stroke meridians. I was also already familiar with acupressure, so this was all second nature to me!

Over time I studied several other forms of energy work. Each has their own beautiful unique aspects that blend perfectly well with the others. Before long, I became certified in EMF Balancing Technique© and found this combination, along with the intuitive energy work Spirit was showing me was very effective! It was years later when I finally decided to get certified as a Reiki Master that I discovered that what Spirit had been teaching me, and I had been calling "intuitive energy work" was in fact, advanced Reiki!

It was the intuitive aspect of healing that really made the difference. Not just in energy work, but in other forms of Lightwork as well. One afternoon I received a phone call from a client I had been working with. She was a single mother of two beautiful, bright-eyed children living in an apartment in an old boarding house. She was highly clairvoyant and her children, being very young themselves were still naturally so themselves. Unfortunately, the night before, the tenant living next door to them had gotten murdered. He was a young man, maybe 18 or 19 and a gang member.

After he had been murdered, he had no concept whatsoever of what to do! He was scared and confused. Once the police entered his apartment, my client's children, who were standing in their open doorway, saw him standing over his own deceased body. He saw the children and could immediately tell they could see him, even though the police could not. So, naturally, he went to my client's apartment where "mom" acknowledged his presence as well. This was when she decided to give me a call, since I was the only one she knew who did any of this kind of Spiritual work.

When I got there, he had returned to his own apartment and the body had been removed. My client explained that she just wanted to protect her children and not have them exposed to this type of situation. She wanted to know if I could help him move on. I told her I could assist, but it wouldn't actually be me doing the work!

The first thing I did was sit on the floor with her and set up a sacred space. Not just in her apartment, but in the entire building.

After I set up this sacred space, I called in a "White Tornado"! This may sound rather silly to some, but one of the first things you learn about working with energy is that "energy flows where the mind goes"! (All energy is conscious, so it reacts to consciousness and intent) I called in a White Tornado with the focused intent to sweep (or should I say vacuum) up and clear all lower frequency energies within the entire building! I closed my eyes and guided it throughout the building until it felt clean. This had actually caught our deceased friend's attention and he came back into my client's apartment to see what was going on! I followed the White Tornado with what is known as the "Platinum Net". I asked that a huge Platinum Net be lowered through the entire building, clearing any and all remaining lower frequency energies into the Earth to be cleansed and transmuted. I do this three times as a general rule. It is a very gentle and nice feeling, but quite powerful and effective.I then focused my awareness on our "friend" who was quite bewildered and standing about 10 feet away from where we were sitting. I could feel his fear, confusion and anxiety. I talked directly to him. I introduced myself and explained that we only wanted to help. I got a brief insight into his mental and emotional state. I saw how he had never been exposed to anything spiritual in his brief life. I introduced him to the beings of Light who were still present from when I set up the Sacred space. I informed him that we were offering him the chance to "Go Home"! I explained that this world had nothing else to offer him but the cold, lonely confusion and frustration he had been experiencing. I told him that all he had to do was make the choice to go with these wonderful, beautiful beings of Light, and they would gladly take him Home!

He did not hesitate! There was an immediate sense of joy that filled the room and we knew he had chosen to go! It was without a doubt the fastest clearing I have ever done.

This is an important concept I hope people will understand. The Light does not "judge" you and bar you from entering the higher realms of Love and Light that have come to be commonly known as "Heaven". There is no Angel guarding the "Gates of Heaven"! Once you do go "Home", you will go through what is known as the Bardo experience. This is a life review. It takes about 3 days of "Earth" time and is why funerals are performed 3 days after a death has occurred. This allows the "deceased" an opportunity to literally go to their own funeral and visit with their loved ones while they are all together! This life review is also why many discarnate beings fear "going home". They know what they have done and do not want to face it in the blunt clarity that exists in the higher dimensions of Love and Light!

The light however, does not judge! One of the Universal Laws is the "Law of Transmutation" which says: "Higher vibrational frequencies will always transmute lower vibrational frequencies"! Anything lower than the frequency of Love cannot enter the higher realms. It is simply transmuted into Love! Damaged souls are taken home and healed in the presence of special Angelic beings who are created perfectly for this purpose!

Think of this…if an old-time shepherd had a flock of sheep on a nice grassy hill and one of the sheep wandered down the hill and got itself hurt, the shepherd would not run down, yell at it, condemn it and throw it in a burning fire! No, he would go pick it up gently, return it to its rightful place with the herd, and heal it if it needed healing. If a shepherd would do this for a sheep, why do we keep telling ourselves that God wouldn't do this for humans? This is effectively saying God has fewer morals and less conscience than we humans! The parable of the prodigal son was trying to tell us this. Anytime you are ready to go home, you can. It is actually inevitable, for all things must return to their Source. This is ultimately the only thing you do not have free will on. The amount of time it takes for you to make your journey home is really the only choice you have. The real question you need to ask yourself is, how much pain do you need to endure before you choose to ask for help?

On another earlier occasion, my dear friend, the Angel Reader mentioned earlier, called me to ask me if I would do a clearing for her daughter who was having a serious problem with some dark entities. My first question was "Why me? Aren't you better suited for this?" She replied quite matter of factly that "Spirit told me you were supposed to!" I knew that her integrity was beyond reproach and I also knew arguing with Spirit was not going to change anything. So, we made arrangements for her, my fiancé at the time (now my beloved wife!) and myself to meet at her daughter's home, which just happened to be very close to where a hospital had been for many decades.

We came to find out, her daughter had been having problems for some time but things had recently escalated dramatically. The incident that had initiated the phone call I received had begun with her having a nightmare. She had a very vivid nightmare that she was being hung by the neck from the rafters above her own bed! She could feel the rope choking her and as she struggled, she woke herself up. The problem was, that waking up did not stop the choking!

She could feel the weight of "someone" sitting on top of her and hands around her throat, choking her. She was starting to pass out and in one final fit of desperation broke herself free and jumped out of bed – yeah, it was time to get some help and do a clearing!

I must say at this point that it was Spirit who taught me how to work with the dark side and those who have not crossed over. The morning of the day I was supposed to do the clearing, I told Spirit: "If you guys are going to put me into these situations, you have to teach me how to do it! That's only fair!"

That day I received a very clear sequence of thoughts or ideas, over several hours that ended up being detailed instructions on exactly how to do this. They are SO AWESOME!

When we got to the house, we all could feel the presence of several entities. It was not a good feeling. I got right to it, and quickly set up a sacred space. I spoke to the entities and discarnate beings present. I introduced "myself" to let them know by what authority I was speaking to them. I then told them to go and round up every discarnate being and entity they knew of because this was extremely important! We gave them about ten to 15 minutes to do so. By the end of that time, the room had such a tight, congested, heavy feeling that it was literally hard to breathe; It felt like there were thousands of them! I asked the others with me if they were having a hard time breathing and they all said they were. My Angel reader friend remarked "Yes, this whole area, even outside is packed! I think you can start now!"

I re-introduced myself to all in attendance now, and explained to them, "You all have noticed a sense of agitation and discomfort recently. There is good reason for this! The vibrational frequency of this planet is increasing, and there is absolutely nothing anyone can do to stop it! This means that it is only going to get more uncomfortable for you the longer you stay here. We are here to offer you the greatest gift any being can offer another. The opportunity to go Home, into the Love and Light of the higher dimensions! You, who are not just discarnate beings may have reservations, and doubt what I am saying, but you do not have to just take my word for it. I now call in my beloved friend Archangel Azrael whom some of you may know better by his former name: 'Azazel'!"

When I said this, there was both an audible and physical sensation that took place in the room! I didn't have to ask if anyone else felt it, I could see their reaction as well! It was a gasp of shock, stunned silence, awe, and amazement all at once! I could feel Azrael's divine presence to my left. I then said "Now you know for a fact that I speak the truth! I now call forth to Archangel Michael and his Legions of Light, to surround us!" There was another uneasy stirring of the "crowd". I said, "Be at ease. We are here to offer you the opportunity to go Home! All you have to do is choose to go willingly and you will be taken by one of the angels in Michael's Legions. We are not forcing anyone to go into the higher realms as that would be a violation of your free will. We are however, setting our boundaries and telling you that while you do not have to go into the Light, you cannot stay here. Again, this planet is ascending. It will only get more and more uncomfortable for you to stay here. If you do not choose to go into the Light, you will be taken to a place that is right and appropriate for you. You cannot stay here! Your time to choose is now!" Within seconds the whole place emptied out. We could all breathe again and there was a sense of relief in all of us! My clairvoyant Angel Reader friend remarked that there were only a small handful that did not choose to go Home. The vast majority accepted this truly golden opportunity. To this day, there have not been any recurrences of disturbing or dark issues at this wonderful lady's house!

I have been involved with many clearings, but this is not the work I choose to do, unless directed by Spirit. In all reality, anyone can do this work. You just have to develop your relationship with Spirit! Again, invite them into your life, talk to them as you would anyone else. Be specific in what you ask of them and pay very close attention to the feelings you get and the synchronicity of events that take place throughout your day.

Then, trust it! Don't let the propaganda of the unconscious people in the world cause you to doubt the experiences that you have. Your experiences are yours forever – own them!

The general technique I use now to do a "Clearing" is as follows:

Create a Sacred Space. (A more complete explanation of creating a sacred space follows later)

Call forth the White Tornado.

Call forth the Platinum Net.

Talk to the beings/entities who are present and explain the current situation with the Shift, why they cannot stay without increasing discomfort, and that they are being offered the opportunity to go Home. Free and clear.

Then ask the Angels to take them Home, or to wherever is "right and appropriate for them".

Then, you can burn sage, palo santo, sweet grass, or whatever your preference is.

(Many people have been taught that you can "drive out or clear out" entities and discarnate beings by using white sage, salt, drumming, rattles, salt and other methods such as these. These methods are actually for restoring good clean energy and inviting Beings of Light, after the dark ones are cleared! Truly dark entities will literally laugh at you and your attempts to drive them out using these things. You really need to call in the Angelic Realm!)

An incredibly powerful __final__ cleansing of the energy, is to pour Epsom salts into a heat/fire resistant container and then pour 90% rubbing alcohol over it until it covers the Epsom salts.

Place this on another heat resistant baking dish and put this on the floor, in the middle of the room. (Preferably on a towel)

Light the alcohol on fire and observe the change in the energy of the room as it burns. By the time the alcohol burns up, the energy will be clearer than you have ever experienced!

The important thing to remember is that you are never alone. Spirit is always with you and ready to help if you give them permission by inviting them and/or asking them to help.

Then learn to stand in your own light and work with them, no matter what you are doing!

One final note on those people doing dark magic, you know, playing on the "dark side":

Everything in this universe is raising in vibrational frequency, even on this planet. The "top echelon" of the dark side started their journey back into the Light almost 20 years ago! Their minions do not however, know that the ultimate joke is on them. All things travel in a circle, and that includes souls and energies/entities on their journeys. Returning to the Light is inevitable because it is Universal Law!

So, play there if you must...until it hurts bad enough that you hit rock bottom, and learn the painful lessons you apparently haven't learned yet.

Don't worry, – we'll leave the Light on for ya!

CHAPTER 6

ON DEATH AND DYING

"There is no such thing as death,
There is only the transition of the soul
from this dimension to the higher ones –
I call it: Going Home"

– Marty Rawson

I have had far too many experiences with those who have crossed over to have any doubt whatsoever about whether or not our souls and consciousness continue on after our transition from these mortal lives in physical reality. These have even occurred with people who were agnostics, people who truly had no belief one way or the other concerning an afterlife.

Let us start off by saying, there is no such thing as death. There is only an event where the Spirit leaves the body. It is the transition from this temporal world back to the Eternal higher dimensions. It is a rebirth and reunion with all the Beings of Light that are your true family. I believe those of us with truly Spiritual understandings should change our funeral rituals to reflect a much higher standard of consciousness and understanding. As for myself, I do not want my funeral to be like any I have attended or witnessed. A Ceremony celebrating the life that was lived is much more appropriate.

One evening a few years after the trip to Egypt, I received a phone call from an acquaintance whose wife's mother was on her death bed. His wife was quite distraught about her mother, and whether or not she would "go into the Light" as we say. I made the quick trip to this neighboring town where they were, and joined them at the retirement home where her mother was at.

As soon as I walked into the room, I sensed an angelic presence hovering at the foot of her bed and at least two other beings waiting there beside her. His wife asked me frantically if her mother had anyone with her or waiting for her and I did my best to calm her down and assure her that "Yes, she did indeed have loved ones with her" and all was well. I was not there too long that evening once she calmed down, but they did ask me to come back the following day.

I arrived the next day, in the early afternoon. Her mother was definitely very close to passing. I was quite surprised she had held on this long. There was a knock on the door and two men entered in suits. They introduced themselves as clergy with the local dominant church and my friend's wife then told me that she had invited them to perform the equivalent of a "Last Rights" ceremony. They stated that we were welcome to stay and observe the ceremony. I was quite interested to see what this ceremony entailed. Especially since I had been informed prior to this that this woman was not "in good standing" with this same church. It seems that since she could not afford her tithing and did not attend services regularly, she had been openly ostracized by them for many years. They did however conduct themselves in a professional manner while they were there.

We stepped back as these two men approached the bed and one of them began a prayer speaking to "Our Father in Heaven" on this woman's behalf. I knew from previous conversations with my friends that he had never met her and did not even know her name, yet he took it upon himself to intercede on her behalf as though she needed his help in order to go home! He spoke of her as if he knew her personally and implied things in this "prayer" to God that he could not possibly know about this woman. He then proclaimed that by *his* authority she should be allowed to enter "heaven". By the time it was done all sense of divinity had been sucked out of the room entirely and I had the most hollow, empty feeling I think I have ever had in connection with anything that was supposed to be a religious rite. This entire "ceremony" had been so totally devoid of anything remotely approaching love, compassion and sincerity, let alone Divinity! There was nothing "Spiritual" about it!

I asked the angels to please be with this woman once again and take her home into the Light. I immediately received a confirmation and knew they already had it all under control, long before *any* of us had arrived. I left shortly afterwards because I was concerned I might say something that would be unflattering towards what had just taken place. I went home and wondered what should really be done when a loved one passes? I wasn't concerned with the pompous actions of clergymen who were only concerned with impressing others with their imagined status and "authority". I was concerned with finding out what Spirit actually recommended that we should do to help our loved ones make a loving transition, that honored them and their lives. I stewed on this for several days, maybe a week and suddenly one day I got a sudden knowing that I had to go to a particular store at the other end of town. I called to my wife and told her we needed to get ready and go to this store, and she asked why? I simply laughed and told her that I didn't know yet, but that I had to go and she was more than welcome to join me. So off we went.

This was a store we had not even been in before. We walked in the front doors and stopped several feet inside and looked around. My wife saw something off to the left she wanted to check out so she went that way. I had no idea what I was looking for so I just basically wandered straight ahead. I wasn't really paying any attention and was just looking around as I strolled. When I got to the back of the store, I found that I was at the edge of the "Books" section of the store. I took a right turn and headed towards the end of the back shelf and stopped about four or five feet from the end and looked at the section I was in. It was the "Spiritual and Self-Help" section which I found slightly humorous at the time. I then knelt down and noticed a book on the bottom shelf directly in front of my feet. It was "Shaman, Healer, Sage" by Alberto Villoldo. I looked at it briefly and put it back, wanting to look around more. Nothing else caught my attention. I picked it up again and checked it out a little closer. It looked interesting. Pretty much right up my alley, but again I didn't want to be hasty. I mean, I had literally just walked into this store, for the first time, walked straight to the back, went to the end of a book shelf, knelt down and picked up this book that was directly in front of my feet! I put it back a second time to give myself a chance to look around more. I wandered about for some time, but nothing else appealed to me even remotely. I found myself back at this book's location when my wife found me. She asked me if I had found anything and I told her of my little adventure so far, but added that I didn't know If I should get it. She gave me "the look" and told me without any hesitation whatsoever to get it – it was obviously what Spirit had sent me for! I must admit, I felt a little silly at that moment because I knew she was right, but I was also amazed at the lengths Spirit will go to – to give you confirmation of something. I also have to wonder how many times they are standing there shaking their heads in loving disbelief and wonder at how dense we humans are on this side of the veil? Thank "God" they are truly Beings of unconditional Love and Light, with a great sense of humor!

I absolutely loved the book and it is still one of my favorite books in my rather large collection. I read the entire book and loved it. Lo and behold…It just so happens that there was a chapter that was concerned with death and dying. Taken in context with the whole book, this was exactly the information I had been looking for. It covered the entire spiritual process of what takes place when we leave this life and the proper warnings and admonitions towards actions to be taken for our loved ones. It had honor, Love and dignity and it was clearly working with Spirit, or "Luminous Beings" as they are often called in Shamanic terms.

I highly recommend this book for many reasons, but this section alone is worth the price. This process provides three major steps in assisting a dying person in their passage from this world. These are things that should be common sense, but we don't tend to think of them by ourselves.

The first is Recapitulation and Forgiveness. Many people die without ever having the opportunity to tell their story, to just actually be heard one last time. This gives closure to the person who is transitioning and gives them the opportunity to forgive others and ask forgiveness one last time before they go. This is invaluable to those who take advantage of this opportunity. It can literally make a huge difference in the life review a soul experiences – shortly after they go Home. This is one of the greatest gifts a human being can give to another. Just listen to their story, however they wish to tell it and perhaps occasionally point out opportunities for forgiveness. It isn't often you can touch another person's soul in such a meaningful manner.

The second step is granting them permission to die; to go Home. Let them know that they are loved and they will be missed, but that it is okay for them to go Home. Assure them that all their loved ones still here will be fine. Many times people will cling to life longer than is good for anyone involved, out of fear that their loved ones need them and won't be taken care of in their absence. They need reassurance that everyone will be okay, even though they will be missed by everyone. You can ask them to come to you every time you think of them with love in your heart. You can even ask them to give you signs they are there with you after they go. If you think about this step, you will realize how important it will be for you to know your loved ones are going to be okay!

The third step is the actual Final Rites that take place immediately after the person passes over. This can be done by anyone actually, but preferably by someone familiar with chakra/energy work and a person of a spiritual nature. When done with love and compassionate intent for the deceased, in coordination with the Angelic realm, it is very, very effective and spiritually fulfilling in that it provides assurance that the soul is not still attached to the physical body or this 3rd dimensional reality, which can happen. In fact, it happens more often than people would care to know, especially in our current culture.

The technique is to start by calling forth the Angels and Beings of Light that feel right to you and of course, those held dear by the deceased, if you know who those are. You need to ask them for their loving support in assisting with guiding this beloved soul back home, into the Love and Light of the Higher Realms. Then, holding your right hand a few inches above the 4th chakra, begin a counter clockwise spiral motion that expands outward from the center, and goes down to the 3rd chakra, then up and around to the 5th, then back down and around to the 2nd, back around and up to the 6th, down and around to the 1st and finally circling up to the 7th, then lifting your hand upwards as you bring it back to center. All the while giving your loving intent to draw forth and release this beautiful soul into the presence of the Angels you have called forth. You may even want to add verbal comments to the departed to "Go Home now, into the Light, with these beautiful Angels." They will take it from there. This does not force the individual to "Go into the Light", it merely gives them one last opportunity, in the presence of Angels, to make their own choice.

Unfortunately, many of the world's organized religions and their clergymen have totally forgotten, or are never even taught, why they perform various actions during the "Last Rights". This can be quite alarming because some of them are literally sealing or binding a soul to the deceased body without even knowing it. When a priest draws a cross over the 6th chakra (Third eye) and then another cross over the 4th chakra (Heart Chakra), they can confine an unconscious soul to the body. This can also happen if a soul has not quite realized yet that they have died, and the Clergyman is too quick to administer Last Rites.

I am sure this may be upsetting to many people and I am also quite sure that it will be disputed if brought to the attention of the various organized religions, but then again, what else would you expect? These souls can still be helped, it just makes things more difficult for everyone, especially the deceased.

I was very glad to learn of these things a couple months later when I was informed that my father was not expected to live much longer. I took a week off from work and went to visit him. I had plenty of time to visit and ask him questions and got him to tell me as much of his story as he wanted to share. I just talked to him, but mostly listened. I tried to recommend forgiveness when it seemed appropriate. When the nurse told us that he would probably not last another day I made sure to let him know how much we all loved him and that we would all be okay. It did seem to provide him peace and comfort. I was with him that night when he passed. I lovingly called to Archangels Michael and Azrael, and to All Beings that could assist with this transition, and with great compassion and sincerity, immediately performed the Final Rights as described above, to release his soul to the Angelic realm and ensure he was free of this physical world and his body. The entire room was filled with loving energy and I could feel his presence. He seemed more at peace than at any time in his mortal existence and I knew – that he knew – how much I loved him!

The main thing to remember is this: There is truly no such thing as death, not the way we think of it... The body dies and decomposes.

But the soul, the being, the consciousness – lives on as an eternal Being of Light. In fact, going Home is quite liberating, when your time is up.

The admonition against suicide is because these lives are considered to be an incredibly sacred aspect of our Spiritual journey back to total unity consciousness with Source. There are countless souls lined up to take this "crash course" in emotions, and to throw it away is a slap in the face to Source and all of those still waiting. You also have to start it all over again and go through all your lessons and experiences that you failed to learn this time.

So not worth it! But, contrary to popular religious dogma, and generational indoctrination, souls who have committed suicide do indeed go to what we refer to as "Heaven", aka the 5th dimension! They go there, as long as there is nothing else holding them back (like their beliefs, attachments to this material world, etc.) They are tended to and healed by groups of Angels who are specifically created to do this type of soul healing. God is Love, and he doesn't throw his children away, or burn them in a pit of fire, just because they had a nightmare and couldn't handle it.

No, he loves them and heals them when they wake up "at Home", and then when they are all better, lovingly allows them to carry on with their eternal journey of growth and learning.

While we can truly say there really is no death that does not lessen the pain of losing a loved one, for those still in these physical lives. This loss is very painful and it hits us deeply, to the very core of our beings. The physical loss of a loved one is truly a devastating thing to go through.

When this happens, allow yourself to go through the stages of grief. This is a natural process of letting go and getting closure, and it should be allowed to progress by honoring the emotions as you go through them.

Honor them and let them go as soon as you are able. The important thing is to not "stay there", emotionally. Extended grief that leads to depression only harms yourself, and in many cases, inhibits the departed souls from moving on. When carried to an extreme, it can be an incredibly selfish act that harms both the living and the souls who are trying to move on.

Try to understand that the departed soul is going, or has gone – Home, and is literally with the Angelic realm, healing anything and everything that they need healed. They are in the thickness of Divine Love that only exists there, in the higher dimensions. They are happy and want you to be happy and continue your life with joy. Think about what you would want for the ones you love most dearly, after you go home. That is what they also wish for you!

Also remember, that while you may miss their physical presence, they were not always readily available to you while they were physically alive. Now, they are! All you have to do is feel all the Love you have for them. When you think of them with sincere Love, they are instantly drawn to you through the magnetic attraction of Love! Loving, conscious energy is the very fabric of this multi-dimensional universe and it transcends all dimensional boundaries. Practice expanding your awareness and your sensitivity and you can spend even more time with them than ever. Please be courteous though, as they still have things to do, just like you do!

If you have a loved one who has passed on, watch for clues and signs that they may be trying to communicate with you. Some of the favorite ways they do this is by causing the lights to flicker in the room you are in. Sometimes, they will leave pennies or other coins as a sign for you. Sometimes feathers are left or they may cause you to smell a scent you would associate with them, such as perfume or even cigar/cigarette smoke. Other times, they may actually come to you in your dreams! This is my favorite way, and how many, many family members and dear friends have contacted me to let me know they are doing fine! Many times, I have even been able to have conversations with them, and sometimes they are just there, at a bit of a distance, looking straight into my eyes with a knowing smile of contentment on their face. A smile that says "I made it and you know what? You aren't as crazy as I thought you were! You were right!"

As mentioned above, I hope that we can make changes in the way we conduct our funeral services to reflect our change of consciousness. Funeral services do, of course, vary – depending on who is conducting them, but for the most part, they are sad, solemn events. Have you actually thought about what you want at your funeral? It is one of the very few things you can count on happening in the future. Do you want professional mourners to be hired so others can witness people wailing and crying over your passing? Or do you want a gathering of friends and family remembering your life and their experiences with you?

Let us speak to the Creator and address our prayer for the departed in a dignified manner.

"Beloved Creator, as you know, _"Name"_ has come home to you. We ask that you cradle _"him/her"_ in the arms of your Angels, heal them and welcome _"him/her"_ home. May _"he/she"_ always feel the Love of the ones they leave behind and may they come to visit us on occasion in our dreams, as we miss them dearly."

Then, as far as my own funeral is concerned, let there be a feast and a Celebration of Life with the people who care enough to be there, sharing their memories of me that are significant to them.

As for my body, cremate it. We do not need to fill this planet with acres upon acres of decomposing bodies that are boxed up and incapable of returning their elemental composition back to the Earth. You know, that whole "Earth to Earth, ashes to ashes, and dust to dust" thing that modern burials do not allow.

The bottom line is, these physical lives are a drop in the bucket compared to the life of your eternal soul. You leave when your learning is done in that particular lifetime, although not finished as far as your soul is concerned! You simply go home, heal as needed, and celebrate your accomplishments with your true family. You then prepare yourself for your next grand adventure, whatever it is. This could be another lifetime on a physical world of dust, or some other experience that suits the desires of your soul from its renewed, enlightened perspective.

From the perspective of a soul in this world, where we literally perceive less than one billionth of "What Is", the possibilities are truly endless!

Those who choose to lie in a black box for eternity and experience "nothing" – good luck with that. Let us know how that works for you. I have much better things to do.

CHAPTER 7

THE KALEIDOSCOPE OF ENERGY

*"The grandeur and intricacy of this Universe
belies its fractal, holographic nature.
Such is the beauty of the Mind of God!"*

– Marty Rawson

My intent for this chapter is to explain some of the topics that people seem to have questions about, and doing so in the way that Spirit has explained them to me. The connection between the various topics is "energy" itself, and the vast diversity in which it reacts and manifests.

Let us first discuss the phrase "fractal, holographic Universe". There seems to be some confusion created by this intimidating phrase. First off what does "fractal" mean? A fractal is a repeating pattern that has the same appearance and likeness regardless of scale. It looks the same when you zoom in as it does when you zoom out.

A hologram is a 3D image created from light (lasers) aka energy, which consists of fractals. In other words, every part of a hologram contains the entire "image". A part of the hologram contains all the information as the entire hologram does.

Since everything is living, conscious energy, and energy is Light, this physical 3D universe is ultimately a manifestation and expression of the higher dimensions, and everything in it is a fractal and holographic play of Light and Consciousness. This is where Sacred Geometry and the Golden Ratio/Fibonacci sequence comes in. In essence, you are a fractal of God, The First Source and Center of All That Is. You are a Fractal of the universe. Later on, we will discuss how astrology works and I will show you the fractal holographic relationship I am talking about.

Our souls have a specific anatomy, just like our bodies do. In order for our souls to inhabit these suits of flesh, there has to be an intricate and complex connection between the two, including and most importantly, the wiring system!

The chakra system has had much written about it. I will not go into great depth on this subject but will give a sufficient overview for our purposes. Each chakra is a complex energy center that governs many aspects of our humanity and controls many functions, while simultaneously providing the majority of the prana required, especially for the endocrine glands each one is associated with. Each chakra is also associated with specific emotional issues and aspects of our lives. The chakras are reservoirs of energy and doorways between the physical and the higher, etheric worlds.

Every chakra can be overactive or underactive. Either one is an aberration, and with each chakra, will cause their own unique mental and emotional issues, or possibly even physical diseases.

The First Chakra, formally known as Muladhara, is associated with the adrenal glands and is related to how grounded you are in this world. It is also intimately connected to your survival instincts. This chakra is affected by your relationship to your "tribe", whoever you consider your tribe to be.

The Second Chakra, formally known as Svadishthana, is associated with our testes or ovaries, and is related to your relationships in life. It is also the primary chakra connected to your creativity, in both the usual artistic sense and the pro-creative sense. This chakra is most affected by the honoring or dis-honoring of others and/or them honoring or dis-honoring you.

The Third Chakra, formally known as Manipura, is associated with your pancreas and is related to your personal power. This chakra is connected to your ambition, achievements and success in life. This chakra is affected by you honoring or dis-honoring yourself.

(Notice the lower three chakras all relate to life in this physical world, while the higher 4 chakras are concerned with higher, more spiritual aspects of our Being.)

The Fourth Chakra, formally known as Anahata, is associated with the thymus and the heart, and is related to your ability to love. This chakra is connected to the emotions of love and or hate. It is negatively affected by anger and hatred, and these will in fact weaken your immune system. The opposite is true as well though. Love strengthens your heart chakra and your immune system!

The Fifth Chakra, formally known as Vishuddhi, is associated with the thyroid and is related to your communication abilities, or the lack thereof. This chakra is also directly connected to your emotions, and can be affected negatively if they are suppressed and withheld, or expressed to the point of being overactive.

The Sixth Chakra, formally known as Ajna, is associated with the pineal gland and is related to your intuition and even clairvoyance. It is related to your willingness or unwillingness to face reality, and is also affected by your willingness or unwillingness to seek higher truths.

The Seventh Chakra, formally known as Sahasrara, is associated with the pituitary gland and is related to your spiritual quest for self-realization. It is affected by your embracing of, or rejection of, higher spiritual truths.

There are actually many other chakras in the body, mostly minor ones. This does not mean they are unimportant; it simply means they are not as large as the major ones most people are aware of. Many of them are found in the joints of the body and facilitate the proper flow of energy through the limbs of the body. You can actually detect the presence of all the chakras and their state of "flow" with the use of a pendulum. A full circle indicates good energy flow, a straight line "to and fro" indicates a partially blocked flow, and no movement at all indicates a total blockage of energy flow! Once you get sensitive enough to energy you can detect these states of energy flow by scanning with your hands. There are however, two more major chakras that are important to the main anatomy of the spirit, that are usually ignored in the mainstream dialogue. These can also be felt and/or detected using a pendulum.

These are the "Earth" Chakra, which is below the feet, and is the primary grounding force to the Earth itself. This works in harmony with the First Chakra.

The other one is the "Star" chakra, which is above your head, and is a portal to the higher realms once the other chakras have been mastered.

Running through these chakras and connecting them is the pranic tube, formally known as the Shushumna nadi. This is a tube of light that exists at the center of your very soul. It is from the pranic tube that the antahkarana extends to your higher self. The Shushumna or pranic tube is the aspect of your soul that can never be disturbed.

Have you ever been in a situation that terrified you, and your body went into a panic, – but then, a still, peaceful, part of you somehow "knew" you were going to be alright? That was this part of your own soul communicating to you!

Out of the root chakra, to each side of the Pranic tube, two more major nadis (for our purposes, let's call them "etheric channels for energy") weave their way upward through the body. These are the "Ida" (masculine and heating energy), and the "Pingala" (feminine and cooling energy). As they weave their way upwards through the body, they cross each other. Where they cross, the chakras exist. (Most depictions of the chakra system portray these two nadis as erroneously crossing between the chakras.) These two nadis do not extend all the way up to the seventh chakra however. Once they depart the fifth chakra at the throat, they come up to below the eyes and bend back down towards each nostril. To those with clairvoyance, these appear as being similar to two serpents, and are usually depicted as cobras in art work. These two nadis, along with the pranic tube, are the basis for the ancient symbol for medicine; the caduceus. It has been used since the most ancient of times and still is to this day. Most, even in the medical field have no idea of its origin. This symbol was given to humanity by the ancient wise men and women who could "See", in other words, they were clairvoyant. When this system is truly healthy, the person is healthy!

There are seven more major nadis in addition to these three, and a total of seventy-two thousand minor nadis that branch out to bring prana to every cell and part of the body. When viewed all together, these resemble the branches of a tree.

Around this anatomy, there exists what is called the koshas, or sheaths. These are sheaths that encompass the energy body. The first sheath is the physical body itself (Annomaya kosha), then, etherically, there are the Breath sheath (Pranamaya kosha), the Emotional sheath (Manomaya kosha), the Intellectual sheath (Vijnanamaya kosha) and finally the Bliss sheath (Anandamaya kosha). These are more and more subtle as they progress outward and are in fact what is seen as a person's "Aura".

This is not a complete description of the anatomy of the spirit, but should more than suffice for our purposes.

Let us now move our attention to one of the ways disease forms in the body. We all know that toxins in the body weaken our immune systems and that other things, such as viruses can cause disease. That is obvious, and not what we are going to be talking about here. The other way to form disease in your body, is through the misuse of thought and emotion. I say misuse because whether it is intentional or not, it is still ultimately wrong use of these powerful aspects of ourselves that tend to cause the majority of our health problems through stress.

Part of this is due to the fact that we, as a civilization, are not taught, nor do we teach our young, how to deal with emotional trauma. More on this later.

As it is, we go through life experiencing many traumatic experiences from the time we are very young to the end of our lives. There is a wonderful book called "Feelings Buried Alive Never Die" by Karol K. Truman. It is not only a highly recommended book; it is an indisputable fact. (Buy the book!)

As we go through life and experience these emotional traumas, our culture in the west has historically disapproved of the expression of emotions. We tell our children all sorts of things just to shut them up and hold their feelings in. It was worse in generations passed, but is still not where it should be. Many times, we stuff our feelings inside ourselves, mostly because we don't want to feel the pain. Whatever the reason, the result is the same.

Thoughts and feelings are energy and energy carries information. Every time you bury negative thoughts and emotions inside, they go straight to the chakra that is related to that emotional issue. If and when the chakras actually fill up and overflow with negative energy, these energies will then continue on to the various organs and bones associated with their chakras. When the lower chakras are full, the hips, being the largest bone mass in the body, serve as the final repository for negative energies.

When the chakras fill up with negative energy, it usually tends to slow the chakra down. It will become sluggish and it will not be able to provide the good clean energy to the glands and organs that rely on it. As the situation gets worse with more and more negative energy accumulating, the chakra can become so clogged up with this tar-like energy that it will stop the chakra from spinning and working at all. When this happens, disease is already formed in the body. The organs themselves have had nothing but thick, heavy, polluted, toxic, tar-like energy to live on for far too long! If it is caught before this, disease formation may be stopped or reversed as the case may be. If not, you are already in pain and have developed disease. This is the arena of the Energy worker.

While I am a Holy Fire® III Karuna® Reiki Master, I am also trained in other forms of energy work and more. A perfect complement to Reiki is EMF Balancing. The reason it compliments Reiki so well, is that it teaches you how to pull congested energy out of the chakras and body, rather than just channeling energy.

I offer this analogy: If you are trying to empty a bucket full of mud, you could do it by standing over it with a hose, and pour the water into it until eventually all the mud is slowly flushed out over the sides of the bucket. This is going to take a while, and it is extremely inefficient. Myself, I prefer to empty the bucket of mud and then fill it with clean water. This is much more efficient, and works like a charm when you transfer this concept to clearing chakras! THEN, you can provide your client with the beautiful, clean and vibrant energy your client so richly deserves. You will find this much more efficient and effective! My students have dubbed this "The Marty Method"!

Okay, so we have covered the formation of disease caused from congested chakras. If you noticed, the lower three chakras deal specifically with issues related to these physical lives.

What happens when a person has truly severe issues and aberrations regarding the topics of Earthly attachment or a totally materialistic mentality? How about extreme sexual perversions and/or addiction to power, greed, or domination over others?

When these issues are carried to extreme lengths, they create an attachment to this materialistic, physical world. Ever hear the saying that you create your reality absolutely? Well, that doesn't change just because you pass on from this physical life! Your consciousness goes with you, and as anyone with any experience with the Law of Attraction knows – the universe or whatever you want to call it, does not judge what you choose to focus your attention on. It merely responds by delivering energy "like unto itself". In these cases, the individual souls have chosen by their own attachments and willpower, to stay in this reality. This even extends to people who are atheists or people who are extremely angry at God for something that happened to them during their life!

In case you were wondering, this is how souls become Earth bound and become discarnate human beings, otherwise known as "ghosts". Those souls that are set on their negative ways, often continue to prey energetically on humans who are alive, who have the same "issues" that they had.

Others may learn from their errors and ask for help, and heal themselves with help from the Angelic realm. Still others may dwell in their mental and emotional prison for as long as they will, their ego not allowing them to see their errors in judgement, and not realizing they literally created their own prison -in their own minds.

Crystals, Color and Sound Therapy

"Crystals are living beings at the beginning of creation."

– Nikola Tesla

Crystal, color and sound therapies all work on the same fundamental principle. As you may have figured out by now, that is "vibrational frequency".

Let's say you decide to go to a crystal therapist for your chakras. You get there and they have you lie down on a massage table or whatever, put on some relaxing music and put stones and crystals of the appropriate color on your chakras. You don't really feel much of anything, but you slowly relax into it.

Depending on your issue(s), you may or may not show some improvement after the session, but you more than likely will feel more relaxed. If you go to several sessions, you probably will notice improvements. The question is – why? How does this work?

As we have said, everything is energy, and the only difference between energies is the vibrational frequency. In color we measure vibrational frequency from the infra-red to the ultra-violet, a system obviously based on our human eyesight. In sound, we have developed the musical scale and have created machines to detect sounds both above and below our hearing range. Both color (Light) and sound are the two primary characteristics of "Energy" because of the friction generated at the most basic level in the quantum field; the Planck scale. These infinitesimal particles of energy are packed so tightly together that they cannot do anything but vibrate.

Vibration creates friction, and friction creates light and sound. Now, let's bring this up to our level in the universe and realize that because of this, we have the Universal law of Vibration, that simply states "Everything Vibrates"

So, here we are, electromagnetic fields of individualized awareness, temporarily couped up in a meat suit, with amnesia, and in the Emotional University of the Galaxy. Yeah…we fluctuate. A lot. All over the place actually. We are not taught how to deal with trauma or deeply emotional issues and so we bury them inside of us until they kill us. Or… we go get help, which brings us right back to the massage table with your crystals laying on your chakras.

Now these chakras may be hyperactive or hypoactive, in other words, they may be going too fast or too slow. Typically, the vast majority of the time, they are hypoactive; that is slowed down or stopped altogether.

So what good does a stone or crystal do?

That stone or crystal does one thing, and it does it very well. It just stays being itself. It cannot change. It cannot fluctuate or vibrate or have an emotional breakdown! Its stability is its magic and its blessing to us. When you put a red stone on the root chakra, the stone simply stays consistent in its vibration. Your chakra wants to be at its original optimum "setting", and it is the only thing that *can* change in this scenario. The electromagnetic field of the chakra will then self-regulate itself to its optimum, healthy vibrational frequency.

It is not woo-woo hocus-pocus, it is 8th grade physical science.

Color therapy works the same way. The only difference here is that it is your eyes that take in the frequency of the color. This is an important point to remember, everything you take in, through any-and- all of your senses, has an effect on you and your vibrational frequency. It either raises it, or lowers it. This means everything you experience – what you see and watch, what you listen to, what you feel through your touch, what you eat, and what you smell. It is all information about your environment, so you can make wise choices concerning what your true goals are.

Colors have a great impact on us emotionally. This has been a science for many, many years. Even the staunchest of scientists cannot deny the effects that color has on the human psyche. This is used by hospitals, mental hospitals, doctors' offices of all kinds, as well as fashion designers, interior decorators and advertising companies.

Of course, sound therapy comes in many forms. From music to mantra, binaural beats to subliminal messaging and many, many more. The chakras also are affected by sounds. Your psyche and emotions are as well. Each of the chakras have an optimum tone that coincides with their appropriate frequency. So, from the root chakra on up we find that the chakras have both color and sound that corresponds to their frequency:

Root Chakra: Red, C Note
Sacral Chakra: Orange, D Note
Solar Plexus: Yellow, E Note,
Heart Chakra: Green, F Note,
Throat Chakra: Blue, G Note,
Third Eye: Indigo, A Note,
Crown: Violet, B Note.

This is, of course, what the Singing Bowls and Tuning Forks are for.

The reason you want your chakras working at an optimum efficiency is because they supply the energy to your organs, including the very important endocrine glands, which govern your body's processes. Yeah, you want them working for you and bringing in clean, vibrant energy, instead of being all clogged up with dark, heavy, sticky, sludge for energy. As an energy worker with over two decades of experience, I can tell you that this dark, heavy energy can even be painful for us to pull out of the chakras when they are overly congested. I have often felt the heaviness and discomfort all the way up to my elbows before getting rid of it.

A couple of words concerning chakras. If anyone offers to "open" your chakras for you, run. Do not let them work on you! They are either too ignorant to know what they are doing and do not know the correct terminology, or worse, they are going to hurt you – permanently. What an energy worker does is "clear" chakras, of old, heavy, sludgy energy that doesn't serve you anymore. This restores them back to optimum working capacity. To suddenly have any of your chakras "opened" before you are actually and naturally ready for it would land you in a mental institution, and the people there could not ever help you. They wouldn't have a clue how to.

Now, while Crystals, Color, and Sound are all excellent Tools to use for your benefit, please understand that they are subtle therapies. Here in the west, we have been programmed into thinking that in order for something to work, or have value, its effect must be immediate and powerful. The problem with this is that most people don't ever heal the problem at its source, they mask the symptoms of the problem with a pill. Eventually the side effects of that strong pharmaceutical causes other diseases and they take another chemical pill for that. It goes on and on, and it has been shown that once you are taking 5 prescriptions or more, you are severely reducing your life expectancy.

Subtle therapies do not work by force, but they do not mask symptoms either, nor do they have side effects – except better health and happiness.

I would be negligent if I failed to mention the incredible work of Masaru Emoto. His book "The Hidden Messages in Water" is a must read for anyone studying spirituality and metaphysics. He proved that water retains information and can be "programmed". He conducted scientific experiments in controlled environments using frozen water, emotions and a microscope equipped to take pictures. He proved that the crystal formation patterns generated by emotions were repeatable and distinct. He showed that emotions like Love, compassion and gratitude created unique, beautiful crystal formations while negative emotions and even words created deformed, globular, unsymmetrical messes.

He conducted experiments involving Buddhist Monks who prayed over polluted water and many more, very interesting experiments. He wrote many books, all of which are worth owning! Unfortunately, we are no longer graced with his loving and wise presence, but his work will live on forever. They are one of the most powerful and clear collections of proof of consciousness affecting matter, and the crystalline nature of water!

Astrology

And now, let us move on to astrology. This is included because this entire chapter has been concerned with some of the lesser talked about aspects of energy. I received this information in a literal vision, where Spirit walked me through the specifics as it went. I have been told that the standard theory concerning how astrology works which is most commonly passed around, is that it is the moon causing a pull on the water in the body, just as it does the Earth's tides. I don't buy into that one. I don't doubt the pull of the moon has an effect. I doubt that it's the effect on the "water in the body", that is what causes the unique effect on our mental/emotional/spiritual aspect of our very being – that we call "astrological".

Now, have you ever seen the electromagnetic field of the Earth and or the sun, or the Galaxy, or the Universe? They are the same as a magnet. There is a toroidal, electromagnetic field with a pole at each end of its axis. Energy and Light carry information. This toroidal shape provides a feedback loop for outgoing and incoming energy/information – on all scales. The human electromagnetic field is exactly the same. The incredible difference with the human energy field is that those with the highest level of clairvoyance can actually see the Pranic tube, or pillar of Light that exists at the center of your very being!

(Can you say fractal, holographic? – I knew you could!)

If you can shift your imagination to an energetic view of things, you can envision the entire solar system as a huge electromagnetic sphere where the sun is being orbited by all the planets which are also electromagnetic spheres. You can zoom out farther and see the same thing at a galactic scale. The greatest minds in Quantum theory now strongly believe the shape of the Universe itself is a Torus. The same shape as your magnetic field!

As you now mentally zoom in towards Earth, you will see about seven and a half billion or more little toroidal, electromagnetic fields scurrying about on the surface of this electro-magnetic planet.

Now, if you watch closely as the moon orbits the Earth, you will see that the moon actually causes distortions in their electromagnetic fields. The amount of distortion is in proportion to their location on the planet and how directly the moon is in line with the sun. When the moon is directly opposite the Sun, the pull of the electromagnetic field of both is the strongest, and has the most effect on the magnetic field of the humans scurrying about on the surface, going about their business. Of course, if you warp the electromagnetic field of humans, their mental and emotional stability is going to be affected!

Every employee of every police station, hospital and nursing home in the world will testify to the fact that full moons affect people, and not usually in a positive way. If this fact dealt with any other topic than astrology, it would be listed as a scientific fact. When science is no longer controlled by the status quo in power and starts to study observable phenomenon like this, instead of childishly denying the facts – maybe we would learn a great deal more about how our world and universe really work!

Now, let us back on out from our close-up view of Earth and take the entire solar system into account. There are many planets each orbiting the sun along with Earth, each at their own speeds and masses, and therefore, their own unique gravitational pull.

We need to remember that the void of space is not actually a void. At the Planck scale there is no such thing as empty space. The void of space is actually full of not only many smaller physical "items", but also Energy at its most fundamental state, which provides zero resistance or interference to the pull of electromagnetic fields in relation to one another. This means the effect of the gravitational pull of the planets is instantaneous! This also explains the instantaneous travel of information at the speed of "thought", across the Universe. The matrix at the level of the Quantum Field is the unified field of consciousness!

Now, as these planets orbit, the distortions created on any specific human being is slightly different from any other, depending on their location on the planet. The constant motion of the planets provide an ever-changing dynamic situation for maximum and unique variation. Now let's look at the electromagnetic field of a baby being born at any specific location. At the moment of its birth, there is a unique electromagnetic "warpage" or "stamp", if you will, on the very DNA of that child. It is the "warpage" of the DNA that is specific to the exact location, at that exact time, of birth of that child. This will forever define how this individual's energy field reacts, in its own unique way, to the electromagnetic pull of the solar system's astronomical bodies.

What most people here in the west are familiar with, is called Tropical astrology. This has gotten a bad reputation because of cheesy newspaper columns. Many years ago, a friend of mine took me over to a friend of hers who she wanted me to meet. When we got to his house, his wife invited us in, as he happened to be in a back room at that moment. He greeted us as he entered his living room, and we were introduced. He immediately asked me what my birthday was, where I was born and the time of day of my birth. I did happen to know this information, so I told him. For the next four hours, he told me my own life story. It was as if he had a script of my life in front of him, or as if he had witnessed the entire lifetime for himself! On a later occasion, he did the same thing with my father's information! I have never doubted since then that there was validity to astrology, when it is done by qualified people.

Remember that there is more than one type of astrology. In the East, they generally practice what is called Sidereal Astrology, sometimes referred to as Vedic Astrology. This type of astrology has been used for thousands and thousands of years as a means of knowing when a person has medical vulnerabilities in specific areas of their being. I am sure it is used for many other purposes as well, but this one of its documented purposes that goes back as long as history has been recorded. Sidereal Astrology has to do with our relationship to the galaxy and the Galactic Center, not our solar system and its Sun. (Remember our earlier "zoomed-out" picture of the galaxy as an electromagnetic field?)

This brings us to an interesting side note concerning the Mayan T'zolkin Calendar. The interesting thing about the Mayan T'zolkin calendar, is that it tracks a thirteen-day "galactic cycle" or "Tones of Creation", in relation to a twenty-day cycle of "Solar Seals". This combination of cycles carry on for 260 days before they both come back around to their original starting point of "Day 1" – together. The Tzolkin holds a 13:20 ratio reflecting the natural cycles of galactic and solar energies that affect Earth, day by day. They observed the unique energies of both the solar and galactic cycles on a daily basis! Our entire Universe is cycles within cycles. The Mayans had over 20 calendars, all of which are incredibly accurate. This knowledge is still very important today, even though most people in the west lost interest after the absurd debacle of 2012.

Conclusion

As you can see, the anatomy of the Spirit plays a significant role in our health, and conversely, in the formation of disease. It is affected by many things and particular, specific mental and emotional obsessions can have a huge impact on this etheric anatomy as well, and can even cause a soul to be bound to this material world, after they cross over. Furthermore, the very planets in our solar system and its orientation to the galactic center play a key role in the mental, emotional, spiritual and physical aspects of the people on this planet.

When you put all of this together, along with the Science of the Rays, you can begin to attempt to fathom the complexity that exists in what makes each of us a truly unique being. For those who are unfamiliar with the Science of the Rays, suffice it to say that your Higher Self was created "from" one of the first 3 primary Rays. Your soul comes into each specific incarnation "from" the Ray that serves the highest good for the Life contract of that soul. This provides the soul with a unique combination of characteristics and strengths that will aid it in its lifetime. It also greatly determines many personal characteristics and driving factors as well.

Yet, we are provided with natural cures like crystals, herbs, sound and Light, that work on the fundamental level of all problems – energy. You are energy, so you can harm yourself with energy or you can help yourself with energy – the choice is up to you.

As I said, when you put all of this together, we are very complex and interesting beings, living in a very complex and interesting multidimensional, fractal, holographic ocean of Divine Energy, which is:

"The Mind of God"!

CHAPTER 8

THE NATURE OF THE UNIVERSAL LAWS AND MULTI-DIMENSIONALITY

"The Universal Laws govern Energy and Consciousness, because ultimately, that is all that exists!"

– Marty Rawson

If you are not familiar with the Universal Laws, you need to be. You are using them whether you understand them or not. They are the Laws of how Energy operates within this Universe, in all dimensions.

If you have not read "The Light Shall Set You Free" by the esteemed Dr. Norma Milanovich, you should. It not only has a wealth of Spiritual wisdom within it, but more importantly, it contains the most succinct and thorough, examination and explanation, of the Universal Laws!

The Universal Laws are basically the Owner's Manual for the Universe! Once you understand them, you should be able to apply these laws to your life and your actions. You are indeed using them whether you are aware of it or not! The problem is, we often cause ourselves harm due to our own ignorance of how these Laws work.

Drs. Norma J. Milanovich and Shirley D. McCune in "*The Light Shall Set You Free*" (1998), state there are 12 Universal Laws that describe ways in which cause and effect are related. The Universal Laws can also be viewed as guidelines for behaviors that will enhance our physical, mental, emotional and spiritual growth.

The Universal Laws are all inter-related and are founded on the understanding that everything in the universe is energy, including us, and that energy moves in a circular fashion. At the microscopic level, we are a whirling mass of electrons and energy atoms spinning rapidly. In fact, everything in the world is comprised of energy and we are intimately connected with this sea of energy, this sea of whirling electrons.

Our thoughts, feelings, words, and actions are all forms of energy. What we think, feel, say, and do in each moment comes back to us to create our realities..Energy moves in a circle, so what goes around comes around. The combined thoughts, feelings, words and actions of everyone on the planet creates our collective consciousness, it creates the world we see before us.

The exciting news is, because our thoughts, feelings, words and actions create the world around us, we have the power to create a world of peace, harmony and abundance. In order to do this, it is essential that we learn to control our thoughts and emotions. Understanding the Universal Laws help us to do this by living in harmony with the cycles of the Universe. Below is a brief summarization of the 12 Universal Laws. They are definitely worthy of deeper reflection than a simple cursory read-through.

The 12 Universal Laws – Simplified

1. The Law of Oneness

The Law of Oneness explains that every individual, every situation and everything else in the world is connected to each other. What someone else thinks or does may affect your life in some way and vice versa, even if you don't know the person at all. This law states that there is only one energy flow and one mind, so everyone is connected to each other.

2. The Law of Energy

From thoughts to people, everything is made of energy, and that's what this law stands for. The Law of Energy is also known as the Law of Vibration, and this means that energy comes in countless frequency levels. Energy and vibrations are being sent out into the Universe constantly, so the Law of Energy is always in motion.

3. The Law of Action

According to the Law of Action, you need to take action steps towards your wants in order to manifest them. An example of the Law of Action in natural motion is when a person gets angry and slams a door. The person is feeling angry, so his/her action is to slam the door to show that he/she is angry. Even if the person doesn't want to be angry, he/she supports the emotion by action.

4. The Law of Correspondence

A very popular quote from the Emerald tablets states, "As above, so below", and this means that whatever happens inside your mental space is reflected on the outside. The Law of Correspondence proves that what you think and feel in your conscious and subconscious minds is what you create on the outside.

5. The Law of Cause and Effect

The Law of Cause and Effect says that events don't happen coincidentally. Everything happens in your life for a reason, no matter if you see how or why it happened. The Law of Cause and Effect can also be related to the concept of karma.

6. The Law of Compensation

This law is like an extension of the Law of Cause and Effect, and it means that what you put out is what you'll get back in abundance. If you do random acts of kindness and good deeds often, you'll receive good things back. The same can happen with negative actions as well.

7. The Law of Attraction

The most well-known universal law out of all 12 is the Law of Attraction. From the words you speak to your beliefs, you attract everything in your life through energy. You can even attract people into your life who have the same energy frequency as you. Like attracts like, so whether it's negative or positive, everything you see in your life is what you've attracted.

8. The Law of Perpetual Transmutation of Energy

This law basically means that you have the ability to change your life into anything you want. It's your responsibility to transform your life, and it's your choice to accept or reject the opportunities that the Universe gives you. Energy is always in motion, and you get to choose whether you want to go with the flow or not.

9. The Law of Relativity

Every life obstacle is an opportunity for people to change their perspective and life so that they can continue to improve themselves. These tests from the Universe also helps us learn to let go of judging events and people as good or bad, nice or mean, etc., which we do when we compare ourselves to others. Everything in the Universe is just existing, and that is what the Law of Relativity means.

10. The Law of Polarity

This law states that everything in the Universe has an opposite. The Law of Polarity helps us understand the difference between positive and negative thoughts so that we can change thoughts we don't want into thoughts we do want.

11. The Law of Rhythm

Everything in the Universe has a unique rhythm that it beats to, and these different rhythms develop into patterns, cycles, etc., in life. The Law of Rhythm encourages us to follow the natural flow of energy and harmony of the Universe.

12. The Law of Gender

The Law of Gender is commonly related to the concept of Yin and Yang, and it states that there are masculine and feminine energies in life. It also tells us that everything needs time to nurture and grow in order to balance and master the masculine and feminine energies within ourselves.

From the Law of Oneness to the Law of Gender, each **universal law** has its own meaning and purpose in the Universe. When used together, harmony and balance in the Universe is always constant. If you're very familiar with the Law of Attraction, you'll now have a better understanding of how the Universe works and how LOA fits right in with the rest of the **universal laws**.

This simplified version of the Universal Laws are Courtesy of Victoria M. Gallagher, LOA Hypnotist www.hyptalk.com, www.victoriamgallagher.com (Thank you!)

Remember, all of these Laws are constantly working. The key is to understand them so you can use them wisely, instead of suffering the consequences of their effects due to ignorance!

In order to really understand Spirituality and the universe, you need not only an understanding of Energy, but the multi-dimensional nature of All That Is. Everything is energy. What we call matter is simply frozen energy. Einstein proved that. Matter is energy that is vibrating at a slow enough rate to condense into dense, physical matter.

Our scientific community has been trying to comprehend the nature of consciousness since they began to call themselves scientists. They have insisted that the brain generates consciousness despite ample evidence to the contrary. The main problem with the scientific establishment, in all fields, is they get stuck in their dogmatic approach to problems and will not allow anyone to challenge fundamental concepts even when the evidence stacks up against those concepts. The status quo gets set in their ways and those who control the dialogue in the hallowed halls of academia maintain an iron-fisted adherence to what they will allow to be said and what is allowed to be studied, and especially what is allowed to be published! Just another example of the petty tyranny that we have allowed to limit us.

Anyway, everything is energy. Energy is conscious. From the tiniest Planck scale particle to the grandest manifestation (the Universe), energy is conscious. There is only one mind, the universal mind, and you and I are Individualized Awarenesses, swimming around in it, just like drops of water swim in the ocean.

Again: Everything is energy. Energy is conscious. Consciousness is life.

God is the sum total of all consciousness experiencing itself in the countless forms that energy and consciousness can manifest in, in this multi-dimensional, fractal, holographic "Universe".

God is consciousness. God is Life. God is within All That Is, and All That Is – is within God.

This means you too. You have never been separate from God, and no part of God is unworthy of God!

What the mystics have referred to as Unity Consciousness is the stripping away of all false notions of separation to the point of gaining back the level of consciousness you have in the higher dimensions, when you are not incarnated in a physical life, with spiritual amnesia. This is like the drop becoming aware, once again, that it is the ocean and the drop – at the same time.

So, how does this multi-dimensionality stuff work?

First off, let's get one thing out of the way. We are not talking about the mathematical – geometrical dimensions of points, lines, planes and cubes with Cartesian co-ordinates. That is a mathematical construct that has nothing to do with multi-dimensional reality. People who try to force this narrow definition onto this topic will remain confused concerning anything involving this subject. They usually try to explain the 4th dimension as being "time" and then their attempts to explain the 5th dimension and above fall further and further into a confusing disarray of hyperbole, the higher they go.

I am going to give you what I consider to be a more straightforward explanation of this concept than *some* are giving nowadays. Some time ago, someone decided to muddy up the waters by adding "densities" to the explanation of dimensions. It is my opinion that this is totally unnecessary, and accomplishes nothing, other than making things more complicated than they need to be, with more "facts" to remember. For those of you who prefer to delve into densities, fine, have fun. Densities are merely a natural function of vibrational frequencies, just like everything else. Density is also relative to the vibrational frequency of the dimension in which you currently reside. In other words, the 5th dimension seems to be etheric to those of us in the 3rd dimension. However, the beings in the 5th dimension manifest objects that are "dense" to them, in the 5th dimension. Density is relative and therefore not of valid use or necessity in the discussion of dimensions.

That which differentiates one thing from another is, of course, vibrational frequency.

Levels of consciousness are also directly related to, and dependent on: Vibrational Frequency.

The higher the vibrational frequency, the higher the consciousness, and the higher the ability to perceive and comprehend more complex issues and higher concepts. (This is why it is more important for Humanity to focus on Spiritual growth than hardcore technological advancement. The ego wants all the coolest toys, but these toys all end up being bigger guns or bigger bombs due to our current mentality/vibrational frequency. If we were to focus on Spiritual growth, we could comprehend concepts that are currently beyond our capability, which would resolve humanity's current and dire issues! This would open up our collective creativity to things beyond simply killing one another!

For our purposes here, we shall concern ourselves primarily with the first dimension through the 5th dimension and the consciousness/levels of perception of each one. In truth, the differences between the sixth through the tenth dimensions are not really of much concern to us in the 3rd dimension, as they do not have significant meaning or usefulness – for humans at our level!

Simply put, the differences between the 6th thru the 10th dimensions are the levels of perception and comprehension that is enabled through the increased rate of vibrational frequency of each successive dimension. There is also an increased ability to influence energy at primal levels, and therefore influence "what is", purely my means of one's own consciousness.

The 1st dimension through the 3rd dimension are dense "physical matter". Above that, the vibrational frequency is too high for matter to form "as we know it". Again, each dimension is relative to its own self.

The 1st dimension is the densest level of this physically manifested universe. This is the level of energy and consciousness that vibrates at the level of rocks, crystals and other matter we generally have referred to as "inanimate". The mystics, shaman and other holy men and women throughout the ages have known that consciousness exists at this level. It is only "modern man", who got too arrogant for his own good, who relegated everything to being dead and "less than". Even in the Bible, God said "Split open a piece of wood and I am there!" The Native Americans and indigenous peoples all over the world have tried to tell us about the "Stone people", The "Cloud people" and suchlike. They knew that the "Great Spirit" inhabited All That Is, at various levels of consciousness. If you can attain the right state of mind, you can have some level of communication with anything. Lower levels of vibrational frequency and consciousness do not necessarily equate to darkness and or what we call evil. That is programming and propaganda from this dimension. However, they do allow for the existence of forms of consciousness with "less light".

The 2nd dimension is the level of consciousness that inhabits the plant kingdom and some of the more simple forms of animal life. There is discernable life here. Our own science has finally developed to the point that we can now detect communication and even emotions that plants not only have, but transmit to one another. Again, the indigenous people tried to tell us of the "Tree people". Every physical form that matter can take has its own energy, its own vibrational frequency, its own level of consciousness and therefore, its own "spirit". This is why the wiser, and truly more conscious and civilized cultures of the world have always lived in harmony with nature and only took what they actually needed. I have always found it fascinating that they have understood and truly lived and practiced the concept of "Being good Stewards of the Earth" without having the benefit of having that spelled out for them in a book.

If we want to survive as a species, we will have to "go back" to the wisdom of the native/indigenous peoples and return to a harmonious way of life with nature and Mother Earth herself!

The 3rd dimension is this dimension of consciousness that we are aware of inhabiting, as humans. It too, has quite a wide range of vibrational frequency. As humans, we tend to reflect and express these frequencies through our emotions. The lower frequencies are those that are fear based, such as anger, hatred, greed and the like. The higher frequencies are those that are based in Love, such as gratitude, compassion and the many forms of love humans have for one another, from their brother to their parent or child, to their friends and lovers. Earth is the Emotional University of the universe and there is nowhere else that can assist in soul evolution quite like this planet can. The question is, can humanity grow up enough as a species, to get beyond our base emotions of fear and separation, to continue our soul evolution into the higher dimensions of Love and Light?

Have you ever heard of the Sanskrit term "maya", meaning illusion? The ancient Vedic texts tell us this entire 3D physical world is an illusion. Quantum physics is now proving this exact point!

This world suffers from entropy or decay. Everything here in this physical world is temporary. You, the mountains, the continents, even the planet itself, is temporary. This is part of what we have come to call the "cycle of Life". We come into these lives, in the physical world, knowing that each life is a fleeting moment in the larger scheme of things.

We know this because in the dimensions beyond and above the third, everything is constantly renewed through Centropy; the constant renewal of "matter" (again, a relative term). This is why in the fifth dimension and above, everything is considered perfect and eternal. Beings there create through Love, and their "creations" remain in their perfection until, or if, they have a desire to change them.

Entropy is the name of the game in these worlds of dust because they are meant to be short-term (comparatively) arenas for the purpose of soul growth.

Why is Earth the hardest? Because we incarnate here in a state of spiritual amnesia on a planet designed to be the Emotional University of the Universe. We forget who we are. We temporarily forget our connection to Source, or "God". This brings about a low vibrational frequency to start out with. Add to this mix, domination over the entire planetary society by dark beings who hi-jacked the planet long ago and you have one hell of an emotional university. This is a great place for younger souls to learn, also for more advanced, experienced souls who can bring enough light within them to notice and feel the emptiness inside them. They are soon drawn to seek the only refuge they can find: Love and Light and their connection to Source! This raises their frequency and they are soon on their journey home!

The 4th dimension is the "bridge" that spans the transition between the physical 3rd dimension and the etheric 5th dimension. It is also the only dimension that I divide in half in order to illustrate its nature. The Third dimension is one of dense, physical matter. It does allow for non-physical aspects such as thoughts and emotions, etc. The Fifth dimension is the frequency of divine, unconditional Love. Nothing below this frequency can exist there. If, hypothetically say, a being who had anger within them, were to try to "crash the 5th-dimensional party" – the Universal Law of Transmutation would instantly raise this lower vibrational frequency to that of divine, unconditional Love! After all, it states quite simply and eloquently that "Higher vibrational frequencies will always transmute lower vibrational frequencies."

So, the 4th dimension consists of those frequencies of energy that are not dense enough to become physical matter, and not high enough to qualify as divine, unconditional Love. Yet, we are beginning our journey through the fourth dimension right now, while in the physical form. That is why this part of Earth's "shift" is so incredibly uncomfortable.

Think for a minute, since energy cannot be destroyed, where do you think all the negative, untransmuted negative energy is, that humanity has ever created, throughout our entire existence on this planet? That's right! It's all around us, vibrating at that low frequency of the lower 4th dimension. All the hatred, all the anger, the violence, all the jealousy, contempt, betrayal and greed that humanity has ever felt, that has not yet been transmuted, is the sewer swamp we have created for ourselves to live in.

This is why this current "Shift" in consciousness is so difficult right now! This is why there is so much negativity coming to the surface and why so many unconscious people are committing insane acts of violence, hatred, selfishness and greed. This is why people who are awakened to higher consciousness are having such a rough time! As the energy of the planet itself rises with the assistance of the higher realms, "**_WE_**" have to transmute the energetic mess "**_we_**" made, as "**_we_**" traverse through "**_our own_**" energetic sewer-swamp! We all have had our part in this, if not so much in this lifetime, then in others.

All of these energies are painful and unpleasant. Pain is a great motivator! Unfortunately, humans are usually not bright enough to learn without the motivation that extreme pain provides. The Earth and this civilization would not be in the state it is in, if that were not true. (Even more unfortunate is the fact that it seems that humanity is not smart enough to learn, even when severe pain is abundant.)

This is also why All Things eventually return to God! The absence of Love and Light is painful and empty and inspires one to seek out Love and Light. This is what causes entities and souls that are stuck in the lower fourth dimension to seek out the higher frequencies! While God has no preferences, All things do return to God, or Source. This is the one thing for which there is truly no free will. It is not because God forces anything or anyone to return to Source, it is because energy, which is Living Light and Love, has a natural bias towards itself: Life, Light and Love. The absence of Light and Love are not comfortable or conducive for Life and it will, eventually, as it gains higher cognitive capacity, seek out, and return to, the Source of Light and Love!

As this continues, the process naturally takes the being through the higher Fourth dimension and eventually into the Fifth dimension of Divine Love and Light.

This has been called many things, Heaven, Nirvana, Paradise and so on. I simply call it Home.

The 4th dimension consists of a wide variety of beings and entities, from those of a very low vibration to beings and entities that are on the verge of "going Home" into the 5th dimension. This is what I call the Astral realm. There are indeed energies and entities that have some higher wisdom here and will even aid humanity when approached. These are the Beings contacted through the use of Shamanic Power plants. Sometimes the Star Nations or even the Angels and Ascended Masters will venture into this dimension to communicate with, or protect an individual who has journeyed here. The problem is, there are many beings and entities that are of lower frequency that love to trick people into thinking they are actually Beings of Light! It isn't always dangerous, but it can be. These are the Djin of ancient lore, that are said to be both good and evil. Always ask your Angels to guide you and protect you anytime you venture into the Astral Realm. The lower aspects of it will drain your energy, which is why those who astral travel are usually tired and drained of energy after doing so. It's like running a marathon at the dump. Why?

While some of the beings there may be working on developing enough Love and Light to "Go Home", they have not made it yet. Therefore, their consciousness level is obviously not as high as the fully realized "Beings of Light" in the higher realms! If you are seeking council, why not go to a source of divine Love and Wisdom rather than to those who haven't accomplished that level yet?

The 5th dimension is indeed the abode of the Angelic Realm and All Beings of Light who have attained the vibrational frequency of divine, unconditional Love. Their wisdom is unmatched within the lower dimensions because their perception, comprehension, and consciousness level itself is that much higher. This is why wisdom here is defined as "Doing that which is in the highest good of all concerned". This should be our definition as well, but not all of humanity has grown sufficiently yet to grasp this. Many seem to have confused "active intelligence" for "Wisdom". They are not the same. Hitler had a substantial amount of active intelligence, but no wisdom whatsoever. Jesus had both active intelligence and wisdom. Notice the difference?

As we go higher and higher through the dimensions, from the sixth through the tenth, the changes can be summarized fairly briefly. With the attainment of higher vibrational frequency comes an ever-increasing perception of All That Is, and a greater comprehension of the mysteries that are the Creator; First Source and Center of All That Is!

After the 10th dimension, all facsimile of a physical body is discarded and beings of pure consciousness exist in the form of truly Sacred Geometries of Light, each according to their own unique vibrational frequency! Their ability to influence and manipulate energy are enhanced so greatly that there is no need for a body of any kind.

All of this, and much, much more is here. Now.

There are as many different types of energies, entities and Beings as there are frequencies! This means that there is indeed a "dark side". The dark side must exist in order for the contrast between the Light and the dark to exist. We could not know the Love and bliss of the Creator if we could not have the absence of it, to compare it to! The dark side is not necessarily evil, but it can be. It is unconscious. It lacks the comprehension, the love and the compassion that exists in the Light. It is therefore, empty and painful to reside there. It serves the Light, without most of its residents ever being aware of it!

CHAPTER 9

A CONTROLLED ENVIRONMENT

*"The ultimate tyranny in a society is not control by martial
law. It is control by the psychological manipulation of
consciousness, through which reality is defined so that those
who exist within it do not even realize that they are in prison."*

– Barbara Marciniak

This planet has one of the most controlled and, let's face it, uncivilized
"civilizations" there is. Maybe not the worst that has ever been, but
definitely found wanting. Here in the U.S., where people have been
literally spoonfed propaganda since the day they were born, they talk
about how free it is, while the government, corporations and others
openly, clearly dictate what dialogue is considered "acceptable" within
our society. Increasingly, what is deemed acceptable is a perversion of
logic and reason that has upended our society! This is not an accident!

This is a world where lying, deceit, and corruption are not only expected,
but actually praised and even rewarded. This is part of what Krishnamurti
was referring to when he said:

*"It is no measure of good health to be well adjusted to
a profoundly sick society!"*

121

Control of a society is accomplished in several ways, the most common of which is, as I said, by controlling the dialogue and therefore the thoughts, through peer pressure. All they have to do is put whatever ridiculous spin, on any topic they want, and put it on *all* the news channels and in the printed media, online and off! They even do this verbatim, on all the news reports simultaneously, and yet many people are too brainwashed to notice it, even when it is shown to them! I have seen several times, when clips from news station after news station has been shown using the exact same phrasing for the same stories that are being spoonfed to the masses.

One of their favorite tactics is to come up with a derogatory catch phrase so they can label the ones who are not yet mind-controlled, as being stupid. Their favorite one for the last couple of decades is "conspiracy theorist". You should ALWAYS be on guard when you see this term or any other term that becomes "mainstream" and is used to label and ostracize some section of society.

Yes, there are some extremely, shall we say, "unintelligent" things that some people believe in, that are beyond credibility. Many ludicrous things have been intentionally put out there as "conspiracy theories" to intentionally exaggerate the absurdity of the so-called "conspiracy theorists", and make anyone who does not conform to the official dialogue, look like idiots. Especially during the last several years, this term is increasingly being used for anyone who does not accept any and all "official" explanations, or mainstream storylines the "Establishment-Elite" is pushing. Yes, there are idiots among us, but, this does not mean that the power brokers behind the scenes don't discuss how to maintain their power and continuously manipulate events to their own benefit. It would be incredibly naïve to think otherwise. It also does not mean that this world is not filled with actual, active, legitimate conspiracies, by the most rich and powerful, to manipulate, control, and dominate this world! How do you honestly think a handful of people ended up with all the money? By accident?

Let's get a little more basic though, and go to the foundation of manipulation and control. There are two systems that have been thoroughly established for the total control of humans on this planet. One is the Fractional Reserve Banking system that is literally designed to transfer the wealth of the nations into the hands of the International Bankers. (You have to admit; it has done a very efficient and thorough job of that!) While we could go quite in-depth on this subject, that is not what this book is about. It will collapse on its own before too long anyway.

I will say this much: long before the current Federal Reserve system was formed in the United States, their philosophy of exploitation was summed up by the French Economist Frederic Bastiat:

"When plunder becomes a way of life for a group of men in society, over the course of time, they create for themselves a legal system that authorizes it and a moral code that glorifies it"

– Frederic Bastiat

Mayer Amschel Rothschild, founder of the Rothschild banking cartel/dynasty, and referred to as a "founding father of international finance", once said: "Permit me to issue and control the money of a nation, and I care not who makes its laws!" Rothschild was ranked seventh on the Forbes magazine list of "The Twenty Most Influential Businessmen of All Time" in 2005. Yes, indeed, we are brainwashed as a society to worship our tyrants! We should have been much more careful about who wrote our history books!

The second system or institution is organized religion. Now, I do not care what religion anyone is. I simply ask that if you claim to be a certain religion, would you please learn enough about it…to live it well?

Much of the following is a reiteration of a concept first brought to my attention through the "Conversations with God" series of books by the wonderful Neale Donald Walsh. I am not quoting him, however he and his work, along with God, deserve the credit for bringing this out into the open for discussion. (I highly recommend all of Neale Donald Walsh's books!)

One of the major issues with organized religion is, that if you go back to the source of all nation's laws on this planet, you will find that they are based on the religious beliefs of the dominant religions of those nations, at the time those laws were written. Not only that, but the laws are still controlled and maintained by people claiming to belong to those same religions. This is an important fact to keep in mind, for it is our belief systems that define our actions and our laws. Most of Earth's major religions have been around for thousands of years, but some of them less.

I believe we can all agree that they have been around long enough to exhibit their efficacy. That is, their ability or the lack thereof, to produce their intended results. I would have to say, that if unity as a whole for humanity (*"**all God's children**"*), all living in harmony with one another (*"**Do unto others**...*") and the planet (*"**Being Good Stewards**"*), was truly their goal, they have totally failed us. **If** creating a society whose systems and institutions work for the highest good of the people, were again, truly their goal, again, *they have failed us! Miserably.*

The biggest misconception and most damaging, is teaching the "Fear of God". This teaches people to fear a God that is wrathful, jealous, and vengeful, and will burn you in hell for all eternity for insufficient groveling! People who believe this way, then project this attitude on others and believe that extremely harsh punishments and belligerent treatment of those who are deemed to be "less than", is acceptable. This inevitably ends up being those who are different from them and don't belong to their religion! No wonder we can't get along.

This may be overwhelming to read, but in order to get a more complete understanding of our state of the world, it is important to read through the following.

Let's look at some of the other accomplishments organized religions have contributed to our society worldwide, after thousands of years of fear, control and domination:

At this time (late 2021), with the best up-to-date information available, we live in a world where 3.6 billion people are living in abject poverty!

Just **62 people**, own as much wealth as the poorest half of the entire world population – or 3.6 billion people – according to the most recent report, released by anti-poverty charity Oxfam.

There are 687.8 million undernourished people in our world, while the rich countries throw away more than enough food to feed them.

Worldwide 218 million children between 5 and 17 years are estimated to be in employment.

152 million of these children are victims of forced child labor of which almost half work in very hazardous conditions.

An estimated 6.3 million children under the age of 15 die each year. That's 1 every 5 seconds. The majority are from preventable causes related to poverty.

There are more people living in slavery today than at any point in the history of the world.

An estimated 40 million people are enslaved. More than three times the total number of African slaves sold during 400 years of transatlantic slave trade!

If earth's history is compared to a calendar year, modern humans have been around for 37 minutes and managed to use up one third of earth's natural resources in the last 0.2 of a second!

The population of 4,300 species of mammals, birds, fish, reptiles and amphibians, have seen a decline of 68% between 1970 and 2016, and populations keep getting smaller.

The world could run out of rain forests in 2100, food in 2050, fish in 2048, water in 2040!

Nearly 90% of the world's marine fish stocks are fully exploited, overexploited, depleted, or in a state of collapse.

The world's oceans could effectively be emptied of fish by 2048.

Over 100 million years of healthy life are lost every single year because of air pollution. That's 1 year and 8 months of healthy life, lost on average, for every single person on earth.

It's the world's 4th most lethal killer.

And all of this is the result of the mindset of thousands of years of organized religion. Yes, the same ones that have caused humans to kill one another in the name of "God", is the single highest cause of death and destruction in human history!

You think we just might have gotten a few concepts wrong? I think so!

The world's religions are worth hundreds of billions of tax-free dollars, yet children all over the world are starving to death, billions are in poverty, millions are enslaved, the Earth is almost destroyed, and so is humanity.

There need not be any further evidence brought forth of the overall absence of conscience in our approach to caring for the Earth and humanity. This mentality that is a direct reflection of the values instilled in humanity by its own beliefs in organized religion! Unfortunately, though, there is more evidence.

Worldwide – $13.6 Trillion dollars was spent on war in 2015! We know that has increased since then!

The United States alone has a military budget that is greater than the next ten countries combined: more than rivals like China and Russia, and more than pretend allies like Saudi Arabia (the ones that helped the terrorists on 9-11!), and the long-term allies like United Kingdom, and France.

At $730 billion in 2019, military spending accounted for more than 53 percent of the federal discretionary budget – That is the budget that Congress sets each year during its annual appropriations process.

The median annual wage in the U.S., in 2019 was $34,248.45.

Let's play a game called fiscal irresponsibility.

Let's say you are the head of your household with this income and you have the typical mentality that led to this "appropriation". You only get this meager income because you absolutely will not tax your corporate masters or the Church's, or the filthy rich, all of whom are also your masters, or should we say; Owners.

This means that your take home monthly pay would be approximately $2,207. This means your yearly income to live on is $26,484.

So, because you are so utterly paranoid that all of your neighbors are out to get you, (probably because of the nasty things you have done...) you are spending $1,169.71 of this income on guns, ammo, Constantino wire, fencing, guard dogs, security forces, satellites, spy equipment, all your "super-secret" black ops, and so on!

This leaves you with a meager $1037.29 for your rent, your food for yourself and your family, upkeep for everything you own, and so forth. This leaves you, just like our country, without the ability to feed or clothe some of your children, and to not be able to get them medical care. It is why you cannot manage the upkeep on your house or save money for the future. So, what do you do? You feed, clothe, and educate only those children of yours that you really like, you know, the ones who look like you, who are utterly obedient, and who repeat your propaganda verbatim. The rest, you let live in the shed eating bread and water. All so your rich gods with already overstuffed pockets, can get richer.

If you actually did this, or had a neighbor that did this, do you actually think anyone else would find it acceptable? Admirable? Sane? I don't. I would see someone who was so delusional that they are neglecting their family and their responsibilities! Small wonder we are the only country in the "civilized" world that pretends we cannot afford universal healthcare, or higher education for our youth, or upkeep for our infrastructure.

No, we have been at war for 93% of our existence and proudly proclaim we are a "Christian" nation, and the loudest ones screaming this are simultaneously swearing allegiance to Fascism, Nazism and White Supremacy. It is past time that some folks need to take a good, long, hard look in the mirror, and re-read some of the books they claim to believe in!

Is there any system or institution that actually and sincerely serves the highest good of the people of this world?

The financial/economic system? No. It serves the wealthy by transferring the wealth of the nations into their pockets and bank accounts.

The healthcare system? No. It is less and less accessible and affordable to those that are not rich. It creates poverty in countries like the U.S. that refuse to implement universal healthcare where people literally lose their homes over medical bills!

The education system? No. Prices are increasing exponentially, again, so only the rich can afford an education. This simply increases the gap between the rich and the poor!

The tax system itself perpetuates this divide by keeping the poorest districts poor – eternally.

The "Justice" system? No. It has been turned into a means of extracting as much monetarily from the populace as possible, with no regard for justice whatsoever.

Organized religions? Oh, Hell NO!

Why? Because again, we are taught to "Fear God". We are taught that God is vengeful, and if you don't do exactly as God wants, he will torture you for eternity! Those who attain positions of power and authority then project this attitude of tyrannical dominion over others!

Now, think about this, according to the Christian narrative, Lucifer's only crime was that he disagreed with God about humanity having free will. For this simple disagreement, supposedly God cast him and everyone who dared to agree with him, out of "Heaven".

Now, think about this; the very ones claiming they are "Christians" are now routinely and deliberately denying their fellow man and woman – free will!

Regardless of the subject, if you are trying to force your dogmatic moral standards on others, you are denying your fellow man of their free will, and you are standing against God. God allows free will because this is all about personal choice and personal lessons for the soul. They are literally acting out "Lucifer's" supposed agenda, going against what God said, in the name of God!

How mentally screwed up can you get?

Now, if this seems like an indictment of the organized religions across the world, then maybe that's because it is! They do not and have not served the highest good of the people of this planet. There are indeed good and wonderful people who are active members of every organized religion, who are doing their best to live their religions well – I salute and applaud every single one of them! Unfortunately, they are in the minority and have never, ever been able to attain any level of influence in order to create a better world.

Some truths about God:

God is Love. God is Life. God has never ordered anyone to kill anyone else.

God does not lack anything; therefore, he does not need anything, not from you, nor I.

Again…God is whole, complete and perfect and does not need anything from us.

Not our worship, not our groveling, and certainly not our money.

God is behind the creation of All That Is, even when God uses other beings as instruments of his/her design. Therefore, everything is created perfect, even when that "perfection" serves the purpose of continued higher lessons.

There is no place called hell. The Catholic Church made that one up. Yes, you can create your own form of "hell" here on Earth, and you can choose to stay in it following your physical demise, but it is not God's creation, it is yours. You are a co-creator, but you choose what you will create.

Although souls do generally in fact, return to the higher realms after each lifetime, that is not to say that there are not consequences for your actions!

A sin, by definition, is "an immoral act considered to be a transgression against divine law". Free Will was established by God so that Humans could make mistakes while having spiritual amnesia and thereby experience soul growth through personal experience. We do not and cannot grow at all in an environment that has no stimulus for growth!

Polarity provides this stimulus. God knows this. There is no sin. There are lessons and the things you do – take you further from God (darkness) or closer to God (Light). The further away from God and Love you are, the more painful your existence becomes! Eventually, even the densest of Beings will get to the point that they realize this direction isn't working for them anymore!

Put another way, everything is energy. Every thought, word or deed has a vibrational frequency. Every thought, word and deed is therefore either taking you higher in frequency, into the Love and Light of the Creator, or it is lowering your vibrational frequency and taking you further into the darkness.

This is why I caution people who overuse the phrase that "there is no good or bad". Ultimately you are correct. God sees it all as part of a wonderful learning process. The question is, and this is something every person must decide for themselves: Which direction do you choose to go ***in this lifetime?*** Because, if you are trying to raise your vibrational frequency, and work with the Beings of Light in the higher dimensions, you cannot harm others and be an all-around "evil-doer", and expect to get there.

You simply cannot support those who control, dominate, and impoverish the world and at the same time, claim you work in the light.

"The inability to experience the suffering of another – as its own, is what allows such suffering to continue. Separation breeds indifference and false superiority. Unity breeds compassion and genuine equality.

A group consciousness that speaks constantly of separation and inequality produces loss of compassion on a massive scale, and loss of compassion is inevitably followed by loss of conscience.

A collective conscience rooted in strict nationalism ignores the plights of others, yet makes everyone else responsible for yours, thus justifying retaliation, rectification and war.

The horror of the Hitler experience was not that he perpetrated it on humanity, but that humanity allowed it to happen.

The shame of the Hitler experience was not just that so many Jews were killed, but that so many Jews had to be killed before humanity stopped it!

The purpose of the Hitler experience was to show humanity to itself!"

— Conversations With God, by Neale Donald Walsh

Humans have an absurd habit of claiming to want one thing and then doing the opposite of what is required to attain that very result.

I believe it is time to change that, before it truly is too late to save our civilization.

"You cannot self-love your way out of systemic oppression."

— Ragen Chastain

"You are in a fight for your very lives... The problem is, you don't know it."

CHAPTER 10

HEALING OURSELVES AND OUR SOCIETY

"Your soul Creates, the mind reacts.
Therefore, get out of your mind. Come back to your senses.
Your Soul is your Truth"

Conversations with God, Neale Donald Walsh

Healing Ourselves

How can humanity heal its mental and emotional issues, to earn its place as a respectable and mature civilization?

We start by being devastatingly honest with ourselves and looking at the reality of our situation. We might want to take a close look at what we claim to want for our world, and what we actually do to accomplish those stated goals. An honest examination will show that we have a close to "zero" rating for effectiveness.

We know what we have done in the past, and anyone with any functioning, cognitive capacity will recognize that it *has not, and is not working.*

Where do we start? With ourselves first. We must start by learning how to control our own emotions, rather than letting them control us. They were meant to be a source of valuable information about our environment and a stimulus for growth, not a fuel for pain, revenge and death. But, how do we do it?

The best advice I can give anyone is to *quit thinking like a human.*

I know this sounds strange, but please hear me out. The first thought most people have is "What do you mean? I am a human!" My reply is always the same, I remind them, "No, you are Spirit, a magnificent Being of Light, having an experience in a physical, human body." By now, this is practically a cliché, but it is vitally important to make this distinction, and take it to heart!

We come into these lives for the purpose of soul growth, and to experience things that can only be experienced here in these physical worlds of dust. Earth is a living library and the Emotional University of our galaxy, if not the universe. We all went through a tremendous amount of effort to get to the point where we could participate in this incredible learning experience. Needless to say, the curriculum at this university is not an easy one, but the potential for soul growth is greater here than anywhere else. Although we may yearn for the higher realms of love and light, there is very little actual soul growth that takes place there, due to the comparative lack of hardships, conflict and opposition. It is only by enduring through all of this that we truly learn and grow.

I am going to suggest methods that deal with both the human aspect and the spiritual aspect of your being. None of this is easy, and some of it may be some of the hardest work you'll ever do. But it can also be the most empowering and rewarding experiences you will ever have.

One of the biggest problems that we face as "humans" on this planet, is that we do not teach how to deal with traumatic, emotional issues in a healthy manner. We are taught to hold it in and not show our emotions. We are often taught that showing emotions is a sign of weakness. This causes people to shut down emotionally, and bury these incredibly painful emotions inside our body. I will stress this again and again – "Feelings buried alive never die"!

Let us look at the physical human aspect of this first. It has long been recognized that humans have stages of grief following traumatic incidences in their lives. These are typically expressed as denial, anger, bargaining, depression and acceptance. If you will look back on your own experiences, you will see that you (most likely) went through these stages yourself. Sometimes people get stuck in the depression stage, and spiral downward from there. We will come back to this in a minute. For now, I would like to stress how vitally important it is to honor your emotions at every stage, understanding that this is a normal part of the process. Do not hold your emotions in, but do not harm others in expressing them either. Find someone, whether it be family or friends that you can talk to and express what you are feeling. Let them know that you just need to vent! (Especially if you are a female and are talking to a male! Tell him you don't need him to fix anything, just listen! If this were communicated openly when it is needed, we could also save a lot of problems.)

On the other hand, if you are the one that someone needs to talk to, you may need to understand that what they need is a good "listening to" in a compassionate manner and a safe environment. I truly believe this is one of the greatest gifts of love that one human can offer another.

So, what do we do when we never had this, or when it simply wasn't enough to get us through the pain? How do we heal from issues that have affected our life for years afterwards, or when it has caused us to go into deep depression?

This is where the work is, and this is where we must quit thinking like a human!

I want you to consider that before you came into this life, you were a spirit, a great being of light in the higher realms. That before you came into this life, you sat in counsel with other very wise beings and laid out your own life plan. This was designed specifically for _you_ to ensure the greatest soul growth in accordance with what your soul needed. You ultimately picked out your parents, you chose your life, you cast the players, and you wrote the script. You worked in the events that would take place at different stages of your life that would provide for the greatest soul growth and that would allow the laws of karma to be satisfied. You did this knowingly and willingly in the understanding that it was all based in love and your soul's desire and need for growth. The catch is – if you do not learn your lessons in this lifetime, you must come back and go through those lessons again! I, for one, have no intention of coming back and going through this again! I will endure whatever comes and have it done with!

Only by taking personal responsibility for writing the script and casting the players in our own life's play can we ever take back our own authority over our lives. This can be very difficult. I myself fought and wrestled with this concept for quite some time. I knew I could fill rooms full of people who could testify that I was the "victim" in many circumstances. I also was quite positive that I would never "do all this" to myself! Then one day in the midst of my own ongoing, internal argument, I had the sudden and incredibly powerful epiphany that it was indeed true. It was simultaneously the most humbling and the most powerful experience I have had. It was humbling in the sense that I had argued so adamantly against it and now I had to put my ego aside and admit to myself how wrong I was. It was empowering because, as soon as a took responsibility for it, I realized how powerful I was. I saw in my mind's eye, the incredible Mount-Everest-sized pile of crap that I had created, that was 'my life'! I realized how much energy it took to build a pile that huge! I immediately thought to myself "What would happen if I turned this around and started focusing my energies on healing my life? If I have enough power to create a mountain that huge, what could I create if I put all this effort into a positive direction?" I did, and I literally changed the world I lived in. I changed my perception and I changed my reality. This all goes back to a spiritual maxim that has been brought to my attention on many occasions, and that is – "_You_ create your reality, absolutely." I saw how my interpretation of events, even as a child, formed lasting opinions, which eventually became beliefs... which the universe showed me over and over... thus cementing them as "facts" in my personal reality and therefore, in *my* world.

Let's take a look now at the next aspect of our process. The hardest lessons we have are those things that we have put in our own way for our soul's growth. These are the ones that change our life profoundly and inevitably cause the most pain. If we have the maturity to be devastatingly honest with ourselves, we will find that the actual source of our pain is that we did not learn the lesson. We stuffed it inside, we buried the pain and tried to ignore it, or maybe we dwelled on it too much, but we did not learn the lesson. There is always a lesson.

This is where you have to detach yourself emotionally for a while, and get into your head. You need to seriously contemplate "Why would I put this event or series of events into my life?" "What could possibly be the lesson at a soul level, that I need to learn?" Do not expect this answer to come to you immediately. It can however come at any time. I have found it usually takes some serious soul-searching before the lesson reveals itself. Sometimes it is extremely difficult to determine the lesson because the entire drama has not yet played out.

Sometimes, we go through a life of hardships – that tempers our souls like steel, so that we can be strong enough for someone else in the future. Sometimes we choose to go through things with others, so we can be there to support one another. Sometimes the lesson can be as simple as "Be careful what you ask for!" This was one of my ***MAJOR*** lessons! *Be careful who and what you invite into your life!*

If you invite the "bad boy" or the "bad girl" into your life, you have to accept this as your part of the situation and accept that whatever happens, you are responsible for inviting this into your life! They are not going to change being who and what they are just because they are around you.

The point is, the lesson can be anything, but only *you* will truly know when you have found it. It is your lesson, and it is your epiphany that will tell you that you have found it. When this happens, ponder this lesson, and appreciate with great humbleness this new-found wisdom that you have just acquired. This is a life lesson and soul growth that comes from learning this lesson will be with you forever. Own it.

Now, get out of your head! You have done the mental work, and it has served you well. Figuratively, take your head off and tuck it under your arm for safekeeping.

Now it is time to honor your original emotions that you buried long ago. You need to allow yourself to feel those emotions, and honor them.

They are valid and they need to be expressed. Once you have truly allowed yourself to thoroughly feel them, and honor them, *release them with gratitude for the lessons they have taught you.*

We are always told that you cannot change the past. I submit to you, that if you do this process sincerely, then you just did change your past. The past is, in reality, nothing more than your memories and the emotions you have attached to them. They are painful when we have not learned our lessons. Once we learn our lessons, we literally change our perception of those experiences, and we can release them with gratitude. This allows us to not only grow, but to take back our own authority over our lives and these experiences will never again have the power to control us.

When this process is done with all your heart and soul, it is very effective. You will still have some of these issues pop up now and again, but they will not have the power over you that they did before. This is why there are cycles in life. Time/Life travels in a circular spiral so that as we progress, we can also come back around to revisit and continue to heal the events of our past, on this "circle of Life". We thereby harvest nuggets of golden wisdom we may have missed in the previous state of consciousness we were in, the last time we worked on that specific issue.

In order to maintain this healing of our past, we must commit to self-mastery over our own thoughts. Much has been said, and rightfully so, about living in the present moment, the "Now". This is absolutely true and valid. I however, do not know many who can do this all the time.

Most people let their thoughts and *"monkey chatter"* run constantly, which triggers a great deal of emotions. They then let those emotions control *them* by reacting to those emotions. Realize this:

How you are doing depends on what you are thinking about!

To help us control our thoughts, and to aid us to quit thinking like a human, let us take a look at two of the yogic sciences. Specifically, pranayama and mantra.

Pranayama is the yogic science of breath control. The reason this is important to our topic is because the breath and the mind are intricately linked. *As the breath goes, so goes the mind.* This is why when people are extremely stressed out, their breathing reflects their mental state by becoming rapid and shallow – thus causing hyperventilation. When this happens, the person needs to consciously change their breathing pattern to one that is slow and deep. This helps to calm the mind which further calms the body. The truth is, we do not have to wait until we are hyperventilating to use this technique. Whenever you notice yourself going to negative thoughts, especially about the past, stop yourself and concentrate on your breathing. Concentrating on your breathing forces you to stop thinking about other things.

One technique is to slowly inhale through the nose to a slow count of one, two, three… up to seven. Hold the breath for another equally slow count to seven, then exhale for the slow count seven, and again holding the exhale for this count of seven. Repeat, repeat, repeat… As time goes on, you may want to increase to a count of ten. Doing this entire process to a slow seven count, a full seven times, is actually a technique used by Inca "shaman" called the "Little Death", to alter perception.

There are many other pranayama techniques that are extremely powerful. It is highly encouraged and recommended that you explore these further and combine them with meditation. This will help amazingly well, if you persist!

Mantra is the yogic science of sound. Let's take a look at why this is so powerful and effective. Ultimately, all that exists is energy and consciousness.

The variation that exists between anything and everything is due in the vibrational frequency of each "thing". All energy vibrates, and therefore, all energy has two characteristics – light and sound.

Now stay with me for a minute, while we touch on a few other concepts that are important. Let us talk for a moment, about the five sacred languages. What makes a language sacred? Languages are sacred when the sounds produced, represent something, match in vibrational frequency – to the item to which they are referring. In ancient times, there were five sacred languages on this planet. They were ancient Chinese (Mandarin), Tibetan, Sanskrit, Egyptian and Hebrew. We will be focusing on Sanskrit, the language of ancient India.

Let us also mention how human neuro-pathways work. The more you think a certain thought, the stronger that neuro-pathway becomes. This is why repeated thoughts become habitual! When those repeated thoughts are about traumatic experiences from our past, we can get stuck in a never-ending loop that keeps playing over and over and over.

The best way to end this negative loop is to replace it consciously with thoughts that are of a higher vibrational frequency. Mantras are either seed syllables or phrases spoken in a sacred language that have the same vibrational frequency as that which they refer to. When we chant these to ourselves repeatedly, they not only take the place of the negative thoughts in our mind, they transmute the energy and raise our own vibrational frequency. You will be amazed at how effective this can be. The more you raise your vibrational frequency the easier it becomes to quit thinking like a human, and commune with Beings of Light on your own. Congratulations, you just used quantum physics, the Universal Laws and the Yogic Sciences all in one smooth shot, to help yourself!

There are many mantras, but the following two are probably my personal favorites and are classics! I highly recommend looking up more mantras and finding the correct translations for them so your intent may have coherence with your words!

Gayatri Mantra:
Aum
Bhuh Bhuvah Svah
Tat Savitur Varenyam
Bhargo Devasya Dheemahi
Dhiyo Yo nah Prachodayat

Om Shanti, Shanti, Shantihi ~ The Rig Veda (10:16:3)

The Meaning:
O thou existence Absolute, Creator of the three dimensions,
we contemplate upon thy divine light.
May you stimulate our intellect and bestow upon us true knowledge.
Om, Peace, Peace, perfect Peace."

Ehyeh asher Ehyeh (Hebrew):
Ehyeh asher ehyeh
Kadoish, kadoish, kadoish,
Adonai Tsebayoth

The Meaning:
I am that I am
Holy, holy, holy
Is the Lord, God of Hosts

A great deal of flexibility in use and meaning can be brought to the world of Mantra by learning to use the seed syllables, in various combinations, of the ancient Vedic tradition. The most common seed syllable is OM/AUM.

There is far too much information concerning seed syllables to try to cover here. I suggest you research this topic for more information if you are so inclined. You may well be glad you did, if you put the information to good use.

The next thing we must do, or should I say "at the same time", is teach all of this to our children! They *must* be taught how to deal with serious emotional issues in a healthy manner. In my opinion, they must be taught mindfulness and meditation, at an early age, like 8 years old. If we want to create a happier, healthier generation of humans, we have to *raise* a happier, healthier generation of humans!

As we change our attitudes about ourselves and our world, we will change our world for the better, so our children and grandchildren can actually live! As for me, I would like to see that!

The beautiful thing about this approach to emotional healing is that it also teaches one how to control their thoughts, or their mind. This too, was meant to be a tool or servant to you while you are here, not your master. This is why meditation is recommended. There are many types of meditation, and we will not be going into any particular forms in depth here, but it is something we should be doing ourselves and something we should be teaching our children. If we taught the children of the world, at the age of 8 yrs. old how to meditate, we could change this world in one generation. The inner peace and clarity in their minds would allow them to see through the façade of this system and they would rebuild it without question. Meditation gets you in contact with your soul, the part of you that still recognizes its own divinity and unity with Source. It cannot be lied to or deceived.

We need to start teaching our children things that will help them in life rather than memorizing trivia they will never need. Things like peaceful conflict resolution, honoring yourself, honoring others, healthy diversity, healthy boundaries and relationships, Free will and doing no harm, horticulture/gardening, protecting the Environment, the relationships between your body, mind and spirit, economics that serve the highest good of all concerned-worldwide, honesty and transparency in all affairs; including business. Spirituality (re-establishing your unity with the Divine) as a way of life. These are just a few that are essential. The list will naturally grow with time.

The most healing practice I know of is to express Love, express apologies, ask for and give forgiveness, and express gratitude. Give these to yourself. Give these to God, Give these to your fellow man and teach these to your children!

Healing our World/Society

The emphasis is on ourselves first, then our children because that is the only way change can happen. After addressing these issues, perhaps we can start taking a look at the systems, institutions, and organizations we have established to "serve" us and see how well they actually work.

I do not claim to have the final answers, but I do have a few suggestions. It would be negligent to raise criticisms without offering ideas to start the conversation off with!

So, let's start with our so-called "justice system". That is, our punitive "justice" system. A system that has failed humanity, and especially the United States. It is based in fear, punishment and profit for the state. Obviously, it has totally failed us. Application of nothing but the threat of jail, fines and punishment has allowed the U.S. to rank #1 in the percentage of its population that is incarcerated. As briefly mentioned above, this has led to some of the most vile entrepreneurs of our society to create "Private Prisons", so they can profit off of the pain and suffering of a broken system in a broken society. There have also been several cases of judges taking kickbacks for sending prisoners and even juveniles to for-profit detention centers! However, threats and post-crime punishment do not create obedience or a better society. If they did, America wouldn't have the most violent society in the "civilized" world and 25% of the world's prisoners!

The entire system is corrupt. Period. The Epstein case proves this all by itself. I am not just talking about how all the cameras in the jail suddenly and conveniently blacked out during his miraculously timed and equally convenient "suicide". I am also talking about how the so-called "justice system" allowed a deal to be made that prohibited Virginia Giuffre from pressing lawsuits against not only Prince Andrews, but also entire categories of sex traffickers, rapists and molesters who were associated with Epstein.

To quote Prince Andrews' attorneys, "Because Prince Andrew is a senior member of the British royal family, he falls into one of the expressly identified categories of persons, i.e., royalty, released from liability under the release agreement, along with politicians, academicians, businessmen, and others allegedly associated with Epstein."

Read that again! The so-called "justice system" of the United States actually allows agreements to be made that prohibit known and suspected sex traffickers, rapists and molesters to go free without so much as a word being said, simply because they are "Royalty, Politicians, Academicians, and Businessmen (Corporate CEOs). This shouts out to the entire world who the sex traffickers of the world really are, and that your government will protect them, not you, at any cost. The fact that "secret deals" can even be made that shield entire categories of criminals from lawsuits, let alone prosecution, is a legal proclamation that says "justice is dead in America". The "America" you have been taught to believe in – is a fantasy… a fiction… and nothing more. We must start over. We must re-build. This must change from the inside, in a non-violent manner. Americans must change the way they think and change the way we teach our children!

We, as a society, have neglected to teach our children *why* they should not do the things that harm themselves and others. We continue to neglect teaching our children the things they need to learn and then wonder why nothing ever gets better! They do not need participation trophies, they need loving guidance and logic. They are young, not inherently stupid.

Some time ago, one of my grandchildren got caught committing a "transgression" that had their mother quite upset. I did not see this grandchild for a few days after this, but when I did, I could tell there was concern over of any judgement I might have. Rather than launch into some pathetic diatribe, I gave her a heartfelt hug and quickly got her away from everyone else. I let her know that yes, I had heard about it, but that I loved her and was not mad at her, nor was I judging her at all. I asked her if she had gotten plenty of that already and she heartly agreed that she had! I told her I would like to offer an approach to this issue in a totally different way and asked if it was okay with her, if I did so. She readily said yes.

I then proceeded to explain to her in very clear and matter of fact language why it was harmful to her, to do this thing. I did this without lecturing or carrying on. By doing this, she saw exactly what I meant and heartly agreed, by herself, that this was not something that was in her best interest, nor was it something she wanted to do again.

Humans are rebels by nature. Threats don't work. That's why little Johnny keeps getting caught with his hand in the cookie jar! Only by showing our children the wisdom behind "why" they do not want to commit certain acts, can you get their voluntary cooperation and "buy-in" on any subject. They must decide they do not want to do something, on their own volition, in order for them to learn and grow.

Part of the healing of our civilization will be the reformation of our so-called justice system. It is currently nothing more than an oppressive and belligerent enforcement arm, and revenue agency for the level of government which it serves. And, it's all about the money.

If you commit any crime, what happens? At minimum, you get a fine. They extract money from you, for your "offense". You may also get jail time, depending on the severity of the crime, but you always get the fine. They will not be denied their money!

How about if you commit a crime that harms another person or their property? You guessed it. You get a fine, that goes to the government. The actual victim gets nothing! Once in a great while, a judge will order some amount of restitution, but have you ever seen anyone actually collect it? Rarely, if ever – Why? Because the courts do not enforce restitution for the common working man. The victim would then have to bring another case before the court just to get what the judge has already ordered. This, of course, costs everyone involved more fees for the government. This is a system designed so that everyone involved, except the court and its agents/officers, are in a lose-lose situation. The flip side of this is that on a routine basis, those who are rich, simply buy their way out of any serious consequences whatsoever, by paying a larger amount which they also conveniently call a "fine", but let's face it – it's a bribe. This is routinely done for crimes ranging from rape to murder to espionage and much more.

Here's an idea, how about we change to a restorative justice system? Anyone caught committing a crime would have to literally restore any damages caused as a result of their crime against another, and pay for their own rehabilitation counseling. Those who cannot afford to pay will work it off as a temporary employee of the jurisdiction involved, doing manual labor. This could include picking up garbage or any manual labor needed.

Those committing violent and/or more serious crimes would also be subject to jail time and rehab and such, but would still have to provide restoration to the victim's family in cases of bodily harm or murder. The guilty party would also be responsible for both parties court costs (the **actual** cost of allotted time and resources) and pre-set attorney's fees. In the case of lawsuits and accusatory litigations, the losing party would be responsible for all the court costs and attorney's fees as well. This would greatly cut down on frivolous lawsuits and free up the courts to actually serve the good will of the people!

You can tell who has the most financial stake in maintaining the status quo by observing who objects the loudest to this suggestion! I am betting on lawyers and judges myself. I believe it is way past time for the actually victims of crimes to have their losses restored by the criminals who caused them! Imagine that…accountability!

Next, let us address the abomination that is Qualified Immunity. This was created by racist judges during the Civil Rights era, to protect racist, violent cops from persecution for violence and murder. It has spread its unconstitutional reach to every citizen of this country. It is a direct violation of every citizen's right to life, Liberty and pursuit of happiness, while declaring some individuals are above the law.

It violates the 1st Amendment by totally denying the victim the right "to petition the government for a redress of grievances". It is a denial of rights for the government to declare itself and its employees to be above the Law and exempt from prosecution. Period.

It is routinely cited to openly and willfully violate the 4th Amendment: "*The right of the people to be <u>secure in their persons</u>, houses*, papers, and effects, against *unreasonable searches and seizures*, shall not be violated…"

In cases of forced confessions, it is used to violate the portion of the 5th Amendment that states "nor shall (any person) be compelled in any criminal case to be a witness against himself, <u>nor be deprived of life, liberty,</u> or property, without due process of law".

It violates the 8th Amendment prohibition of <u>cruel and unusual punishments</u> being inflicted.

It violates the 9th Amendment by denying people the right to not be assaulted and or murdered by the people who were supposed to be protecting and serving them!

This court-created "doctrine" is a violation of everything the Constitution of the United States once stood for. It allows for the willful and total disregard of the rights of all American citizens by the government that these same people established to protect their rights!

Do not be fooled into thinking that your skin color will protect you! This type of tyranny spreads to every and all members of society that any immoral, unethical member of the government chooses, at any time and any place, no matter what you are doing.

The steps toward creating an enlightened society will have to be made one at a time, but if we do not start the process, we will never get there!

Back to our children. What about the "education system"? It is failing for many obvious reasons. Primarily, it is continually being defunded, year after year. Apparently, roughly half people in this country would rather fund eternal war than educate their children. To top that off, school districts are funded exclusively by the taxes of their local community. This is great for the rich, affluent neighborhoods, but it maintains the status quo, and keeps the poorer neighborhoods under-funded and under-educated. Unfortunately, this is absolutely intentional, not accidental.

In addition to this, the rich institutions, foundations and think tanks that control our nation, the ones who, by the way, are not taxed, are also the ones who supply the text books and their content, for our public schools. Imagine that! The corporate "leaders" supplying the indoctrination materials for the masses! How generous of them! No wonder our children are taught nothing but to obey authority figures, fit into the social "norm", and memorize useless facts. Coincidence? I think not! As the saying goes:

"Governments don't want a population capable of critical thinking, they want obedient workers, people just smart enough to run the machines and just dumb enough to passively accept their situation."

— George Carlin

George Carlin spoke more truth than almost anyone else in the public eye, during his life. He got away with it because he disguised it as humor, but he made people think!

Then add to this, the rising costs of tuition for universities in the U.S., and you have a complete system that is designed by the status quo to maintain the status quo. Only the filthy rich can get a decent education, the middle class is disappearing, and the poor don't stand a chance!

We must change this ourselves. We must change this at the local level! It is here that we can actually have a say. We can change the curriculum and teach our children things they actually need to know later in life instead of useless trivia. We can spend time in their early years teaching them how to deal with emotional issues and how you hurt yourself when you harm others. We can give them time to figure out a little bit of who they are and what they want in life.

We can teach them the basics, and when they have them down, we can find out what their natural tendencies and preferences are. Then, when little "Johnny" or "Sally" says they want to be engineers or scientists, we can explain to them what courses they will need to learn in order to accomplish those goals. This way, they will know why they are learning the things they are learning! One of the biggest frustrations for students throughout the decades has been knowing they are learning useless things they will never use later in life! If they want to learn anything later on, there is this phenomenal invention called the Internet that provides instant access to most of the information available to humanity.

When you give them the opportunity to go in their own direction first, they are empowered and have a natural investment in their own future, with much more enthusiasm. This enthusiasm then carries on to whatever learning they aspire to later in life.

So, we can start by taking the control back for our children's education in all these ways and change the financial structure for funding them so the financially disadvantaged get a break and can have hope for their future! Then we can start towards developing an enlightened society, and teach subjects and concepts like those listed earlier.

Oh, how about the "healthcare" system? The current system is out of control financially and is increasing the gap between those who have access to healthcare and those who don't. Over 2/3 of all bankruptcies are due to medical reasons. Over 1/4 of Americans are struggling to pay medical expenses, and that number is increasing rapidly.

The U.S. spends a lot more per person on healthcare than comparable countries. Healthcare spending per person in the U.S. was $10,966 in 2019, which was 42% higher than Switzerland, the country with the next highest per capita health spending. These costs have obviously skyrocketed since then, due to the Covid-19 epidemic. Every study conducted has shown that the "for profit" healthcare system we have is not only much more expensive, but it is also killing us. Especially the poor and the disappearing middle class. This simply proves once again, that profits are more important than people in the United States of America.

This brings us to big pharma. They, along with the other massive corporate entities, literally own and control our congressmen, senators and judges, all of whom will do their bidding at will. This is more than evident when observing the voting records of these "servants". We do indeed have the best government money can buy! Too bad they don't work for people of this country. The very few exceptions that do care for the American people are so ostracized and vilified by the mass media, that half the country hates them for sticking up for the people!

Obviously, and again, we must make drastic changes to the laws concerning corporations and undo much of the damage that has taken place since our country began. As long as corporations own our government officials like they do now, no effective change can take place. Again, we have to start at the local level and hold local officials accountable when they pander to the corporations at the expense of the people. At the higher levels of government, there must be a national movement to eliminate the legalized bribery system that has so eloquently been called "lobbying". After all, if you were so inclined to "lobby" your local policeman to get him to change his "vote" on that speeding ticket, would they call that lobbying or bribery? Isn't it amazing how the terminology changes depending on who the financial beneficiary is?!

You may notice that a common denominator of the changes required for our societies healing is our government and the corporations who own it. Until we address this, nothing can change.

We must take our country back from those who have hijacked it! To start with, we must put an end to the legalized bribery known as "lobbying".

We must put strict controls and limits on campaign finance! Controls with teeth, not loopholes!

We must restructure both political parties and remove their stranglehold they have on the entire system. As it is a third party cannot succeed. This means the most extreme individuals from each of the two current parties win their primaries and we have to pick between these two. Truth be told, both candidates are owned by the same corporations or they couldn't have made it this far in the process! This means the powers that be don't care which puppet you pick, they own and control both of them. This is how they have rigged elections for at least 90 years!

How do you tell which candidates from the original field are not owned by the corporations and the powers that be? A couple ways. First, the media coverage across all major media will be absolutely petty, vicious, and non-stop. Second; they do not make it as the party's candidate for office!

These corporate whores who we have had the misfortune to elect by default have destroyed this country and will not do anything whatsoever to fix it.

What do we do? We go around congress and work at the state level. This is where we can still have an impact. States control the federal elections as well! When enough states pass a law, the federal law is enacted.

We must end gerrymandering! Let cities elect city officials, counties elect county officials and states elect state officials. Count the ballots and announce the winners. One person = One vote, just like in a real Democracy!

We must implement term limits!

We must implement ranked choice voting, and secure at-home voting!

All of this is currently being proposed in the "American Anti-Corruption Act" that the establishment will undoubtedly attempt to kill at any cost. Time will tell. You can Google it yourself or start at: anticorruptionact.org.

As long as America maintains its love affair with corruption, the world cannot heal.

What about manufacturing? The Capitalist utopian practice of building everything to break or wear out, so you can sell more of that product has to end. It has depleted world-wide resources and it is killing the planet. Have you noticed that the real motive for war ends up being for the natural resources of the country that is so conveniently being invaded? What we do to the planet, we do to ourselves!

Now, I believe in supporting our troops. The young men and women who join the military tend to have noble and patriotic motivations for joining. They truly believe in their hearts that they are "protecting Democracy". Because of that alone, they deserve the best of everything we can offer them. The problem is that in the country with the most fanatical military spending in the world, nothing goes towards the troops. In the last 40 years, the war-hawk Conservatives have increased military spending every chance they have gotten, but have blocked every single legislative bill that would benefit the actual troops on the ground. For most of you, that's your sons and daughters, brothers and sisters.

In the immortal words of Dick eternal-war Cheney, "You go to war with the army you have, not the one you wish you had."

Now, consider the following quotes from the legendary Major General Smedley Butler:

"I spent 33 years and four months in active military service and during that period I spent most of my time as a high-class muscle man for Big Business, for Wall Street and the bankers. In short, I was a racketeer, a gangster for capitalism. I helped make Mexico and especially Tampico safe for American oil interests in 1914. I helped make Haiti and Cuba a decent place for the National City Bank boys to collect revenues in. I helped in the raping of half a dozen Central American republics for the benefit of Wall Street. I helped purify Nicaragua for the International Banking House of Brown Brothers in 1902-1912. I brought light to the Dominican Republic for the American sugar interests in 1916. I helped make Honduras right for the American fruit companies in 1903. In China in 1927 I helped see to it that Standard Oil went on its way unmolested. Looking back on it, I might have given Al Capone a few hints. The best he could do was to operate his racket in three districts. I operated on three continents."

— Smedley D. Butler, War is a Racket

"Beautiful ideals were painted for our boys who were sent out to die. This was the "war to end wars." This was the "war to make the world safe for democracy." No one told them that dollars and cents were the real reason. No one mentioned to them, as they marched away, that their going and their dying would mean huge war profits. No one told these American soldiers that they might be shot down by bullets made by their own brothers here. No one told them that the ships on which they were going to cross

might be torpedoed by submarines built with United State patents. They were just told it was to be a "glorious adventure".

Thus, having stuffed patriotism down their throats, it was decided to make them help pay for the war, too. So, we gave them the large salary of $30 a month!

All that they had to do for this munificent sum was to leave their dear ones behind, give up their jobs, lie in swampy trenches, eat canned willy (when they could get it) and kill and kill and kill...and be killed"

— *Smedley D. Butler, War is a Racket*

"There are only two reasons why you should ever be asked to give your youngsters. One is defense of our homes. The other is the defense of our Bill of Rights and particularly the right to worship God as we see fit. Every other reason advanced for the murder of young men is a racket, pure and simple."

— *Smedley D. Butler, War is a Racket: The Antiwar Classic by America's Most Decorated Soldier**

(*for a long time!)

Now, you must remember, Major General Smedley Butler was no ordinary officer!

"Major General Smedley Darlington Butler (July 30, 1881 – June 21, 1940), nicknamed "Old Gimlet Eye", was a senior United States Marine Corps officer who fought in the Philippine-American War, the Boxer Rebellion, the Mexican Revolution and World War I. During his 34-year career as a Marine, he participated in military actions in the Philippines, China, and Central America; the Caribbean during the Banana Wars; and France in World War I. Butler was, at the time of his death, the most decorated Marine in U.S. history. By the end of his career, Butler had received 16 medals, five for heroism. He is one of 19 men to receive the Medal of Honor twice, one of three to be awarded both the Marine Corps

Brevet Medal (along with Wendell Neville and David Porter) and the Medal of Honor, and the only Marine to be awarded the Brevet Medal and two Medals of Honor, all for separate actions."

— Wikipedia.

Obviously, he cannot be dismissed as someone "out-of-the-loop"! All of this was 80 to 110 years ago! Is there anyone alive who really thinks the Corporations and the Governments have become more ethical since then? I suggest that if there is, they could easily be out-smarted by the average clam.

While I obviously have issues with the corruption that is rampant within our Military-Industrial Corporate State-Government, I must say unequivocally that armed insurrection and sedition are out of the question. We must find a non-violent solution to this or it will come back to destroy us. Only traitors and cowards would try to violently overthrow our "government". We must remember who we are first!

I would be negligent if I did not include a few words on the environment. Our environmental laws are killing this planet. That means they are killing us. That means you may have the experience of watching your children or grandchildren die. Was that a little too blunt for you? Well... nothing else has gotten the world's attention, and it is the truth. The sad, disgusting, horrible truth. We only have this one planet. She has supported our species and provided everything we have ever needed, and we are killing all life on her so we can make a few sick, twisted, greedy people even richer. That doesn't sound very sane to me.

We must adopt the wisdom of the Elders. The Native Elders of the world. Without stepping down the mass consumption that is killing this planet, we are doomed. And rightfully so, if we are indeed too stupid to learn.

When I say adopt the wisdom of the Elders, I mean much more than just their environmental practices which apply common sense! I mean their way of life. Their understanding of Unity Consciousness and the practical application of these concepts into their way of life. They understood long ago and still understand today that the "Great Spirit" exists within "All That Is". This, by the way, is the meaning of the verse from the Gospel of Thomas that says "Split a piece of wood: I am there. Lift a stone, and you will find me there." It's amazing what the people of yesteryear (and today) could have learned from the Native Peoples if they would have spent more time talking to them and less time killing them!

The Indigenous peoples of the world were far more advanced than the propaganda our school systems have taught us. They simply did not take from the Earth more than they needed and did not hoard wealth. It was, in fact, looked down upon by their entire culture. This is how they lived on this continent for untold thousands of years and why it was still in pristine condition – when the Europeans deluded themselves by stating they "discovered" the "New World". It would still be pristine if the indigenous peoples had been left alone.

The oceans are either dead or dying, depending on where you look. The land is depleted of nutrients and poisoned with pesticides, insecticides, herbicides, and other toxic chemicals that are also being ingested by all of us, including our children and grandchildren. This doesn't even include the pollution corporations are illegally dumping on land and sea. The air is polluted horribly, as well.

What we are doing is not working. At least not if our goal is to support life, liberty and the pursuit of happiness!

Let's take a quick look at the financial system. The Federal Reserve Banking system is a fractional reserve system. This means that the banks are not required to have cash on hand in order to lend it out.

When the Treasury requests more money be printed from the Federal Reserve, they print the amount requested and charge us face value, plus "prime" interest.

In other words, the request is for $10 Billion, the international Bankers of the "Federal Reserve", charge the American people $10 Billion, plus whatever the prime interest rate is at the time. (Talk about a profit margin! That's 100% total profit!) Now, let's say we are talking about printed money, not the kind created out of thin air by the ones and zeros in computers. In this case it costs the International bankers about 3 cents to print each bill. That's 3 cents for a $1 bill, a $10 bill, a $20 bill, a $50 bill or a $100 bill – plus compound interest.

Talk about a nice profit margin! All this adds to our National Debt. You'll see why you should care about this in a little bit.

Now, let's say you want to buy a house. You go to the bank and they loan you $500,000. Not an unrealistic amount nowadays. The bank creates this money out of thin air on the spot, and this too is immediately added to our National Debt. The Federal Reserve does not have to have any actual gold or money in the bank to back up that loan. (They stole the county's gold back in 1913 to 1933!) This is due to that "Fractional Reserve" system mentioned earlier. When they print the money, or simply transfer 1's and 0's – and give it to you, you take that money and spend it at the store. The store then deposits that same money in the bank. The bank then loans that same money out again and again. They are supposed to have at least 5% of the money in reserve to cover their loans, but the Federal Reserve has never been audited! Why? They own the government. In the case of printed money, they can repeat this process of loan and deposit until there is approximately $20,000 loaned out on an original $1,000 loan! And they are charging compound interest on all of it! This is important to remember, because? Due to this fact, you only have to be in debt, one twentieth of your total "net worth", to be declared insolvent and bankrupt.

So, we have been paying face value for 3 cent pieces of paper, plus compound interest on 20 times that amount, plus the total debt – for over 100 years now. In 1913, when the first Federal Reserve Banking Act was passed, our National debt was $2,916,204,913.66. That's after 124 years as a nation.

The Federal Reserve initially had a 20 year Charter. They were granted a 20 Year "Franchise", because that was the only legal way to get around the constitutional requirement that states *"Congress shall have the power 'to coin money', regulate the value thereof...".* **A franchise by the government allows the recipient to conduct business that would otherwise be illegal and or unconstitutional.**

In less than 80 years, our National Debt had grown to $4,064,620,655,521.66– That's over $4 Trillion.

That also happens to be almost 1/10th of the estimated value of America's Net worth in 1992 of $46.5 Trillion.

That is also almost twice the amount necessary for America to be declared insolvent and bankrupt! Oh, but that's what they did in 1933 when they legally changed the United States of America from a Constitutional Republic to a Corporate State. This redefined life in this "country" for ever more. They did a lot during this time, none of it good for the people of the "country".

As of this moment, we are listed at $28.828 Trillion in debt. Each American citizen owes $86,627, and that breaks down to every tax payer owes $229,000!

Why do they say this is the American people's debt? Because when the Emergency Banking Relief Act of 1933 was rammed through congress in just 45 minutes on March 9th of that year, it was stated very succinctly and clearly, by the Speaker of the House that the collateral for these "New Federal Reserve Bank Notes" is "All the properties and all the possessions of all of the peoples of the United States and her territories"!

In case you didn't get that, this means you don't own squat. That house? That boat? Those clothes? Nope. Nada. None of us do.

Your government sold you out long before you were even born. They can and eventually probably will come and repossess everything they want. Ask anyone who was not filthy rich during the Great Depression!

This information right here is the original "Conspiracy Theory". It is now recognized as fact. Be very careful of what your handlers, the unconscious masses, and the media label as "conspiracies" and "theories"! Some are too absurd to believe, but some, like this – are Law!

I bring all this up so you can see a small glimpse of the corruption of this banking system and the government that coddles it. This banking system must be totally annihilated world-wide and we must start over. The Personal and Corporate wealth of the international bankers world-wide, must be seized through the RICO statutes and put towards mending the world-wide damage they have intentionally done! This can also be done lawfully because they have never, ever informed all the people of the world of all of the contents of the Contracts they have entered into. Any contract that any of its contents are not faithfully divulged to all parties involved is null and void, as if it had never been written. At least according to Common Law, which is the foundation of all laws!

Ideally, I would suggest this world slowly convert to a moneyless society. Jacques Fresco has done an incredible job of attempting to provide working models of how a resource-based economy could work. Of course, there are people who are pointing out the flaws on a regular basis. Perhaps they could grow up a bit and help offer constructive ideas of how to make it work, instead of why it won't. Or perhaps they could come up with any alternative suggestion that they believe will work for the highest good of the people of this planet! The objective here is to start the dialogue.I am not saying this is *the* answer. I am saying this is an interesting concept that needs exploring. We have to start this conversation and replace the culture of corruption that currently exists;

otherwise, your grandchildren that do live, are going to be even more enslaved by their banker "masters".

You may want to search the internet for the history of corporations, especially in the United States. You will see a small portion of how the power brokers of yesteryear have stolen our country.

Without a **_TOTAL_** re-structuring, re-defining and severely limiting the power and influence of the "Corporations", **_we cannot and will not ever accomplish anything_**!

There is a great deal of work to be done in cleaning up the mess we have made and the destruction the filthy rich have intentionally created of this planet.

We cannot expect others to come and fix it for us.

We cannot continue to blame God or the _devil_ for it either.

It is time for humanity to grow up and clean up our own mess.

CHAPTER 11

RELIGION VS SPIRITUALITY

"Spirituality liberates and unites.
Religion enslaves and separates."

– Marty Rawson

The origin of the word "religion" lies in the
Latin word "ligare"

– "to bind."

The origin of the word "spiritual" lies in the
Latin word "spiritus"

– "Breath; the breath of life."

Just looking around you, you can see this world is splitting apart. There are those who are awakening to spirituality and the reality of a higher purpose in life, and those who just are not yet ready for such an adventure. Those that are not ready are the ones perpetuating the status quo with its pervasive culture of corruption and inequality.

People are abandoning organized religion by the droves. Especially the younger generations. Why? Because they see through the propaganda that has no heart. People come into this world with spiritual amnesia and they look around and quickly say to themselves – "This is it?

No... No way. There has to be more... What am I missing?"

This world offers a vast array of physical and mental distractions, not to mention material ones. Eventually, people look towards religion to see what it is about. With the consciousness changing in the world, myths and fables just don't work anymore. Working yourself up into an emotional frenzy is just not being recognized as a spiritual experience like it once was. People are looking to fill the void in their very soul, that they can literally feel. Pompous ceremony in ornate churches or tales of being the only ones with the "truth" are not filling this void. Neither does the blatant hypocrisy between what they claim to believe and what they actually do. No, people are looking for their own connection to God and the Divine and they are not looking for a middle-man go-between.

I would like to start right off by delineating the difference between religion and spirituality. Please understand, I am not against religion. I am also not for it. It has, in my opinion, totally failed, after thousands of years, to create a global civilization that works to benefit the people of this world. It has provided some of the people with comfort and support in times of need. However, it has also been used to produce more death and destruction than any other single cause, except possibly the wars financed by international banking. It has left half of the people on this planet clinging to the desperate hope that things might be better... after they die. That's not much of an accomplishment after thousands of years.

When I say religion, I am mostly referring to "Christianity" as practiced in America, as that is where my experience and observations are located. That being said, this does apply equally to the other major religions of the world such as Judaism, Islam and even Hinduism. The countries where these religions are dominant are not doing any better in this regard. In my opinion, to put it simply, religion is the dogma of man. Religion is what happens to divine teachings after greedy, power-hungry humans have manipulated and aberrated them for their own purposes.

The very act of creating an organized religion is contradictory to its own stated agenda and belief system. It is stating that **"*I* "am 'this religion'** and *"you"*- **are not"** thereby instantly creating separation and division between people, which is the very antithesis of what most organized religions claim they are about!

I have to laugh when I hear people who have been indoctrinated into the various religions arguing! It seems that most of these people think that the Christians are in one place in the higher realms, and the Buddhists, the Hindu and all the rest are all somewhere else in their own little domain, but still fighting and arguing about who is "right"! Do people really think Buddha and Jesus are duking it out in Heaven? Wow!

Every divine teacher has come from the same Source to help humanity wake up and they all serve the same God! They all taught basically the same things!

The West is deeply entrenched in the Judeo-Christian mindset. It demands that you take every aspect of every story very literally and by faith alone, and then demands that you worship someone else who had an experience with the divine. This is all good and fine for those who it works for. The problem I have with this approach is that it doesn't seem to me to be what Jesus himself said to do. It is what the people, the humans, are telling us to do. Jesus said many times that the kingdom of heaven is within you! This was obviously an instruction to meditate and access the divinity within. Jesus also stated very emphatically, "All these things I have done, you can do too. These and more!" He was telling people of their own divine nature, and that to realize this they simply had to "go within" to find the kingdom of heaven, by meditating.

Through meditation, you can attain what is called Unity consciousness. In Unity Consciousness, you are literally "One" with God. This is the highest level of self-realization there is! The realization that you are literally an aspect of God and are 'One' with God. You and God are One, just like Jesus said of himself! Yes, this is exactly why he said this and exactly what he meant. It is also why he instructed you to find the Kingdom of Heaven within you! It is not outside of you and it is not inside a church.

And yet, after all of this, the people pushing this religion tell you to fear God, who supposedly loves you, but will burn you in hell for all eternity if you do anything that makes him angry. You have one chance to make a "perfect" life (this perfection is however, totally dependent on who you talk to), or you are one crispy critter. You should fear God because you are a vile sinner, for something someone else did thousands and thousands of years ago. Your only hope is from Jesus, who was God's "only begotten son", (and apparently his favorite), who was murdered so you could be forgiven for that thing – you didn't do. You however, are still too unworthy to approach God yourself and therefore need a middle-man to handle these affairs for you. Oh, and you have to donate money to the middle-man, lots and lots of money.

I have a particularly hard time understanding why God would only forgive humanity's "Sins" after they murdered his "favorite" son, then claim his blood "washes away their sins" as if bathing in blood is a good thing! They then spend the next couple thousand years conducting weekly symbolic cannibalism ceremonies, with items that literally represent his flesh and his blood. Now they are waiting for him to return as their Savior, and forgive them again for the sins he already supposedly died for!

Ya' know, I love Jesus, but some of his followers are freaking me out! They latched onto the human dogma like a starving pitbull, but never listened to anything Jesus himself taught.

I have had two wonderful experiences where Jesus spoke to me personally, although very briefly. His voice alone was so imbued with such magnificent, divine Love that it was and still is unforgettable. I know Jesus (I prefer his Higher Self's name: "Sananda") to be a very real and magnificently divine Being, beyond any words that humanity has the ability to express. So do not mistake what I am saying as being anything against Jesus or what he taught. I am in fact defending him and what he taught. It is because I truly believe in what he taught, that I cannot and will not call myself a "Christian" and associate myself with the people who have disgraced everything he taught. We all know what would happen if Jesus were to come back and offer his teachings in the "bible belt" today. He wouldn't make it out alive…again.

These various churches tell people they have to believe whatever they tell them on "faith". They teach people that faith is taking their word – for their myth. I offer you this:

*"The purpose of faith is to inspire you
to put forth the effort that will result in
you having your own experience with the Divine."*

– Marty Rawson

(Please read that again!)

Then you will no longer need faith, because then – you will *know*. Once you have your own personal experience with the divine, no one can ever take that away from you. They may be as fanatical in their beliefs as they want to be, but opinions mean nothing compared to firsthand experience. It is evident that a large number of people confuse emotional fervor as proof of the religious convictions they are emotionally attached to. Sorry, but emotional fanaticism does not make you right.

In the East, specifically in Hinduism and Buddhism, they have an approach based on you having your own experience with the divine. They do not proselytize; they do not push religion on others. If you are interested, you simply take up the lifestyle and spiritual practices that are literally the "manual" for accessing the divine. This is why we find that most of the major spiritual techniques come from the East, mostly from Hinduism and the various forms of Buddhism.

If you are willing to spend the time and the effort by diving deep into these efforts, the pearls of wisdom you seek will be within your grasp. Again, once you have your own experiences with the divine, no one can ever take that from you. Having your own experiences with the divine is the very definition of Spirituality. Worshiping someone else who did, is the definition of religion, at least in Christianity as practiced in America, by the majority of people calling themselves Christians. Please understand, that I have no problem with anyone practicing any religion as long as they are not harming others. I just wish those practicing religions, would *stop harming others!*

I also understand that there is a clear difference between members of a religion and the organizational hierarchy that controls it. This organizational hierarchy is where the true problems exist. I would ask that if you are going to call yourself Christian, would you please practice what Jesus actually taught himself and not what humans are telling you to practice that goes against his teachings?!? For those of you who are already doing this, I salute you and I appreciate you. But could you please do more, much more, from within your organizations to influence positive change and growth?

Christianity has fallen so far from the teachings of Jesus it is not even recognizable. Most people who call themselves Christians, in America at least, do not practice anything Jesus taught. This is why it is declining in membership so rapidly. Has anybody else noticed that it has been so twisted and aberrated over the centuries that it is only the Christian nations that have adopted Fascism/Nazism? Has anyone noticed the link between racism and "Christianity", and racism and Fascism/Nazism? Historical evidence is abundant in all of these links. The crimes committed in Jesus' name are a bloodstain that cannot be cleansed by refusing to teach the truth to our children. It cannot be ignored or denied out of existence.

Does anybody talk about or care about the tens of thousands of indigenous children that were put into Indian Boarding Schools and subsequently molested, raped, tortured and murdered by bishops, priests, reverends and nuns who did all of this in the name of Jesus? (Don't think for a minute that women did not play a major role in all of this.) This is not judgement; this is blunt historical fact that illustrates how far

"Christianity" has strayed from what Jesus taught. No, these "schools" run by "Christian" churches intentionally practiced a policy of ethnocide and cultural genocide. ***Genocide that murdered over a hundred million inhabitants that lived in the Americas alone.***

Here are some more hard historical facts that may upset people who don't appreciate the honest reflection their actions have upon themselves.

*"Christians have been desperate to distance themselves from European fascism and Nazism, and apologists like to argue that fascist leaders were not practicing Christians. Yet, all the Nazi leaders were born, baptized, and raised Christian, mainly in authoritarian, pious households **where tolerance and democratic values were not valued.** Catholic Nazis, besides Hitler, included Heinrich Himmler, Reinhard Heydrich, and Joseph Goebbels. Hermann Goering had mixed Catholic-Protestant parentage, while Rudolf Hess, Martin Bormann, Albert Speer, and Adolf Eichmann had Protestant backgrounds. Roughly two-thirds of German Christians repeatedly voted for candidates who promised to overthrow democracy. Protestants had given the Nazi party its main backing leading up to 1933. **Evangelical youth was especially pro-Nazi.** Ninety percent of Protestant university theologians supported the Nazis. Christians were Nazis and took part in Nazi atrocities. Any who turned to outright criticism of fascism made their last appeals from the death cell."*

— askwhy.co.uk

"Not only is Rome the source and centre of Fascism, but it has been the seat of a Pope, who, as we shall show, has been an open ally of the Nazi-Fascist-Shinto axis, he has never denounced the abominable aggressions, murder and cruelties they have inflicted on mankind, and the pleas he is now making for peace and forgiveness are manifestly designed to assist the escape of these criminals, so they may presently launch a fresh assault upon all that is decent in humanity."

— H G Wells, Crux Ansata (1943)

"Since the second world war, there has been a convention that the Nazis were driven either by atheism or by all sorts of sinister occult fancies. Christians have been desperate to distance themselves from European fascism and Nazism. Yet "every tree is known by his own fruit," said the Christian God (Lk 6:44), and **European fascism was the fruit of Christianity.**

Christians were Nazis and took part in Nazi atrocities. Nazi practices pioneered by Catholics included the forced wearing of yellow markers, ghettoization, confiscation of Jewish property, and bans on intermarriage with Christians. Martin Luther's book, On the Jews and Their Lies, deploring Jews and implying they would be better exterminated, inspired many parts of Hitler's Mein Kampf in which Hitler praised Luther as a hero of the Germans."

– churchandstate.org.uk

Do we really need to do anything more than mention the "Christian" embrace of slavery? It's really funny because I do not recall Jesus ever advocating that we should enslave others.

Currently, we have so-called "Christians" openly calling "One nation under God, one religion under God." This should scare the hell out of any and all sane people in this country. Be very careful what you support, condone, and endorse. A tyrannical beast will always turn on its own!

If it seems like I am singling out "Christianity", it's because I am. It is the dominant religion within this country as far as sheer numbers go, and it has become so blatantly hypocritical, as a whole, that it is way past time someone calls it out! The First Amendment states *"Congress shall make no law respecting an establishment of religion, or prohibiting the free exercise thereof"*...This means anyone may freely practice any religion they choose and the government cannot interfere nor declare any religion to be the state religion. This country was not founded as a Christian nation, despite desperate attempts by some, to rewrite history. The official and only 1797 Treaty with Tripoli which was read, accepted, approved, and ratified by the Senate of the United States was the one penned by Joel Barlow in the English language. And, like it or not, *Article 11* of the official 1797 Treaty with Tripoli was in the Treaty in 1797 and is appropriately recorded in the official treaty book:

"The government of the United States of America is not in any sense founded on the Christian Religion." Furthermore, look at the society that has been created which is based on modern "Christian" values and note that there is not one single institution that exists that actually works for the highest good of the working-class people of this country, or the less fortunate.

Another disturbing development in America at least, is an increase in atheism recently. This is largely due to the actions and rhetoric spewed by the Christians themselves. This is combined with a rise in people claiming to "believe in science", as their new religion. Yet these same people refuse to apply the scientific process to spirituality! Nor do they seem to understand that science is a method of exploring "what is", and is always, at any given moment, only a snapshot of humanity's current level of understanding! What we know and understand today will change in the coming years, just like it has in the past.

Being born into a culture whose basis for religious teachings is primarily Christianity, these people's arguments invariably entail disbelief of various aspects of stories that are indeed considered implausible and illogical in a modern scientific world. You know...a virgin birth, a talking snake...etc. Inevitably, they will then carry on with exclamations of disbelief in an "Invisible Man in the Sky." I don't mean to be rude, but I must say, all of this is based on a willful, lifelong devotion to ignorance, and pure laziness. First of all, to say nothing divine exists because you do not believe certain allegorical stories provided by *one religion* – is nothing short of asinine. Talk about throwing the baby out with the bath water! Then, to be so lazy as to believe that the definition of "God" is an "Invisible Man in the Sky", and refuse to even try to learn – is simply a declaration of your own pathetic laziness. I also have met very few atheists that weren't narcissists. Just an observation.

If you are too lazy to put in the effort to have your own experience, at least be mature enough to say "I don't know".

I believe that spirituality is in fact the most scientifically proven experiment ever conducted in the history of this planet! The very definition of a scientific experiment is to attain the same results by following and repeating a specific process. For literally thousands and thousands of years, millions upon millions, if not billions of people have practiced the spiritual sciences that have led to having their own personal experiences with the Divine. This is the very definition of scientific. This is why roughly 95% of the population of the Earth believes in some form of spirituality. Atheists seem to be saying that during their one short but apparently self-proclaimed, "elite" lifespan of 2 or 3or 6 decades, through their lifelong devotion to ignorance and laziness, they know more about "All that Is" than the countless generations who have gone before them, throughout all of human history. They actually believe they know more through their lifelong devotion to ignorance and laziness, than those that have spent lifetimes studying, practicing and experiencing the Divine firsthand!

Sorry, but devotion to ignorance, even for an entire lifetime does not beat the personal experience of billions of people throughout all of recorded history! Personally, I do not care if an individual is an atheist or not. In fact, "God" doesn't have a problem with it either. It's their life and it's their lesson. It's all good in that regard.

The problem lies in the hostility and belligerence of their argument, towards anyone who does not believe the same as them. In this regard, they have truly made a proper <u>religion</u> of atheism.

That takes us to the next argument: Proof.

Let me ask you this: Can you *prove* that you witnessed or experienced anything in your life? Can you *prove* to me that you watched a movie or had a specific dream? Can you *prove* to me that you *feel* love for anyone?

Can you prove to me that you saw anything you saw, or that you heard anything you heard, at any time? You can tell me about it, but that does not prove it! People who pretend they are "scientific" will ask for proof, yet they are so mentally undisciplined and cognitively challenged that they cannot comprehend that the fullness and the completeness of any personal experience cannot be "given" to another person.

Hint: That's why it's called a "personal experience"!

You want proof? – *Earn it.*

Go get it yourself. – By yourself – For yourself.

And please...Try to quit basing your opinions on ignorance, assumptions and hearsay.

As we grow up in our lives, we are given descriptions of this world by those who raise us. They in turn, were given these beliefs by those who raised them. First, it is by our parents and siblings. All well-meaning and appropriate in most cases. Then by our schools, churches, social groups and organizations where "people of like-mind congregate". This is all good and fine for the most part, but when was the last time you actually contemplated your core beliefs to see if you actually still believe them?

Those beliefs were handed to you, and for the most part, were believed without question on your part, because you trusted the people telling you these things. Do they really stand up to scrutiny? It is not inappropriate to question anything! It is your obligation to yourself to sift through all the propaganda of this world to find what is your truth! Seeking Truth is the main quest for any soul. It does not have to be in agreement with everyone else's truth!

Working with Spirit will empower you as an individual and give you the courage and strength to live your truth! It is the toughest path there is in this world, but it is also the most rewarding!

I recommend getting so used to talking to Spirit that your internal dialogue naturally turns to them. Make them a constant part of your life and ask their assistance with anything you do – they can do more than you might think! There is one caveat to working with Spirit. You must always ask for an outcome that is in the highest good of all concerned. Spirit never takes "sides" in human drama. The Angelic Realm in particular is incapable of anything that is not based in Love. Once you get used to asking for outcomes that are indeed in the highest good of all concerned, you will find their cooperation and assistance is increased exponentially.

Please also understand that there are many forms of spirituality from many peoples across this planet. I have spent decades studying all I could find. I have found that although they come from widely different backgrounds and areas of the planet, they all have one thing in common: Love. All the great ones who have been venerated across time have taught Love. The nature-based forms of spirituality teach Love through the honoring of all life. This is the litmus test for Divine teachings (once again): If it is based in Love, it is Divine. If it is not, it is the teaching of man.

If your "God" has you hating others, or has ordered the deaths of others, you are not praying to the God that is the First Source and Center of All That Is. You are praying to and worshipping a dark imposter.

I will also give another word of caution – beware of any person or group that tells you their "way, or church" is the "only true church, or religion, or way"! Don't walk, run!

There are many paths leading home in a universe as varied and marvelous as this one! If someone else is doing it different than you but is not harming anyone, let them be.

Perhaps instead of criticizing them, you may actually want to go learn their ways and expand your wisdom. You will probably find you have more in common than you have differences.

It has always seemed to me that humans have an incredibly myopic view of God and the world's various religions. Let us imagine a family of humans that has 10 children. They raise each of their children, for the most part, in relative isolation from one another. They also teach all of their children different things, in different ways. They then inform their children, whom they have told they love, that each one of them has been taught the "right" way, and that at the end of their training, there will be a test. A test which, only one of them has actually been taught the correct information. Oh, and by the way, every child who fails the test is going to be tortured and then burned alive!

If a human couple actually did this, the entire world would be aghast and up in arms! Yet, this is exactly what many claim God himself is doing with all of humanity! Not with just 10 people, but billions of people! How is it that we assign to God, absurd, negative attributes that are unworthy of us? Then, to add to our apparent mental disorders, we tell ourselves that this God who would do this, is perfect, and we are unworthy sinners! It just all seems a bit too odd for me.

Let's now turn to the concept of judgement for a second. Here in the west, we usually recite the admonition "Judge not lest ye be judged". It doesn't work at all as a deterrent. It is an insinuated threat or warning of a repercussion, on you, for your actions. Yes, karma exists, but humans don't respond to threats and they are obviously poor deterrents to negative behavior. Let us look at this thing called judgement. Judgement lowers your vibration by its very nature. The Law of Attraction will then attract a lower frequency that matches that of your judgement.

If strawberries are your favorite thing to eat in the world, and I hand you a bowl of beautifully ripe, clean strawberries, you will not judge that. You will smile, take the bowl of strawberries and spend the next few minutes enjoying them. If, however, you witness some activity that appalls you, like someone abusing an animal, you will likely judge that activity rather harshly. It is okay to have your initial reaction. The problem comes from allowing this judgement to live inside you and fester like an infected wound.

If you dwell on it, it lowers your vibrational frequency and you attract that lower frequency. The more you attract it, the more the universe shows it to you. The Law of Attraction has no judgement of its own! It will bring to you what you focus on! If you continue down this road, soon you will form a concrete belief that this is the way the world is, because you have witnessed it so often. Before long, you are drawing people to you who feel the same way, and you may even join groups of other like-minded individuals to confirm with one another your mutual beliefs. Since this is all based in a negative judgement in the first place, by this point you are so full of negative emotions, you are spewing it out to everyone around you.

Your bucket is so full of crap you can't help but share it! This is how hate groups are formed.

This is why it is not wise to judge! It will fill *you* up with negativity if you are not careful!

It is far better to use discernment. Discernment is the ability to observe something someone does and say to yourself "I choose to not have *that* in my life! If *that* is *your* lesson, good luck! It looks like it is going to hurt eventually, but if that is your lesson, so be it".

Now, this is far easier to say than to do. Most things on the spiritual path are. You may spend your entire life simply trying to remind yourself to keep trying to do this! That's okay too! It is far better to try, than to not try! Like everything else, if you fail, get back up and try again!

Another concept I would like to touch on is the common saying "There is no good or bad". This is a common phrase in the new age movement. I consider this to be a potentially dangerous statement. This is not a statement anyone should be teaching their children! Especially without a great deal of explanation.

God does not judge. God understands that this material world is where we go to play in a temporary dream state and learn incredible lessons at the same time. Nothing we do can harm God or what is "real" in the eternal sense. God understands that the apparent harm we do to one another, we are actually doing to ourselves. From God's point of view, there truly is no good or bad, there are only lessons.

From a human point of view, in this 3rd-dimensional reality, we need to look at where we want to go and who we want to be. Then, in order to attain these goals, we need to make choices, decisions and actions that are in line with our stated goals. (Humanity as a whole is really, really crappy at doing this!) How well does what you are doing, support what you say you want?

So, what we do here, does matter – it will have repercussions across the world and across the universe! If anyone takes this concept to mean they can do anything they want as long as they get what they want, they are in for a world of hurt and a lot of karma! Anyone who thinks that they can lie, cheat, steal, rape and murder their way into the ascension process, are sadly mistaken.

It really all comes down to where you want to go. If you wish to work with the Light, you cannot do things that promote the darkness to get there.

I see people all the time trying to say there is no God, simply because a "God" who would allow all the evil to exist in this world must be evil himself, or at least apathetic. Again, this is common in people who have only a cursory understanding of certain religions, but no personal experience in spiritual matters. The "First Source and Center of All That Is" or "Creator" created us as Beings of Light in its own self-image, which is the Light! We are beings of Light and literally sparks of the Divine! It is humans who have tried to create God in their image! We have assigned traits that humans are ashamed of to God!

We were originally created to go play, explore and investigate the cosmos. It was a means of the Creator to experience all of creation through the individualizations of awareness that were and still are an aspect of itself. The Creator turned us loose with these instructions: "Go forth and co-create with me, as an extension of me! But be careful to always create everything with Love, because, you will have to experience your creations!" This is the part we have forgotten! We create so much in this world out of fear and other negative emotions and then wonder why we have to experience these very same negative things. Quit blaming God or the "Devil". Start creating with the Divine, in an Alliance with Spirit, and see what happens – you will change your world! If enough of us do this, we will change the entire world!

Part of Spirituality is keeping an open mind. This is not just limited to spiritual matters. We, as humans have been conditioned to never question the status quo. Especially in academic and scientific circles, there is a moratorium on challenging the "accepted" beliefs. There is no end to the lengths those in even minor positions of authority will go to- to maintain their exalted status and positions. Let us remember that science is a method of investigation of our world, and is, at any given point in time, merely a reflection of our current understanding.

Truth itself never fears the scrutiny of being brought out into the light of day and being questioned and or investigated. What could it possibly have to fear? Being discovered?!?

I think not!

Why then do we refuse to study common, known phenomenon that exist in our world?

If you were to proclaim that you were seeking funding to study the effects of the full moon on human psyche, you would probably be laughed out of the building. Yet, at the same time, we could literally fill stadiums full of people who work in the healthcare world like hospitals, convalescent homes, and police departments across the world who will tell you they have to staff up on nights of the full moon! This is known, this is accepted, and it is practiced. It is not however, currently allowed for science to seriously investigate this phenomenon.

Why is that? We could learn so much about ourselves and the universe if we would simply investigate things like this that are known to occur, but are not thoroughly understood. We would literally open up new fields of scientific inquiry that could propel us forward by leaps and bounds! The only other explanation for us not being allowed to study things like this, is that those in power already have that knowledge and do not want anyone else to have it. Either way, we do not need their permission!

What other things are we refusing to study to keep the status quo content?

One thing they cannot control is your relationship with the Divine. This is where your true power lies. This is where *our* true power lies. They may have all the gold and control those with all the really big guns, but they cannot control your relationship with Spirit!

Make your connection to Spirit and keep it alive and active on a daily basis. Being spiritual is not about acting "holier than though" or anything like that. Be real with yourself, establish and nurture a personal relationship with the Divine Beings of Light and do no harm. Many people seem to think being spiritual is always acting like they never have a bad day, or acting as if they are above all the negativity life can ever throw at them. These people are attempting to fool themselves and eventually burn out and usually end up suffering from depression. It is ok to be human! It is ok to have negative feelings and even to express negative thoughts. It's okay to go there, just don't unpack your suitcase. Don't stay there!

It is okay to vent when you need to – there is a reason that a pressure cooker has a valve!

If you need to beat a pillow with a stick, scream as loudly as you can or smash an object to proverbial smithereens, do so. It's okay! Let it out. Let it go! Just Do No Harm to others or their property. It is burying these emotions inside of you that will cause you harm. Please also remember, spirituality is about taking back your personal power, remembering who you are.

Spirit will never tell you what to do or place themselves in a position of authority over you.

If any being does this, or asks for donations of money… you are not dealing with Beings of Light!

CHAPTER 12

SPIRITUALITY

"Be Love"

– The (Entire) Arcturian Ascension Manual

Ever since the fall of consciousness, humanity has been asking the questions: what is the purpose of life, and where did I come from? Spiritual amnesia is a pain in the butt, but great for creating a learning environment!

From what Spirit has taught me, I will offer up a few thoughts on these matters. The ultimate purpose of life is the ongoing evolution of the soul – back to total Unity Consciousness with Source. These lives in physical incarnations are engaged to facilitate learning that could not take place in the higher realms, at least not as efficiently. It is intended that you will not only learn, but experience things in your own unique way and perspective, which allows God to take part in this "new" experience in real time. It is also hoped that you will engage these adventures with the gusto and enthusiasm of an ambitious child, and self-create the best version of yourself that you can imagine. Soul growth and joyous adventure is the intended name of the game.

The purpose of Spirituality is to assist you in remembering who you are by providing you with the tools and methods to do so. Spirituality teaches you the rules of how this multi-dimensional, fractal, holographic multiverse works so you can use these rules/laws to your benefit; consciously. In the higher dimensions, all beings are in unity consciousness, so there is no need for Spirituality, let alone the religions of any particular, individual planet.

The Universal Laws are constantly functioning, whether you understand them or not. Kind of like gravity, you don't have to understand it for it to work, and you might find out how it works the hard way. It is much more efficient and enjoyable to function in this physical universe if you understand the rules. This way you can use them consciously to your benefit, rather than them working to your detriment, unconsciously. The Law of Attraction is one of the Universal Laws and an understanding of it explains a great deal.

What is Spirituality? Being Love. God is Love. Love is the energy that is the unified field that this matrix is founded on. The problem is, it is not easy to "Be Love" in a world literally owned and controlled by Beings of Darkness. Oh! But what a challenge, and what a victory for your soul, if you can!

Before you come into these lives, you take part in creating what is called your Soul Contract for each lifetime. These are custom fit for your very soul, for the perfect lessons for soul growth and for the possible resolving of karmic debt or karmic benefit, as the case may be. The goal here is to provide a lifetime where, at perfect stages of your life, you will encounter people and situations that provide you with the opportunities to learn and grow, that you need. Some of these are designed to happen to you prior to your "waking up" or enlightenment, to true spirituality. These are hard lessons, but they provide great rewards for your soul for all of eternity.

The problem is, you do this with spiritual amnesia, meaning you do not know who you really are, as a Being of Light! You have been taught you are a "human". You have been taught many things, by people with good intentions, but quite possibly, things not necessarily true. You feel alone, because you have no memory of your absolute connection to Source that your soul has grown used to throughout eternity. Therefore, you feel that something is lacking in your life. You feel a void in your life. You look around and you say to yourself "This can't be right. This can't be all there is. This world is screwed up and has no heart! There has to be more." You start experimenting with ways to fill that void. You look outside yourself for everything, because that is what you have been taught. You have been taught that this product, that lifestyle, a form of entertainment or perhaps a drug will make you happy and fulfilled. But it doesn't. Ever. It can't.

Depending how much damage was done to you in your early years, you may have to really hit rock bottom before you wake up. This is actually fine, as it is part of the lesson. This is far better than being one of those who will not wake up at all! Many of the people who start drinking and doing other drugs are actually spiritually advanced souls that have endured such pain, they cannot handle this world. They "check-out" through the use of substances to avoid the pain. If and when they realize the answer lies within them, they will hopefully be inspired to clean themselves up and continue on with a productive, healthy and rewarding life! This is a process some people have to go through to learn. It is also another reason why you should not judge others. The one you are judging just *might* have insights into the spiritual realms that no one would listen to, and they were ostracized for talking about. Even if your journey did not ever reach this level, your seeking to fill the internal void is what will bring you to spirituality.

Spirituality will empower you. It will help you to realize that you are a Divine Being of Light. That is what your soul is. The Angels and the Masters and the Star Nations are in fact, your brothers and sisters. They do not want you worshipping them. They want you to claim your own birthright, stand up on your own two feet, and work *with* them, like an adult. First, heal your own life, then help this civilization and this beautiful, but forsaken planet.

When you realize that you are a Divine Being, and nothing can change that, it goes a long way towards filling that void mentioned earlier.

Nothing can change that, not even your own opinion, because you did not create your own soul. The Creator, First Source and Center of All That Is did, and He/She/It has created you as such for all eternity. You can believe whatever you choose to, at any time. As A Course in Miracles so eloquently states "Nothing real can be threatened. Nothing unreal exists. Herein lies the peace of God."

Once you have accepted who you really are, and realize God is Love, you will begin to open up to the assistance of the higher dimensions. Then you can begin to heal your life. You do this by unlearning most of what you have probably been taught and what you have perceived to be true, but were not. This is most difficult, because the hardest thing for a human's ego to admit, is that almost everything it believes is not true! There is a truly wonderful quote that I feel summarizes the awakening process beautifully:

"Finding yourself is not really how it works. You are not a ten-dollar bill in last winter's coat pocket. You are also not lost. Your true self is right there, buried under cultural conditioning, other people's opinions and inaccurate conclusions you drew as a kid, that became your beliefs about who you are. Finding yourself is actually returning to yourself. An unlearning, an excavation, a remembering who you were before the world got its hands on you!"

– Emily McDowell

Amen, Emily McDowell, amen. I have never had the privilege of meeting her, but I am a huge fan, just from this quote alone! Google her...she is quite accomplished and talented!

As your personal power continues to grow and flourish as you heal your life, you will recognize your karmic lessons for what they are and possibly find the lessons in situations that escaped you before. You will start to create a relationship with the Angelic realm and other Beings of Light.

You will begin to see the sanctity of all life and start to live a life of compassion, with concern for the welfare of others and this beautiful planet which gives us life. You will eventually realize that the definition of wisdom truly is "Doing that, which is in the Highest Good of All concerned."

You will slowly and ever increasingly begin to comprehend what Unity Consciousness truly means. You will realize that if your ego tells you – you have attained it, you probably haven't. That's okay too.

Spirituality liberates and unites everyone, while empowering you as an individual, so you can contribute your gifts to the betterment of All That Is. This will very likely involve assisting those that are following in your spiritual footsteps. Being of Service to Others is the way of true spirituality.

Beings who have been created as souls that are Service to Self, can only progress to a slightly higher vibrational frequency than this world has been at, since the fall of consciousness. They will have to change their very nature and learn how to be of Service to Others before they can ascend into the higher realms as Beings of Light. They chose dominion over the material worlds as their preference, now it is time for their work to really begin. This is what was meant by "The meek shall inherit the Earth". The ascended Earth will not support such low frequencies.

It really is all about understanding how the Universal Laws work. The Law of Attraction that so many have talked about, and taught - is great, but only if you have paid attention to the Law of Vibration and kept your vibrational frequency high enough to attract those things in life that are based on Love!

So, by empowering you to realize who you really are, spirituality gives you the tools and inspiration to heal your life and become the highest version of yourself that you can imagine, while being of service to Life itself. With the assistance of your brothers and sisters in the Light, of course!

Below is something Spirit gave me one night, long ago:

Surrender to the Divinity within you,
and reflect this back onto the mirror of Source.
We've all heard "Be here now."
How simple. How true...
Manifestation starts within.
The world merely reflects what you,
In your own sovereign right, have chosen.
Choose Love. Choose Wisdom. Choose the Heart.
Give Gratitude for All That Is – to All That Is.
See All That Is, – in All That Is.
Nurture All That Is.
Open your consciousness to a universal level
And share the Light within,
With All That Is.
Be Love. Be Gratitude. Be Divine.
Be all of these, and reflect this back onto
The multi-dimensional mirror that is –
All That Is.
Be this here...
Be this now...
Just Be.
— Copyright © 2001 [Marty Rawson]. All Rights Reserved.

When you really understand this, you will also understand what Spirit means when they say there is no right or wrong. They are not saying it is okay to harm others for your own selfish gain, they are saying you have the right to choose your lessons. You will build karma either way. Good karma for an enjoyable life and future, or negative karma for a painful one. The choice is yours. Pain does serve as a wonderful incentive.

Spirituality is healing. It is healing the wrong thoughts and wrong perceptions. It is healing the emotions that have arisen from these as well. Emotional healing is probably the most important, and is often the most neglected. I will say again, your memories and your emotions tied to them are your biggest problem. If you can work with Love, forgiveness, surrender and gratitude – on your memories, while finding the lessons inherent in them, you will accomplish so much! (You might want to re-read that last sentence.) You do need to find the lessons in order to actually heal some things.

Now, what about all these tools? Besides the Universal Laws, there are many paths and many tools to use. No society or civilization has ever been without spiritual guidance. As long as these are methods and techniques that are based in Love and do no harm, they are Divine.

Because humans have reverted to vocal speech due to the Fall of Consciousness, there were originally 5 sacred languages brought or taught to humanity in different regions. A sacred language is one where the sound made by an individual, to represent any "thing or concept", matches the vibrational frequency of that thing or concept. Obviously, there are various vibrational frequency "matches" for any given thing or concept. I do not believe that it is a coincidence that there are 5 sacred languages.

What I offer below is an advanced understanding of the nature of the anatomy of the Spirit, and how the 5 sacred languages relate to it in a very unique way. I will need to start with a few explanations before I can give the actual technique however. This is a very simplified explanation.

The languages of ancient Egyptian and Chinese unify all the bio-chemical energies in the body that work horizontally. The languages of Tibetan and Sanskrit unify all of the bio-chemical energies that work vertically in the body. This forms an energetic grid, that when activated by the Divine Light of the Hebrew Fire Letters, activates the light body and assists with the merging of complex higher dimensional energies.

The higher the attainment of vibrational frequency of the individual, the more these bodies are activated and the grander the spiritual experience and wisdom. When you use the 5 sacred seed syllables together in mantra form, these languages will open channels so that you can work directly ith the higher Intelligences with increased communication. It also assists with eventually anchoring the Light Body, or Merkabah.

Each of the 5 Sacred Languages has a "seed syllable" word that is associated with an aspect of this portion of the anatomy of the Spirit. The 5 sacred languages and their "seed syllables" are:

Egyptian – "Amen-Ptah" – Horizontal – (ahmen p'ta – as in 'top' without the p)
Tibetan – "Phowa" – Vertical – (Po as in potato, wa as in water)
Chinese – "Kwan Yin" – Horizontal – (Kwan – with a as in water, yin same as in Yin-Yang)
Sanskrit – "Buddha" – Vertical – (Boo, - Da as in Dakota)
Hebrew – "Gabriel" (Gavriel) – 3rd Eye (Gab/Gav as in gavel, re as in return, el as in elephant)
Layooesh is another ancient Hebrew word used - (pronounced Lay- oo-esh)

So, you say "Amen-Ptah" and visualize a horizontal grid throughout your body.
Then, you say "Phowa" and visualize a vertical grid throughout your body.
Next, you say "Kwan Yin" and visualize a horizontal grid throughout your body.
Then, you say "Buddha" and visualize a vertical grid throughout your body.
Then you say "Gavriel – Layooesh" (both), while directing a pillar of Light to your 3rd eye to activate this higher dimensional crystalline grid. (Gavriel is the Hebrew pronunciation for Gabriel, and Layooesh is Paleo-Hebrew (ancient) for "energetic pillar of Light")

Results will obviously vary greatly, depending on the person. There are too many variables to tell who this is going to work for, in a noticeable way, and to what extent. It works great for me, but I do have to be focused intently. It can really work up a beautiful and powerful energy that you won't soon forget. Some people simply are not ready for this exercise and some will take off with it. Either way, it's all good. Work with it as much as you feel you should, or are drawn to.

The beauty of this technique is that those who propagate hatred, prejudice, and separation will never use it. The universe has wonderful ways of sorting out those that are not ready.

We must remember that since everything is energy, and since sound and light are two defining characteristics of energy, they are also fundamental ways to influence energy. This is why this and many healing modalities work.

Writing is simply putting pre-agreed upon forms down to express concepts so we can communicate with one another. Letters are signs, or symbols, arranged to express concepts, which we then string together to convey our thoughts. The point is that it is the thought, the consciousness that matters. When you use the Fire letters of the Hebrew aleph-bet (the Hebrew alphabet), you are writing in a sacred language. The same is true for the other sacred languages. The same is true for Runes, for that matter. Old Norse may not be one of the 5 sacred languages, but that does not exclude the Runes from being sacred symbols for the energies they represent. Again, no society or civilization has ever been neglected by the Divine. That would be impossible.

You will notice that the vast majority of traditional mantras in use come from Sanskrit, Tibetan and Hebrew. Ancient Egyptian is quite rare and I am not familiar with any Chinese mantras.

One Egyptian Mantra I am familiar with is for calling forth the elements of Earth, Fire, water, and Air. They are El, Ka, Leem, Om respectively.

Fill yourself with the emotion of gratitude and chant these to yourself. These words represent wave forms that cannot easily be reproduced by the human voice, but the energies themselves do respond to the emotions of love and gratitude. It's all about that Unity Consciousness and remembering who you are.

The interesting thing to me is that the indigenous peoples of the world never lost their understanding of the Unity of all life and how to live in harmony with nature. It was the ones who insisted they themselves were the "civilized" ones, who are having to relearn that lesson.

What about prayer? How do you make sure your prayers are reaching Source?

Did you know there is a 'science of prayer'? If you didn't, don't feel bad, most people don't.

I have to give credit to the wonderful Gregg Braden for his research which turned up part of the following. In his book "The Isaiah Effect" he details how the book of Isaiah was the only book of the bible that survived intact. The interesting thing is, the scroll that survived is about twice as long as the version in the bible! That means someone edited out the last half of the book of Isaiah a very long time ago! Why?

A closer look at what was in the second half of this book showed that it included what was called the "Science of Prayer". It gave detailed instructions on how to make sure your communication (prayer) got to Source, instead of simply, quietly asking for whatever is on today's wish list.

Now, the funny thing about this whole thing is that our dear Mr. Braden found that there was still one Spiritual discipline that taught this very method! It is the Huna Masters of Hawaii. I find that incredibly interesting since these two regions are almost 9,000 miles apart!

Below is a user-friendly version of how to perform this beautiful form of communication with the divine.

I truly hope and believe I have captured the essence of Huna Prayer, but I am not claiming to be a Huna Master!

Huna Prayer:

First off, you must make preparation for an effective prayer. This means carefully deciding on exactly what you want to manifest. Never ask for anything that would cause harm to anyone. Decide what it is you truly are asking for and write it down.

Meditate on this for clarity, and ask your Higher Self for assistance and affirmation of the proper goal.

Re-write your request as needed after meditation.

Second – you need to build up an increase of energy – Prana!

You can do this through breath work or exercise, but the important thing is to be concentrating on your Prayer the entire time so your mind and your emotions are in sync.

I recommend the Wim Hof method of breathing for this, as it is incredibly powerful and effective. Just remember to keep your focus on your prayer with your mind and emotions!

After you have taken your last inhale, pull the air up high into your upper chest and concentrate on syncing mind and emotions.

When you exhale, do so extremely forcefully and powerfully in one great explosive breathe, (like someone punched you in the stomach), while simultaneously envisioning your prayer and emotions shooting up and out of your crown chakra – up to Source!

Burn your written prayer as a final gesture of release and give sincere gratitude, **_knowing_** that your prayer has been heard, and will be answered in Divine fashion.

You then need to follow up by doing those things in the physical world that will enable your prayer to come to fruition.

In other words, if, for example, you want to write a book, you can't just pray for one to land in your lap, you have to write it… But you can surely ask for help in the writing!

The beauty of the Huna prayer is that it provides a practical method to bring your mind, your emotions and your will power into a coherent, focused intent, which is then sent straight as an arrow – to God, which is exactly what is needed to manifest in the quantum field and communicate with Source!

You see, it is difficult, even for God, to know what we really want when our actions say one thing, our thoughts say another and our emotions are scattered all over the place! (Focus people... Focus! Lol.)

As you go forward, please remember to follow your heart and look into the aspects of the metaphysical world that appeal to you! There is truly something for everyone! As you continue to grow, you will become interested in other things that you come across. This is good, as the last thing you want to do is become stagnant and stop learning.

Most of all, remember that you are a sacred being of Light, literally an aspect of the Creator itself!

This planet is a sacred Being itself, and it is high time we started treating her as such! This physical reality/dimension is no less sacred than the higher dimensions that we call "home" and "heaven". We have just trashed this place, and ourselves to the point that we have created hell on Earth instead of Heaven. It is – again – high time we changed that!

Earth (Gaia) is a beautiful, sacred being and she has faithfully and lovingly supported us while we have trashed her in response. THIS MUST CHANGE!

Start by working on yourself and send gratitude to Mother Earth on a daily basis. Spend a little time appreciating her beauty and care for the abundance of life she supports on her! Is that really asking too much? You really can make a difference!

I must also note that there are certain animals that are much more than they appear. We must protect the whales and the dolphins at all costs!

They are incredible beings that possess a higher level of consciousness than humanity does! They are in constant communication with the higher dimensional beings and they are the record keepers for the planet. All whale and dolphin hunting must end now! It is my opinion that the U.N. military forces should be put to use defending and protecting the whales, the dolphins and the rain forests/environment wherever necessary on this planet. It is past time they start protecting what is truly precious on this planet, and that is the life on it!

I hope this helps you gain confidence and empowers you to make positive changes in your life. Furthermore, I highly encourage everyone to joyfully explore any and all forms of spirituality that appeals to you! Simply make sure the teachings and practices are based in love and honor all life. There is a lot of very cool stuff out there! Have Fun and Enjoy!

CHAPTER 13

UNIVERSAL, GALACTIC AND EARTH HISTORY

*"You are on the verge of becoming a Galactic Civilization,
the question is:*

Will humanity choose to destroy itself?

Or will humanity choose Healing and Love?"

– Marty Rawson

It should not shock anyone who actually engages an occasional thought process, that the history of the world they have been taught through the mainstream curriculum, is the farthest thing from the truth. Yet, ever so slowly, the truth is coming out in bits and pieces. The Elite hope you are too stupid to put these bits and pieces together. They surely do not want you to know the true history of this planet, or homo sapiens, and definitely not the galaxy. So, let's go back to the beginning, way back.

The mind of the Creator is infinite. It is… All That Is. However, being in a state of eternal singularity gets rather boring quite soon. The one thing the mind wants and needs is stimulus, even the mind of God. It did not therefore, take long for the differentiation of individualized awarenesses, within the whole, to take place. First one, then another, then a veritable explosion of continuous division and expansion.

For those with mathematical and/or Sacred Geometry leanings, I highly recommend Drunvalo Melchizedek's Flower of Life Volumes 1 and 2 for a little "Light" reading on this.

The individual awarenesses that were created were magnificent Beings of Light created in the "image" of the creator itself; Fractals, if you will. These were without number, especially to the human mind. The Creator said "Go...Go play and co-create with me! I shall experience All that Is through you, for you are all a part of me! Go, play and co-create, but remember – You must experience All that you co-create with me! This is the only way I can experience it! So please remember, create with Love!"

And off they went.

As these magnificent beings of Light ventured out, as much in frequency as distance, they eventually became aware of a difference in their perceptions. For as they ventured on, they were literally increasing the distance from the location where Source had centralized its individualized aspect of its own personal awareness. This radiates the pure Love and Light of Source, and as they ventured on, they were changing in frequency, and experienced their "dimensional" shifts. They went on and on and on and found this to be a recurring phenomenon. The farther out they got from "where" Source had localized/centralized its awareness, the lower the vibrational frequency of the energies became and the shifts in perception continued. Eventually they even noticed their own geometric Light Bodies were starting to change.

Then, after a very long time and journey, the most wonderous thing happened. They discovered a frequency of dimensional energy that solidified into dense, solid, physical matter! This dimension was wonderous indeed and behaved differently from anything they had ever experienced before. There was one problem though. They couldn't interact with it as they were used to. They were etheric Beings of Light and this dense, physical matter required a body of dense, physical matter to interact with it.

Being in Unity consciousness with Source, endless possibilities were instantly comprehended and shortly implemented.

Source would create Lords of Light called the Elohim. They would have the powers and the wisdom to create Universes of this dense physical matter, according to pre-determined guidelines based on Divine Will. God, or Source would also create unique forms of Beings to administer these Universes from the dimensions higher in frequency than these physical realms.

The magnificent Beings of Light that had originally "discovered" this dense physical matter, would then create differentiated, individualized awarenesses that were aspects of themselves, much in the same way as Source did in the beginning.

These souls would incarnate into physical lives on these worlds of dust so they could interact with this dense physical matter, and to experience all the wonders of this new phenomenal experiment. The Beings in the higher realms, created to administer to these worlds of dust, are of course, what we refer to as the Angelic realm, of which there are many types. The angelic beings are created perfect for their divine role and exist in comparative ecstasy. There are many, many types of divine beings throughout the myriad dimensions. They are not all Angels to be exact, but for simplicity we shall limit our discussion to them, the Elohim, and the Melchizedeks, because these are the main types of Beings of Light concerned with administering to these "worlds of dust".

The Order of Melchizedek is an Order of Sonship that serves the Divine plan for this Universe, in a more "hands on" approach. The Melchizedeks are the only autonomous self-governing Order in the Universe. Their number is fixed, meaning there is no ongoing creation of these types of Beings, nor are there any who are initiated into the Order. They are the First responders to any crisis in the universe and the teachers/professors at the Melchizedek Universities in the Higher dimensions. They are also the ones who deliver the original Divine teachings to the lower worlds of matter when these worlds are ready for them. Thus, it was one of the Melchizedek Sons who incarnated on Earth to bring the original divine teachings to Earth. This is why he is noted as the first High Priest, and why he simply seems to appear very sudden like, with no Earthly history.

Please note, this is not to say that the Judeo/Christian teachings are a reflection of these original teachings. They do still contain some of the original truth in them, but humans have grossly distorted everything they have touched throughout history. One of the first things humans did was try to make a priesthood of the Order of Melchizedek. Joining a club or group here on Earth does not make you one, any more than joining the Lions club makes you an actual Lion. You, of course, are free to call yourself anything you wish.

There are many, many types of specialized beings in the higher realms/dimensions that do indeed serve the divine plan for each local universe, but for sake of clarity we shall limit our discussion to these.

Once a Divine plan was approved for a Local Universe to be manifested, the Light of Source itself was refracted by the Elohim Lords of Light, in the higher dimensions using what is referred to as a 5-Pyramidal prism, in a very specific manner which caused an "explosion" of the previously unmanifested potential energy of the "Void". This refracted the Light of Source into the living Cosmic Rays we know of today. Each one being a literal aspect of the higher divinity and wisdom that is Source. Since everything is energy, and energy is light, it only stands to reason that new creations would have to come from Light/Energy, and from the higher frequencies to the lower – "As above, so below". While current popular theory postulates that the universe was created from the explosion of a phenomenally heavy pea-sized piece of matter, no one seems to have ever asked the question: Where did this supposed "phenomenally heavy pea" come from? There was no mysterious pea, it was done with Light!

The exact specific format or programming that the Elohim Lords of Light used determined the structure of the ensuing matter. It is the blueprint so to speak for All That Is within this particular, specific local Universe. Ours was based on the duality of the Inner Light and the Outer Light, the polarity of the Masculine and the Feminine, Service to Self and Service to Others, hot and cold, and so on… and on… and on.

An interesting aspect of this 3rd dimensional reality is the way energy behaves. It is continuously changing form. There is a process of formation of elements into the various types of matter, and then through entropy it will decay and change form, or it can change through combustion or chemical reactions. The higher dimensions have a continuous centropic action going on where forms are created and sustained through energetic coherence, and are eternal, unless acted upon by direct consciousness. This made the higher realms and original Creation both perfect and eternal, while the physical realms were temporary and therefore illusory. A nice, and inherently useful, contrast indeed.

Before long, by divine timing standards anyhow, the physical universe began the long process of taking form. It was and is, itself, a living organism, since all that exists is conscious energy. It gave birth to a wide variety of other forms, galaxies, nebula, black holes and of course the stars and planets that make up the galaxies. The universe has sometimes been referred to as the Mind of God. It is indeed uncanny how the structure of the Universe is virtually indistinguishable from a close up of brain cells! Truly a dramatic representation of the fractal nature of all that is and yet another interpretation of the axiom – As above, so below!

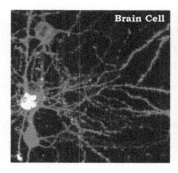 

It was a wondrous feat for the Elohim Lords of Light to program this matrix of energy to create lifeforms that would evolve over time into specific types, yet with a variety that was astounding. The very blueprint for life itself ensured virtually endless variety at every frequency of vibration.

At every differentiation of vibrational frequency, there exist individualized awarenesses that reside there naturally. These may be termed energies or entities. In this 3rd dimension, strong energies are usually the result of physical acts that have taken place in that location. Since energy is programmable, it takes on the "electric" information from the brain and the "magnetic" energy of the heart. This is why some locations where dramatic events have occurred retain that information. Sometimes even retaining the sounds of the event. This phenomenon has been reported many times by various people throughout history.

Entities reside in all dimensions naturally, at their frequency. Thus, the fleeting glimpse of something out of the corner of your eye, may very well be one of these. There is no need to be alarmed, they have always been there. They are as natural in their environment as we are in ours. We are simply raising our frequency at this time, and are starting to notice things that we haven't been able to before. Perception is based on the rate at which you can perceive things. This is why animals can perceive things we cannot. The point is, Life is All That Is. You are an electro-magnetic being of Light and Energy with an individualized awareness that you know as yourself, and you are swimming in a vast sea of Light and energy while interacting with All of it. Hence the saying, "You are a drop in the ocean and the ocean in a drop."

The geometric nature of the universe has been confirmed by scientists from the quantum level to the structure of life on this planet and the larger scale of the universe itself. I highly recommend researching the relationship of the Fibonacci sequence to the Golden Mean. In short, the Golden Mean and the Golden Spiral are the theoretical and mathematically perfect equations. The Fibonacci Series represents the manifestation of how mathematical perfection is expressed in a physical world. It is a beautiful science which is why it is called Sacred Geometry. It governs everything there is, from our physical proportions to the spirals in a galaxy. When you construct anything according to Sacred Geometry it will work better and be more harmonious. The beauty of sacred geometry is that it is the observable, measurable blueprint for this universe.

When the original divine plan for this particular planet was formed, it was meant to be a living library of life from all quadrants of the galaxy and to some extent the universe. It was formed and seeded with a vast variety of life. There was originally a specific form of bipedal hominid that was intended to evolve into a being with enhanced connection to all life on this planet. The plan was to have a beautiful gem of a planet, with lifeforms from all over the universe, complete with living librarians that were spiritually connected to the planet and all life on it. That was the original plan...it didn't last too long.

Before I go any further, let me be very clear. The galactic history I am going to summarize is unabashedly and directly based on the "Prizm of Lyra" by the incredible Lissa Royal Holt and Keith Priest. I will be adding some information, but much of this will be a summary of their work. The reason for this is because it was Spirit that led me to the Prizm of Lyra and I received both visions and memories from reading several sections of it. I still have relationships with many of the Star Nations talked about in it, and several that are not mentioned in it! I am firmly convinced that this is the most precise accounting of galactic history available to us, at this time. Now, let's also be clear, it doesn't matter who you are, no one can fit billions of years of history into a format concise enough for humans to read in one lifetime! So, while I am going to greatly summarize much of their incredible work, I highly recommend that you get it for yourself, find a nice, quiet place and read it to your heart's content. Their version is much more thorough.

One of the concepts that need to be understood, and most of us get, is that this universe is based on polarity. Polarity is expressed in every aspect of its existence, especially in the 3rd dimensional worlds of dust. One aspect of polarity that is not discussed enough is the polarity of soul types. What I mean by this is those that are "Service to Self" and those that are "Service to Others". There are advanced species that are predominantly one or the other of these, and there are beings of both types within those species.

"Service to Self" types have perhaps an excess of masculine energy and are very materialistic. They are greatly concerned with power, influence, dominion over others and the accumulation of wealth, material goods, and status. They believe that by taking care of themselves, first, last and foremost, they somehow make the "whole" stronger. This is your "dog eat dog, every man for himself, survival of the fittest" mentality. Basically, they are your type A personalities and tend to be the ones to run things in this world, whether they are competent or not.

"Service to Others" type of beings, have a more feminine energy comparatively speaking, meaning that they are more nurturing to those in need of help or assistance. They are concerned with the welfare of "the whole", their entire society, and realize that only by doing what is in the highest good of all concerned, can everyone win! These are your type B personalities and tend to be those serving others, in many capacities.

There are many, many types of lifeforms in this universe. I guess that should be no surprise. And just like any play, there are actors that play the dramatic roles. In this universe, at least in our little drama, the two life forms/roles are the Reptilians and those of us with what is referred to as the "Adam Kadmon" body type. We will simply refer to them as "Human" from here on.

The Reptilians actually evolved prior to the emergence of the Humans, and with their predominance of Service-to-Self mentality, they have, ever since, regarded the universe as their dominion. They have been very devoted to dominance over the 3rd dimension and all life that exists within it. This is not to say they have all been like this. There are in fact entire races of Reptilians that have shifted in consciousness and ascended into higher dimensions! Please keep in mind that much of this dialogue is from a mindset of galactic "history".

Sometime later, beings of the Adam Kadmon, or Human type evolved on a planet orbiting the star we call Lyra. Once they evolved sufficiently, the conflict that was inevitable between the two types of beings (Service to Self and Service to Others), reared its ugly head. The Service-to-Self types eventually chose to leave and relocated on Vega.

Sometime later, and more significant to our story, another group left Lyra and ended up on Earth. They found the planet beautiful and full of life. They stayed here for some time before realizing that Earth was not quite as perfectly suited for them as they had thought. There were several types of bipedal hominids present at the time, and they chose the one they determined to be the best fit, for an experiment, with hopes of helping themselves adapt to life on Earth.

They conducted a genetic modification experiment on themselves and their chosen hominid. They took specific genes from the indigenous hominid and spliced it into their own DNA. They also took some of their own genes and spliced it into the hominid. As for their part, they were hoping that the genes from the hominid that evolved naturally on this planet would allow them to live here more comfortably. To what extent it worked, we do not know. What we do know is that they were eventually followed here by the very ones they were trying to get away from. Before conflict started, they decided to leave and try their chances elsewhere. They did move on. Far away from everyone. They ended up in the star system we know as the Pleiades and are indeed the ones we now call, the Pleiadians.

Somewhere, at some time in all this, more beings split off from Lyra and inhabited other planets, including Sirius. Sirius already had a very diverse amount of higher life forms, and now had another. In the Sirius sector, the drama between the two "soul types" raised to heights not experienced before. We will not go into specifics here, but let us just say they were eventually booted out of the region and told to take their drama elsewhere.

From Sirius, they went on to the Orion sector. This was the last major experiment in cohabitation of the two soul types within the same star system. It was also the most drastic and traumatic for those involved. It does not take a genius to figure out the social structure of a system where Service-to-Self types cohabitate with Service-to-Other types. The pecking order quickly sorts itself out.

However, even the most subservient-minded beings can only take so much abuse and torture. This culminated in the largest and worst "war" to ever take place in this galaxy. Even the horrors that Earth humans have committed against one another do not hold a candle to the atrocities that took place during this horrible time.

(One of the ironic things about this war, being the worst that has ever taken place, and the fact that it took place in the Orion sector, is that in the fifth dimension and above, the Orion sector is the location of the Universal Council of Light! This is why it was so revered by the ancients and why the Great Pyramids of Egypt were laid out in the pattern of the stars that make up the Belt of Orion.)

Eventually, even this conflict ended (for the most part) and many of the souls involved incarnated on Earth.

Now, interesting things were happening on Earth. Several civilizations had come and gone during the vast amount of time that had passed. Some of the Star Nations came to visit and even colonize the planet. A few hundred thousand years ago, more came. A specific group of them were looking for gold. They found it in good quantities in southern Africa. They started mining it and continued to for quite some time. Eventually their own people started to rebel from the hard work and demanded something be done to change their situation.

Their scientists conducted experiments and actually created a hybrid being from the most advanced bipedal hominid on the planet. (Remember the one the Pleiadians did their little gene swap with?) This specific group of Star Nation were not really all that much further advanced than humans are now, and they conducted this hybrid experiment of creating an entirely new species without consulting with, or getting approval from, the Spiritual Hierarchy. Their first attempt did not work out so well. It could not reproduce and was unable to evolve and grow spiritually. This was a big problem to the Spiritual Hierarchy, who, of course by then, knew all about what was going on!

At this point, the Sirians were called in to help fix this problem due to their expertise in genetic modification and their advanced spiritual status as a civilization. They knew the history the Pleiadians had on Earth, and asked them for their assistance with this issue. The Pleiadians are also a very advanced civilization – spiritually. They both agreed that they could meet the Spiritual Hierarchy's primary concern that this new life form be able to evolve spiritually.

They started with some of each of their own DNA and created yet another hybrid. This one was smarter, could form complex thought and speech, could reproduce and could evolve spiritually. Soon after this took place, another couple of dozen other Star Nations decided they wanted to get in on the action, and they began conducting minor genetic alterations to various groups of this new species. This is in fact how the various races of humans came about. Each of these Star Nations contributed DNA which contained some of the special gifts they had naturally developed over time. These contributions made each race unique and would provide further gifts as each race evolved spiritually. Kind of like a delayed, spiritual, coming of age gift! Thus, we now have a planet populated by one body type, with wonderful variations on that theme. The problem is...we have to wake up!

This clears up two mysteries that are currently being questioned. One, why there is no such thing as a "missing link". The evidence of our genetic modification is present in the fact that we have one less chromosome than the other hominids, because our second chromosome is fused, end to end!

Two, this is why, when we tested DNA from the skull of the Star Child project, The Sirius body, and the Nazca mummies – all had DNA almost indistinguishable from ours, by our current level of testing! We are in fact hybrids ourselves and our DNA is basically the same as our progenitors!

Before some of you go off about how the "experts" working for the status quo have continually put out statements that these were all humans with bizarre deformities, let me remind you that you are talking about the same people who have continuously lied to and deceived the American people and the world for the last 70 plus years on this subject. The ONLY thing you can actually count on is that they are lying! These are the same government organizations that have ruined the lives of many of the members of our armed forces and even threatened the lives of their families, simply for telling the truth of their own experiences. So, no…I do not trust, nor do I believe, anything they say! There may be trustworthy individuals, but as a whole…nope.

This brings us to the current time and situation. These same people have planned for several decades to create a mock invasion of Earth by using reverse engineered craft, so they can get a total "buy in" of "money and fortune" from the people of the world for an interstellar war. Their agenda of eternal war is obvious and this agenda was leaked decades ago. The government has recently released three videos of UFOs taken from fighter jets that they admit are not "ours". However, in every show, in every depiction, they always emphasize the danger to national security that these craft present!

What threat to national security? They could have conquered us at any time, if that was their intention. Also, they have shut down our nuclear missiles on several occasions and stressed, to those who will listen, that they will not let us destroy this planet! Earth is NOT our planet to destroy!

As usual. The only ones we need to fear are those running and controlling this planet, and their unconscious minions that are still controlled by them.

Now let us move on to another hybrid program taking place currently. This is the one involving what most people call the "Greys". The Greys in general, have gotten a bad reputation because a relatively small faction of them have broken away from the majority to work with and trade with the Military-Industrial Corporations that actually own and control this planet. (I am not against those in the Military, I am against those controlling it and the Corporations that actually run this world! Huge difference! The higher you go up this particular "ladder" the lower the vibrational frequency of the beings you encounter.)

In order to understand the real hybrid program, you need to understand a little of the history of the Greys themselves. They used to be very, very much just like us! Although they were more advanced than us mentally at the time, they were still unconscious enough as a civilization that they let fear and their emotions get out of control. They almost didn't survive. They had a nuclear war on their own planet that wiped out the majority of their population and most life on the surface of their planet. The survivors were those who were able to hide deep underground. Even those were made sterile by the radiation. Their only chance for survival as a species was by cloning, so that's what they did. When they did this, they made the observation that it was their emotions that had gotten out of control and they blamed them for their having almost totally destroying their planet and their civilization. So, in a knee-jerk response, they cut out their emotional capabilities through genetic engineering.

What they didn't quite understand at the time, was that without your emotional body intact and functioning as originally designed, spiritual growth and progress is stopped. Over time, their bodies adapted to the underground environment with little food and little to no light. They were making a copy of a copy, for thousands and thousands of years. (Science has proven that genes do change in the course of a single lifetime!) This is how and why they developed thin, frail bodies with such large eyes consisting almost totally of the light-seeking, black pupil. Without their emotions, they devoted themselves to the mental aspect of their beings. They are indeed very intelligent, but not all of them have wisdom, just like us! They realized the huge mistake they had made in eliminating their emotions, and after so many generations of cloning, they were dying out as a species.

To make a long story short, they eventually heard about Earth and its inhabitants. Through others, they actually did petition the Spiritual Hierarchy and got permission to create a hybrid program, with one primary condition.

They could not violate a human's free will by forcing us to give up our DNA or other bodily fluids and such. Being as crafty as they are, they readily agreed to this. They simply arranged for souls to be approached prior to incarnating here on Earth, have the situation explained to them, and asked them if they would be willing to participate in an experiment that would save an entire civilization. Obviously, compassion is a high virtue and most who are approached, say yes. What these incarnating souls may not have thought about, or possibly realized too late, is that they would not remember making this agreement once they incarnated. That is however, irrelevant. An agreement by the soul is an agreement, even if the conscious human mind does not recall it. This means, that the vast majority of those people who have been "abducted" by these beings, have agreed to this beforehand and are in fact helping this civilization survive.

There was a small faction of this race that broke off from the main group, as mentioned before, that have abducted people without their prior agreement. These are the ones working with the Black Ops groups of our Military-Industrial complex. Many of these abductions are carried out by humans alone, in order to generate fear of any and all extraterrestrials! Remember, only in a state of perpetual war can they totally control society and hoard all the riches and power for themselves!

As humanity grows up and evolves spiritually, many beings of this new hybrid race will be making more and more contact with us. In fact, this has already been happening. They are incredibly wise and magnificently spiritual beings and they have great love and compassion for us as a species, because we have in fact, saved theirs! They will in turn, assist us in saving ours from going down a path similar to what they did. That is in fact, what might make some people nervous. The best way for the Human/Grey hybrids formally known as the Essasani and the Yah Yel, to help us, is for them to live on this planet with us. Possibly even interbreed with us. This means we could advance our civilization by leaps and bounds in the span of a single generation. But we would have to let go of the death grip we have on our own fear, to do that. The course we are on is basically a death wish waiting to happen, so could this be any worse? We already _are_ a hybrid race, so what do we have to lose?

Unfortunately, between the propaganda spewed by religious fundamentalists, Hollywood and the government, most people on Earth have a fear-based belief system with regard to the Star Nations. Yes, there are a few who have not evolved much past the point that we are, and are still backwards enough to play the childish games of fear, control and domination, but they are the vast minority. The majority of Star Nations have evolved spiritually far beyond this limited, pathetic mentality.

Let us take a look at a few of them. We have already spoken of the Sirians. Earth is in the Sirian sector of this galaxy, as they are the closest major conglomerate of advanced civilizations. There is a wide variety of advanced life forms there. There are aquatic beings and human-type beings amongst others. They have watched over Earth and humanity for thousands and thousands of years and are one of our main progenitors! They have no interest in "conquering" us! They have nurtured and protected us on many occasions, and we literally would not exist without all they have done for us!

Another group already mentioned is the Pleiadians. They are literally our primary progenitors! They too have come here many times to nurture us along. They, along with the Sirians and a couple others, have been watching us for a long time wondering if we are going to destroy ourselves or if we will grow up and mature into a mature civilization that can join them peacefully.

Have you ever noticed that every indigenous people from every single part of this planet, speak of the Star Nations that taught their ancestors practically everything? Ever noticed that the vast majority of these legends and the temples and monuments of these people are oriented towards Sirius, the Pleiades, and Orion? Now you can see why; Sirius and the Pleiades are our primary progenitors and benefactors and Orion is the seat of the Spiritual Hierarchy where, from time to time, great beings are sent to Earth to assist.

Many people discount these legends and stories of the indigenous people. This is simply foolish. The indigenous people have an entirely different culture from modern "civilization". Lying and deceitfulness was not acceptable actions in their cultures. They understood the harm these actions bring upon the people who would do such things. It is also absurd to think that all these different cultures all over the Earth could, or would, focus and coordinate the majority of their "false" legends on these three areas of the stars!

Yes, there are temples such as Angkor Wat that are oriented towards Alpha Draconis, but like we mentioned earlier, there have been Star Nations from all over that have come here and assisted humanity. The three mentioned above do however, cover the majority.

There are several other Star Nations that we must introduce and mention here. One is the Arcturians. They are the most advanced civilization in our galaxy and reside in the fifth through the twelfth dimensions. They have watched over this planet's formation for over 10 million years. Theirs is the benchmark civilization for others to aim for, in the attainment of Spiritual growth. They are so advanced that their "spacecraft" are living beings themselves. They do not like to lower their vibrational frequency enough to manifest in this lower 3rd dimensional reality, but they are very, very active in assisting humanity in many ways. They are masters of emotional healing among other things. Since emotional issues are the foundation of most of humanity's problems, this works out well for those who are intelligent enough to call on the Arcturians for help! They are willing and able to help all who call on them, whether those people are conscious of it or not. Work on raising your vibrational frequency and you will eventually be able to perceive them! To know an Arcturian is to love Arcturians! They do in fact have the shortest and most concise manual for ascension in the Galaxy: "Be Love".

Another group well worth getting to know is the Hathors. The Hathors are not actually originally from our local universe. About 20 thousand years ago, one of the great Arcturian elders, Sanat Kumara journeyed out of this local universe and came across these beings of Light in their own native universe. Sanat Kumara was able to scan the probable timelines that existed and knew Earth humans were going to need all the help we could get. He invited a group of the Hathors to our universe, specifically to assist with Earth and they agreed. It is said that the single ship they sent resembles a nautilus shell and they came through the stargate near Sirius. They took up residence on Venus and are located there to this day. They are incredibly loving creatures and so advanced that if they are threatened by beings of a lower conscience, they simply shift to a higher dimension. These beings are true masters of sound!

Why is that so interesting you may be asking? Well, let's look at the nature of the Universal Laws once more. One of them is the Law of Vibration, that simply states that <u>everything</u> vibrates. The most basic particles of energy vibrate! Two characteristics of energy therefore are the sound produced by their vibration and the light produced by the subsequent friction of the tiniest particles at the Planck level. Therefore, if you want to manipulate "reality" at its most basic and fundamental levels – do so through sound and/or Light! An understanding of the Universal Laws is truly key to understanding how everything in this universe works. They are all concerned with the fundamental aspects of energy, because that is – All That Is.

The Hathors were a major influence on the formation of the ancient Egyptian culture. Their temple at Dendara is one of the best-preserved temples in all of Egypt. Modern archeologists and such really have no understanding of our ancient cultures! The reason the Hathors were associated with the cow, was simply the gentle nature of the cow. Others have associated them with the energy of the dolphin. Loving, peaceful, and nurturing energy is the hallmark of the Hathors. If and when they do lower their vibrational frequency enough to appear physical in this dimension, they appear just like the sculptures of them in Egypt. They do however stand from 14 to 18 feet tall!

The Hathors will also work with anyone who calls on them. For those interested in learning more about them, I highly recommend the work of Tom Kenyon. He channels the Hathors and others. He is, in my opinion the most accomplished sound therapist in the world, and its foremost leader in psycho-acoustic therapy. For those interested, expect to spend a fair amount of time on his website! He has many books and a large number of CDs, and MP3s and MP4s for sale, and a large amount of samples you can download for free! I simply cannot speak highly enough of him and his work, especially with the Hathors and Arcturians!

The Lyrans and the Vegans, and many others also have a presence here on Earth, but not as pronounced as the others. The truth is, the eyes of the universe are upon us! The entire universe is ascending in vibrational frequency, which is why the "shift" simply cannot be avoided. But no other planet has spent as much time in such an unconscious state and attempted to ascend as a civilization while still maintaining physical form. This has never been done exactly like this before, and many didn't believe it was possible. Now, we are very close to accomplishing it and every civilization in the universe that has the ability, is watching with trepid anticipation. The unfortunate aspect of this is that due to our density compared to most of this universe, we are still the "anchor" that is holding it back!

So, ever wonder why the "dark" side has held humanity back so aggressively for so long? It is simply this: They are the densest of the Service-to-Self souls. They have invested all of their existence in fear, domination and control and cannot proceed beyond the 4th dimension in their current state. They have convinced themselves that the 4th dimension is the highest dimension and to go beyond it is to basically annihilate your own soul. The only way for these souls to actually proceed is for them to grow spiritually to the point that they willingly change to being of Service to Others. This is something that cannot be faked. Energy doesn't lie!

So, from their point of view, our "ascension" is destroying both our Selves (who have unwittingly served as their mindless minions) and their entire existence as they know it. This is why they fight so hard to maintain the status quo! From their point of view, they are protecting their life of luxury and dominion over this entire planet, while refusing to go to their own death.

Ever wondered why they have discouraged inter-racial marriage so strongly, for so long? Because each "race" of humans has those "special gifts" they received from the genetics of their specific (additional) progenitors. If humanity ever gets to the point where all the races are combined, we would have the gifts of all of our combined progenitors and would eventually join the higher dimensions as Galactic Royalty. We would leapfrog over them spiritually, so far that they could not even fathom it!

If we can indeed pull this off and succeed in ascending with this planet into a higher frequency, we will also heal the wounds that our souls have endured throughout this drama of polarity in our galaxy!

Thus, I offer you a statement from the esteemed Nassim Haramein, that reflects my hopes as well:

"It is time for humans to rise above their animalistic territorial disputes, realize we are all one and that our reality is but a mere fraction of a greater whole supported by higher consciousness."

– Nassim Haramein

CHAPTER 14

BEINGS OF LOVE AND LIGHT

"The Higher Realms are teaming with Life.
In fact, "Life" is all that exists.

God has created Beings for every purpose imaginable,
and for every adventure and experience to be had."

– Marty Rawson

Throughout all of recorded history, humanity has recorded encounters with Beings of Light in the higher dimensions. These beings are of countless sizes and shapes and go by many names. The term angel, which means "messenger" has become a catchall term for most beings of light. In order to assist in clarification, we will attempt to use additional terms and definitions. Regardless of what we call them, these beings are not of human form; they are distinct life forms of their own, residing in other dimensions of time and space.

In Sanskrit, one word summarizes the entire range of these beings. That word is *Deva,* meaning "heavenly, divine, (anything of excellence)". Recently, the term "Devic Realm" has come to signify those beings commonly referred to as fairies, sylphs, elves, gnomes, and any little people – depending on the culture. These beings are indeed a significant and important aspect of the higher dimensional beings of light.

While many people say that "seeing is believing", the fundamental truth of working with the Devic realm, the angels, or other beings of light, is that you have to believe before you can see. The reason for this is because "You create your reality, absolutely". You cannot have a fundamental, core disbelief in the higher realms – and expect them to reveal themselves to you at the same time. We will call this rule number one.

In the ancient times of Lemuria, the beings that resided there were in fact etheric beings. Because the descent into the lower vibrational frequencies, often referred to as "the fall", had not yet occurred, interaction with these beings of light was a normal, everyday occurrence. Beings who resided in this civilization had no sense of separation from unity consciousness at all.

As time went on, more and more beings chose to incarnate into physical bodies in order to increase their ability to interact with the third dimensional physical reality; duality slowly began to take hold. By the time of Atlantis, duality in third dimensional form and consciousness had a much stronger hold, but interaction with the divine beings of light was still matter of fact, and commonplace. What actually led to the downfall of Atlantis was in fact the same age-old struggle that caused the Orion wars. This is the struggle between those who practise "Service to Self" _over_ those who practice "Service to Others".

The reason this little-known aspect of our history is so significant to this discussion is because it verifies that our natural state is to be in communion with the divine. It is in fact unnatural to feel separation from the higher realms and unity consciousness. It is this sense of separation that brought forth the fearful aspects of the lower ego in man. It is high time we turn the "ship" around and get humanity back to its natural state of communing with the divine.

It has been suggested that there are four critically important steps we need to take to prepare ourselves for working with the Angels.

First, you must forgive yourself for your past errors of thought and the negative things you have created in your life. You can't get where you're trying to go if you are consumed with guilt and other low frequencies. You do this by Loving yourself and Loving God. By surrendering to God's will and apologizing for the times you failed to understand or remember who you really are. By asking for forgiveness and by giving gratitude and appreciation in response to that forgiveness.

Second, evaluate yourself. Take an honest look at yourself. Your personality traits and your attitudes. We're not talking about trying to be perfect. We are talking about being honest with yourself about the direction you want to go in your life. Do you compromise on issues of integrity or morality? Do your actions line up with the goals that you claim you want to attain?

Third, If you truly want to commune with Spirit, you must surrender yourself to Spirit. You must want a relationship with them – as much as a man who is drowning wants air.

Fourth, Meditate, bringing your awareness into the presence of God; First Source; the Divine.

The Elohim; Lords of Light

Many people take the references from ancient texts concerning "Elohim", to mean literally "God".

God is "All That Is".

"All That Is" has the ability to create Individualized Awarenesses of whatever capacity is desired, in order to fulfill the Divine Will. The Elohim Lords of Light are not God itself, but from our small view point, we could not tell the difference. They are created Beings in perfect and absolute unity with Source, so that "God's" Divine Will is perfectly implemented in every way. These are the Beings who understand through the Divine Mind, how to program the unmanifested, potential energy we call the "Void" into new universes that are designed to function in perfect harmony with Divine Will!

Since they are in perfect harmony with Divine Will, they often reside in a local universe of their making and serve as, shall we say, advisors or consultants, of the truly highest order. One such Being, who is often erroneously relegated to the status of Archangel, is Metatron. He is a phenomenal Being of magnificent Love and Light and is far beyond caring about which title humans use for him. He is however, correctly given credit for his role in the creation and programming of the cosmos through Sacred Geometry. Sacred geometries of Light at the most fundamental levels of energy, are how the programming is accomplished!

It was Metatron who assisted in creating this Universe according to God's will by using the Divine Light of Source/God. Metatron is of great wisdom and authority, being the Lord of Light entrusted by the Creator to bring this universe into physical manifestation. He is the embodiment of Love and Light beyond mortal description, although he can be very intimidating due to the fact that when he has appeared before humans, he is said to stand around 55 feet tall.

The Angels

Angels are perfect spiritual beings whose purpose is to administer to, help, protect, and sustain everything in God's universe. Everything, even a humble rock or a cooling breeze, has an angelic intelligence guarding it to ensure that God's will be done. Angels can be found in Judaism, Christianity, Hinduism, Islam, Zoroastrianism and Tibetan Buddhism. The fact that angels are known through all forms of earths religions as well as forms of traditional spirituality, proves that humans everywhere and through all time have been experiencing interactions with these wonderful beings.

There are many types of angels. There are Angels, Archangels, Principalities, Powers, Virtues, Dominions, Thrones, Cherubim, and Seraphim. Although this is classified as a hierarchy, it must be understood that each type of Angel is created perfectly for its specific role. Therefore, there is no "ego" involved as there is with humans on Earth. Each performs their duties in perfect harmony with the "whole" while in the ecstasy of divine bliss. A few of the Archangels are listed below with some information concerning them.

Sandalphon is not as well known to most people as some of the others, however I personally hope this changes. Sandalphon has a soft, extremely gentle energy of love and compassion. In my experience his presence is felt mainly in the plant and animal kingdoms and with humans who are in the most need of healing compassion and willing to accept it. He is one that will literally cradle you in the Arms of Spirit! He is the living embodiment of the compassion of the Creator. He does not seek to be known, but I think sending a loving, heartfelt energy of gratitude once in a while is the least we can do!

Archangel **Michael** is the living embodiment of the Will of God. He is often depicted with his flaming blue sword of Truth. This blue flame is the Flame of the Creator, signifying the creation of the higher realms of Love and Light far above our own dimension. This is why only the personification of the Will of God is entrusted with a tool of this magnitude. Beloved Archangel Michael is the guardian, the protector, and the valiant hero of the legions of light. While he is often depicted as a warrior, let us always remember that he is a being of Love and Light.

Archangel **Raphael** means "God has healed". Raphael is the living embodiment of the healing power of God. Just as it would be appropriate to call on Archangel Michael for protection, it is equally appropriate to call on our beloved Archangel Raphael for healing of all kinds. He not only helps people in the physical world, he also provides invaluable assistance to souls who need it when they go home, into the higher realms. As one may imagine, he is not only the personification of compassion, but also the original teacher of the maxim "Laughter is the best medicine". As with all archangels, to know him is to love him.

Archangel **Mary**. Many people are surprised to find out that the beloved being known as Mother Mary is one of the very few archangels to ever incarnate as a physical human being. In order for an avatar of Jesus's high consciousness to be born on such a low frequency planet, Jesus needed a being that was truly 'Angelic' to bear him as his Mother! She is sometimes referred to lovingly as the Queen of Heaven. She works very closely with Archangel Raphael in healing people due to her unfathomable love and compassion. She is the living embodiment of the divine feminine as expressed in the Mother archetype. She is caring, nurturing and supportive of all who will accept her loving energy! Make no mistake though, she is as powerful as she is loving. She once graced me with a small touch of her energy to my back, which sent such a wave of ecstasy through me, it dropped me to my knees.

Archangel **Azrael** is "(the) Help of God". He is the living embodiment of that aspect of the Creator that is sent to help others. It is for this reason that he is the Archangel who greets people when they pass on from this life, and go home. He is typically the great being of Light who stands with a person's loved ones to greet them when they cross over. He is the one who puts his arm around you and lovingly guides you home into the higher realms of Love and Light, when your consciousness has not yet regained its unity with the higher realms, and may still have some confusion present. Obviously, his devotion is endless. He has a complicated history though, as he was also the one banished to the "Dark side" for teaching humans knowledge they were not ready for. He led the charge of the "Dark side" back into the Light and has since been fully reinstated in his role mentioned above. He is a fantastic Archangel to call on if you have issues with the dark side. They still know who he is and he has great authority.

The Angels are here to help humanity ascend back into the Light. They are of great assistance but they cannot do things for us. One way they assist us is by literally adjusting the frequencies of thought patterns to allow us to hear the messages from themselves, the Ascended Masters and our spirit guides. They do much more than this, but this is an aspect of their assistance that is vital to our success! Please remember in your work with spirit to always pay very close attention to how things are worded. If you have a thought that is phrased in such a way that it sounds as if someone is speaking to you, it is because someone _is_ speaking to you! Always pay close attention to this! Trust it! Also pay close attention to feelings that you have, especially ones that won't go away!

Most of the Angelic Realm has not ever incarnated into a physical body. They are created perfectly for their role in the higher realms and function in a state of ecstasy and bliss while in full connection to Source! It is we who incarnate for the purpose of soul growth who suffer from amnesia and therefore have an innate sense of emptiness within us that drives us to seek fulfillment. As soon as we come into these lives, there is a disconnect from the higher realms. As we grow older and accept the version of reality that people here force upon us, our connection dwindles further. Over time, this emptiness within us grows and our dissatisfaction with life increases. We tend to seek forms of sensory stimulation by which to entertain ourselves. This comes in many forms, but is never truly fulfilling! That's because what we are missing is our divine birthright which is our connection to Source! Our interrupted connection to Source leaves us feeling incomplete and this cannot be "filled" by mere sensory stimulation! This is why Jesus taught "The Kingdom of Heaven is within you"!

You must "go within" in meditation to find your connection to Source while in the physical! The Angelic realm is right here to assist you along the way!

The Masters

The Ascended Masters are those who have gone before us on this very same path to enlightenment and have made it! Some choose to stay in the Higher Realms (Ascended Masters) and assist us from there, while others incarnate into the physical again (Living Masters) to teach humanity on our own "turf". They can relate to us better than the Angels can because they have actually lived through and experienced many lives, along with the full spectrum of feelings and emotions that we humans go through! This puts them in a much better position to assist us with the daily trials and tribulations of life. They have been through the full gamut of human experience. They have had totally unconscious lives where they were the murderers, the betrayers and the deceivers. They have also been the murdered, the betrayed and the deceived. This ensures that they do not judge you. They've been here, done this! They went through it all and still managed to reestablish their connection to the Divine and fill themselves so full of Love and Light that they attained enlightenment and escaped the wheel of incarnation.

There are many Masters whom you can call on. I highly recommend that people do their own research in order to discover which Masters they have an affinity for. The Masters over the Cosmic Rays are particularly active on Earth and are always willing and able to provide guidance and assistance. There is some discontinuity regarding which Masters are over which Rays. At first this can be a little frustrating when one is seeking the truth of these matters. I follow the teachings of Djwal Khul, "the Tibetan" who was the original source of this information. I suggest meditating on any ascended Master you feel drawn to, regardless of what they are "over". Expand your horizons and work with all of them over time. You will find they each have their own personality and special forms of wisdom!

A few of the favorites are St. Germain, Kuthumi, Hilarion, Lanto, El Morya, Serapis Bey, and Kwan Yin. There are more, but this short list will definitely get you started in the right direction!

The Order of Melchizedek

Lord Melchizedek, a true Lord of Light, was one of the first beings brought into existence within this local universe. This "Father" Melchizedek, known simply as Lord Melchizedek, subsequently collaborated with the Creator Son and Creator Spirit to bring into existence the entire group of this name, the 'Melchizedek Sons'. Being an Order of Sonship wherein one of their own number functioned as Co-Creator, Melchizedek's are, in constitution, partly of self-origin and therefore candidates for the realization of a supernal type of self-government. In other words, they are the only truly autonomous "brotherhood" in the universe. The Archangel Gabriel oversees Universal "policies", while Lord Melchizedek oversees the logistical aspects of this Universe. Gabriel presides over the regularly constituted tribunals and councils. Melchizedek presides over the special, extraordinary, and emergency commissions and advisory bodies. The Melchizedeks are in essence the Universe's First Responders, teachers and counselors.

The following is from the Urantia Book. The only source of factual information available on the Order of Melchizedek.

"Melchizedek's are the first order of divine sonship and function directly in the ministry of the worlds of matter. They also assist with higher education in the higher dimensions through the Melchizedek Universities. They are natural intermediaries between the higher and divine levels of existence and the physical beings on the evolutionary worlds. The angelic realm delights to work with the Melchizedeks; in fact, all forms of intelligent life find in the Melchizedek Sons understanding friends, sympathetic teachers, and wise counselors. The Melchizedeks are a self-governing order. With this unique group we encounter the first attempt at self-determination on the part of local universe beings and observe the highest type of true self-government. It should be recorded that they have never abused their prerogatives. Not once throughout all the super universe even, have these Melchizedek sons ever betrayed their trust. They are the hope of every universal group which aspires to self-government; they are the pattern and the teachers of self-government.

The Melchizedek Order occupies the position, and assumes the responsibility of the eldest son in a large family. Most of their work is regular and somewhat routine, but much of it is voluntary and altogether self-imposed. A majority of the special assemblies which are convened from time to time in the higher realms are called on motion of the Melchizedeks. On their own initiative, these Sons patrol their native universe. They maintain an autonomous organization devoted to universal divine intelligence. They are by nature unprejudiced observers;

they have the full confidence of all classes of intelligent beings. The Melchizedeks function as mobile and advisory review courts of the realms; these universal sons go in small groups to the worlds to serve as advisory commissions and to act as counselors, thus helping to compose the difficulties and settle the differences which arise from time to time in the affairs of the evolutionary worlds.

There is no phase of planetary spiritual need to which they do not minister. They are the teachers who so often win whole worlds of advanced life to the final and full recognition of the Creator. The Melchizedeks are well-nigh perfect in wisdom, but they are not infallible in judgment. When detached and alone on planetary missions, they have sometimes erred in minor matters, that is, they have elected to do certain things which their superiors did not subsequently approve. It should be noted that these minor mis-adaptations in Melchizedek functions have rarely occurred. It should also be noted that, the Higher Beings "treat a Being who has given up their place in the higher realms, to serve others here on Earth, with reverence. Such a Being carries more weight with their prayers and intentions because they are serving while dealing with an increased sense of separation that is inherent in being incarnate."

Their number is fixed. That means that the original number of Melchizedeks that were originally created, are the constant number there is in existence. Many people have attempted to claim initiation into some type of Priesthood, but that does not make them a true Melchizedek by lineage. These priesthood formations on the worlds of matter are finite and have no impact on the higher realms whatsoever, but it is recommended that they observe universal truths such as equality. True equality, across races and genders. Any person or group who does not recognize the divinity and spiritual equality of all, racially, gender-wise and all other ways, is displaying their total lack of understanding of the Order of Melchizedek and that which is Divine.

(It should also be noted that when terms like "Sons" and "Brotherhood" are used in reference to any groups of the higher dimensions, this has no bearing or implication on gender in the higher realms. In the higher realms, beings are truly androgenous and may present themselves as they desire.)

"It is the responsibility of the membership of the Order of Melchizedek in embodiment to make the connections to the angelic kingdom and begin to coordinate with them to bring God's plan to earth. That is why both groups have come. They have come to unite to do God's will before the will of the ego. All have come to raise the vibrations of the planet into the stream of consciousness that will eventually catapult into the higher dimensions of the new millennium."

– Kuthumi

We see then, that there are Melchizedeks incarnated on Earth at this time. They are here to serve and assist humanity in establishing its connection with the Angelic Realm and the other Beings of Light. It is an autonomous Order of Sonship that serves many aspects of the Divine Plan throughout this universe.

The Great White Brotherhood and The Law of One

The Great white Brotherhood is an organization that is comprised of Beings of many types. The only prerequisite for membership is that they are beings devoted to working in the Light in accordance with Divine Will. In other words, they follow the Law of One.

The Great White Brotherhood brings together Angels, Melchizedeks, Elohim, and Ascended Star Nations to work together for the highest good of all concerned. They are the guiding force for the many Councils that are formed at local levels. Their headquarters, so to speak, is the Great White Lodge on Sirius. It is fortunate for us on Earth, as we are in the Sirian Sector of this galaxy, and Lord Sirius is truly Galactic royalty. We, as a species are only here due to the benevolence of the Sirians, Pleiadians and a few other Star Nations, as mentioned earlier.

For those who have studied the Law of One, they know that a vast amount of information has been written about it and a lot can be said in discussing it. I am going to do the opposite. The Law of One simply states that All is One. There is only one mind, the mind of God. All that is, exists within "God" and "God" exists within All That Is. Everything returns to its source to become 'One' again.

The Galactic Federation

The Galactic Federation is an alliance of Star Nations that also works in accordance with Divine Will. It is under the command of Commander Ashtar. The Galactic Federation was formed millions of years ago, when a coordinated response to the encroachment of dark forces became necessary. It serves to protect the entire galaxy and is also directly involved in aiding Earth in its current ascension from darkness.

There have been many false rumors and misleading statements concerning the Galactic Federation and even Ashtar himself. He is however, a being of impeccable character and has proven himself to be beyond reproach. It is unfortunate so many people have succumbed to such negativity and gossip.

Sanat Kumara

A short bio for Sanat Kumara is necessary here. Sanat Kumara is mentioned in almost every ancient sacred text, including the Bible and the Vedas. In the Bible, he is referred to as the "Ancient of Days".

He is in fact, an Arcturian Elder who first came to Earth over ten million years ago. He is also the one who first contacted the Hathors in our neighboring universe, and brought them here to assist with the problems he could see Earth was headed for, long ago. A little-known fact is that it was also he who bestowed Reiki and its teachings to Master Usui on Mt Kurama in Japan. Reiki is in fact, an Arcturian Healing modality and is just one such modality they have to offer. The Japanese have a spaceship and a temple on Mt Kurama dedicated to Sanat Kumara's first landing here. According to Sanat Kumara himself, this initial landing took place ten million years ago, but the Japanese have mistakenly dated it to a mere 6.5 million years old.

He has been watching over Earth and humanity for a very, very long time. Long, long before our species was even here. I cannot express my own affection and respect for him sufficiently, and I do call on him regularly for many purposes.

The Flower of Life

This is probably as good a place as any to add a few words concerning the Flower of Life. As I stated earlier, it was the Elohim Lords of Light who were tasked with creating this local Universe according to the Divine Plan and program.

When they refracted the pure, clear, white Light of Source into the unmanifested potential energy of the void, many things happened simultaneously and instantaneously. Besides the refraction of the Light of Source into the Cosmic Rays, the unmanifested energy of the void was programmed through the sacred geometry of the Flower of Life, at its most fundamental level.

It is not only responsible for the underlying geometry of all matter in this universe, it is responsible for the very life force within all energy itself. I highly recommend you study sacred geometry in nature and the universe. Below we find the words of Chequetet Arelich Volmalites, better known to most people as "Thoth", and/or Hermes Trismagistus.

Deep in the Earth's heart lies the flower,
the source of the Spirit that binds all in its form.
For know ye that the Earth is living in body
as thou art alive in thine own formed form.
The Flower of Life is as thine own place of Spirit

and streams through the Earth as thine flows through thy form;
giving of Life to the Earth and its children,
renewing the Spirit from form unto form.
This is the Spirit that is form of thy body,
shaping and moulding into its form.

He also follows this up with more sage advice:

He who would follow the pathway of wisdom,
open must be to the Flower of Life,
extending his consciousness out of the darkness,
flowing through time and space in the ALL.

You may think of the energy of the Flower of Life as the higher dimensional form of prana or chi.

Getting to know the Beings of Light that serve this Universe and understanding the primal Divine forces that are at your disposal, is a fundamental aspect of spiritual growth. It is fun, informative, inspirational, and provides the necessary support for your journey!

CHAPTER 15

THE STAR NATIONS

"Your older brothers and sisters in the Star Nations are watching very closely, with trepid anticipation to see what you will choose next"

– Marty Rawson

With so much life in all dimensions, it is quite reasonable to say that there is life at many stages of evolution throughout this vast Universe. The one thing about the Light is, that no matter what level or dimension you are on, it is your duty and your privilege to assist those who follow behind you. Everyone in the Light reaches a hand down on this proverbial stairway to heaven – to lift up those following behind. Those that are not working in this manner are not worthy of associating with!

The fall of humanity's consciousness is a long and detailed story if told comprehensively, but suffice it to say that our older brothers and sisters are indeed here to help. Since they work within the Divine Plan and also follow the "The Prime Directive" of never interfering with "Free Will", they are limited in what they can do. It is also a matter of dealing with the backwards and unconscious individuals controlling and dominating this planet. These beings do not work in the Light and are constantly violating humanity's Free Will. It is no coincidence that the only Star Nations in contact with this world's governments are also as backwards and unconscious as the heads of our governments are. (Another bit of proof that like energies attract!) At this point, the government has actually released videos of UFOs that the pilots themselves are saying are UFOs; not from this world. Yet the upper brass of the military are still actively covering up and lying about the whole thing. This simply illustrates the division within our society,

The Star Nations worth associating with are those who have evolved to a higher consciousness as a species, and therefore as a planetary society. What does this mean? It means, in part, that they understand that they are all one species that wants to live in harmony with one another, and with the environment/planet on which they live.

No one hoards anything on their planets. They would never even think of hoarding so much wealth that others of their own kind starve and go without – anything. They have evolved to the point that they understand that there is "enough" for everyone. Instead of worshipping and idolizing the biggest hoarders within their society, they would council them long before they could harm themselves and others. Then again, they teach their children not to be this way, and all about the higher concepts of love, unity and true compassion for life, at an early age. We tend to teach our children prejudice, greed and violence from a very early age. Just an observation based on historical fact.

The Star Nations not only teach Unity with one another as a species, but also as a part of the web of life on their planet, and within the entire Universe. They understand that as the primary sentient beings with higher cognitive capacities on their planet, it falls on them to maintain the harmonious balance of all life on their planet. A few have gotten to the point that their entire species lives on ships orbiting their planet, so they can visit it in the divine beauty of its purest and most natural state! Now, this may not be the norm, but it does show the level of love and compassion they have for life. Again, they comprehend the meaning of true spiritual wisdom, which is:

"Doing *that* which is in the Highest Good of All Concerned!"

This also means they have a long-term outlook concerning the consequences of their actions with regard to their world and their descendants. This means they would never allow a "corporation" to exist that would pollute the planet and destroy the environment while poisoning its employees and the population, all for the short-term profit of a few. They would be intelligent enough to see that there is no profit whatsoever in this scenario for the species and the planet. They actually DO what is best for their progeny even though they know they may not be around to experience life with them! Humans seem to have a total disregard for the lives and environment their children and grandchildren with live in, simply because they won't be around to see it! To be willing to sacrifice the world and the lives of millions, if not billions of lives, for the short-term monetary benefit of a few greedy people is not just sick, it is beyond evil.

The beauty of the higher Star Nations is their comprehension and actual living of Unity Consciousness. Survival of the individual is insured because they concentrate on the survival of the whole, not just the "strongest one" among them. They practice co-operation throughout their world, not competition within it.

This is what happens when you honor all life. This Unity with All Life is the foundation of their culture and all of their social systems that we would call economics, spirituality, manufacturing, and so on. Nothing that violates this premise is actually even thought of, let alone given any consideration. Violating Life itself is simply not acceptable to beings of higher consciousness.

In higher civilizations, the wise elders and teachers are held in higher esteem than individuals who play sports games with various types of balls. They put more emphasis on teaching their young and healing their people, than on giving outrageous rewards to "actors" and athletes. They put more time and effort into ensuring that every individual in their society is fed and clothed and cared for, including a top-grade education, because they know _that_ will have the most positive, long-term advantage for their entire civilization! If everyone is taken care of to this extent, no one has any thought of harming others. They also are taught that to harm others is to harm themselves and the entire society. They teach their children by example and their entire society is based on honesty, awareness and responsibility. They observe what works, and what does not, and have abandoned what does not work, given the stated "goal".

If and when a transgression were to occur, the offending party would typically be brought before a Council of Elders and the source of the aberrant behavior is discovered and *healed*.

This is why I stress the education of our children in the higher truths, and things that will assist them in life! In the Star Nations, they teach how to deal with emotional trauma from an early age. They continue with things like peaceful conflict resolution, the Art of Listening, spiritual sexuality, understanding the Divine nature of Energy, Being Good Stewards of All Life, Honoring One another, honesty, awareness, personal responsibility, and much, much more! They understand that when children are properly cared for and taught to Love and nurture, that is what they will do, and that is how they will continue to live.

In many of the Star Nations, it is the grandparents who are the primary caretakers of the young children. This does not mean the parents are absent, it just means that the wisdom and experience of the elders is not only respected and appreciated, it is utilized to the greatest advantage for the newest generation. This way, those that are still trying to figure out life are not the ones attempting to teach another generation what they do not yet know themselves. Of course, these families have a very strong bond and often live together anyway. Their cultures do not have the egoic issues and conflicts our juvenile species has.

Like it or not, our species is comparatively at the pre-school level and these other civilizations are at the Multiple-Master's Degree level.

This is another reason why we have to raise our vibrational frequency. If we ever want to make contact with these Star Nations and their wisdom, individually or in mass, we must reach for them! You do not need either the government's approval or any religion's approval. Neither one of these is interested in relinquishing control of your mind.

We have so much potential and so little foresight. Spirit looks at us as their greatest hope and their biggest concern – both at the same time! While some of us are attempting to reach out to the higher realms, some are actually helping the dark side destroy our species and all life on our planet. Some humans are willingly condemning our children and grandchildren to slow, miserable, agonizing deaths. We must stop this, and heal ourselves and our planet – soon!

We have to continue to raise our frequency and raise our consciousness! Then, more of us will make contact with the Star Nations and Beings of Light. The original plan was the lovely rose-colored and compassionate idea that eventually we will hit critical mass in our vibrational frequency and lift our entire species into the Light. Then, anyone of lower consciousness who has survived, would be lifted with us. Basically the "Hundredth Monkey Effect". That is not likely anymore, because the dark side has put up such an incredible fight. Both those following them in the physical, and those beings not in the physical.

We, however, cannot change who people are, and if some choose to continue to play in the dark, we must honor that, regardless of how painful it is for us or them. It is their lesson. This is especially upsetting when we see friends and family who have refused to abandon their fear-based beliefs and practices, but again, it is their lesson.

There are many eyes upon us, waiting and watching. Many who are here to help if you will only ask their assistance. Just remember to set your boundaries and **_only_** work with Beings of Light that work within the Divine Plan. They can and will help, but they will not do it for us! The question is, are we mature enough as a species to take responsibility for our own actions, to clean up our own mess, and to join our older brothers and sisters on a galactic level? I hope so.

If you wish to work with the Star Nations, you can start from where you are. But, you will need to raise your vibrational frequency as you go. To start, you simply need to seriously set your intention and keep at it. Persistence pays off. Whether you are working with the Star Nations or the Angelic Realm, the rules are the same. ***Invite them in, pay close attention*** and ***TRUST!***

There does seem to be quite a few people who are confused about Star Nations verses the Angelic Realm. It seems that some people who believe in the Star Nations, have not yet experienced an angelic presence and try to label every encounter ever recorded as being an "alien". Sorry guys, *they are not the same*, but they do work the same way and in accordance to the same plan (At least the higher Star Nations). Lest we forget: "There are more things in heaven and earth, Horatio, than are dreamt of in your philosophy"!

The Ascended Masters are also in this same category. They are doing their part in helping those of us following in their "footsteps" up this stairway to Heaven. The "Masters" are called masters because they have mastered their own "Self" to the point of ascending from this physical world into the Light and Love of the 5th dimension. It has absolutely nothing to do with them being our masters. I have found that the people who try to push that twisted theory are actually revealing much about their own mentality, and their (learned) need to demonize anything they don't already understand.

The Star Nations I am most familiar with, as I have already mentioned, are the Arcturians (the "benchmark" civilization we should strive to emulate), the Pleiadeans, the Sirians, the Lyrans, the Hathors, the Higher Orions and the Andromedins. Recently, I had assistance from and experience with a wonderful being from Tau Ceti! He was from an ascended race and has been a dear friend for a long time! I had totally forgotten our relationship, as is common in these physical lives. I had the opportunity to experience the wonderful and incredibly advanced energy work of this wonderful being first hand. I immediately began to recall our friendship afterwards! One of the students in this particular session had quite an experience working with him as well. There are many more star nations out there, and no one can claim to know the names of all of them. I have seen several in the higher realms whose names I do not know. Many, especially the Pleiadeans, Sirians, Arcturians and the Lyrans have a great deal to do with our planetary history and the genetic modifications that created us as we are.

The Sirians in particular have protected us on many occasions and have assisted us in more ways than we can count. We truly owe them gratitude for our continued existence. The Pleiadeans also have helped greatly and the Hathors were invited by the Arcturians to help us out. The Hathors are not even from this local universe; they are Masters of Sound that helped raise and teach the ancient Egyptian culture.

The cosmic drama being played out here has a long, long history. It is the story of the histories of these Star Nations, and it is what is happening here and now. Again, I highly suggest reading the Prizm of Lyra by Lyssa Royal Holt. It is a summary of the events that have transpired to bring us to where we are. As I read it, I received so much divine inspiration and information it was incredible. I saw the events unfold from a higher perspective and knew exactly which ones I had been involved in physically. I give my sincere appreciation and gratitude to the wonderful Lyssa Royal Holt for gifting this wonderful bit of galactic history to humanity.

The Service to Self folks have dominated the banking and political aspects of this planet for hundreds of years to say the least. Some started long before that. They have almost succeeded in accumulating all of the wealth of the planet through their banking and political schemes. In some cases you can add control of entire religions to this as well. Control of a planet's natural resources and its currencies tends to make one very powerful. You have to admire their active intelligence though. They have convinced most of the population of the world (minus those already in poverty) that they are benevolent masters and that they are trying to create a sustainable economy. Nothing could be further from the truth. The economy is not broken. It is functioning exactly as it is designed to. It is and always has been a system of wealth-transfer, from the nations of this world to the international bankers, who are your "Owners". If that is news to you, you either have not been paying attention at all, or have swallowed the spoon-fed propaganda that has been delivered on a daily basis, your entire life.

We are at a major crossroads here and now. Most on this planet now have had many lifetimes on these other various worlds, and have taken part in the conflicts mentioned. This is why people are so incredibly stubborn when it comes to political beliefs. Their cellular memories plus their DNA makes them unable to see the "other" point of view. Again, nothing so trivial as facts, proof or evidence will change their minds. Not even the fact that they are condemning their future offspring to death will affect them! If we who work in the Light (Service to Others) can pull this out and save this planet and most of our species, we can take as many as are ready and willing, with us.

I used to get upset with Spirit when they would tell me that the only way to proceed with this was to work on myself and that as I did this, it would be like one candle lighting another. To be honest, I considered this to be a "namby-pamby" approach! I wanted to take this fight directly to "them". I have grown a lot since then and now see the incredible wisdom in Spirit's approach. If you remember from earlier, I mentioned that you should never fight the dark side! You will only feed them. There is really no sense in talking to them about any of this either, it will only aggravate them. Share when, and to what extent, the information is requested.

We must continue to work on ourselves continuously. We should gather with like-minded individuals to exchange ideas and conduct group meditations. We must change how we raise our children and introduce them to meditation from a very early age. We must share our spiritual wisdom with those who are waking up and help them along their journey in a compassionate way. As we do these things, more and more people will awaken! We can and must create a revolution through the use of Love and the Universal Law of Transmutation. We must create an Alliance with Spirit on a personal level, then on a larger group level. Eventually we will hit critical mass and the consciousness of those who are ready, will shift. When that happens, it will not only be a victory for Love, Light and Life, it will heal millions of years of conflict and pain within billions of Souls and the entire Universe will raise in frequency! The Earth is the anchor holding it back right now. Yes, the goal is to literally bring the dark side into the Light using the Universal Laws to our advantage. This is truly a cosmic drama of universal proportions. This is why there are so many eyes on us. The Star Nations and the Spiritual Hierarchy are watching with trepid anticipation to see what we will do...

Failure is not an option!

CHAPTER 16

CONCERNING STAR NATIONS AND DISCLOSURE

"We have met the enemy, and he is us!"

– Walt Kelly

For as long as we have existed, man has been looking to the stars for answers. But not everyone has had the same questions. It would seem that our ancient ancestors knew a lot more than most people currently believe. Every indigenous culture on the planet has attributed either their existence or their knowledge to beings from the stars. All of the ancient temples and monuments were aligned in some fashion with the Pleiades, Sirius, Orion or perhaps Zeta Reticuli in the Alpha Draconis constellation.

The most ancient written documents in the world from the Vedic texts, to the Enuma Elish of the ancient Sumerians, to the Emerald Tablets of Thoth, all state as a matter of fact, that the Star Nations used to come here routinely and even lived here with us.

Petroglyphs, geoglyphs, mummified remains, and ancient oral traditions from every ancient civilization all attest to their existence and their presence!

How could all these ancient accounts be coordinated to match, if all of this were indeed some elaborate hoax? More recently, we have had eye witness accounts of millions of people, military videos released by the government itself, and televised disclosure testimonies of many high-ranking military officers, scientists and airline pilots and many other "reputable" people!

For the last 70 to 80 years, the United States Government has vehemently denied the existence of anything to do with this. And, when military personnel have dared to speak out about incidences that occurred while they were on duty, the military has ruined many of their careers and even threatened the lives of them and their families.

Recently, a few years ago, the government released 3 videos taken by our own military jet pilots that the government itself admits is not ours and is most likely, not from this world. Then silence. This follows, by many years, the most substantial release of documented information in current history that was "The Disclosure Project", organized by Dr. Steven Greer. He arranged for the televised disclosure of testimony by military officers, politicians, police officers, airline pilots, and many, many other people. He released the videos, transcripts, everything. The majority of the people in the U.S. gave a collective yawn and carried on as if nothing occurred at all.

In the meantime, we have a rock star, Tom Delong, from Blink 182 who has used his time and money to investigate these matters up close and personal. He made the phone calls and knocked on the doors of enough people that he got the attention of some people in the know, who would like to have the truth divulged. He has assembled a team of what appears to be, very reputable people that he calls his "To the Stars" team.

The "To the Stars" team consists of:

Lou Elizondo: former DIA military Intelligence who headed up the AATIP. (Advanced Aerospace Threat Identification Program)

Chris Mellon: former Deputy Assistant Secretary of Defense and Intelligence.

Steve Justice: Retired Program Director for Advanced Systems at Lockheed Martin's Skunkworks.

Hal Puthoff: CIA Researcher and Quantum Physicist

Jim Semivan: Retired Senior CIA member

This would appear to be a dream team. This team, or members of it, have made and been featured in many television shows and documentaries. They go over the same 3 videos released by the government over and over ad nauseum.

In today's climate of subterfuge and mis-direction, we cannot know how legitimate these people really are, as far as truly wanting to reveal the "truth" is concerned. It is unfortunate that our government is so deceitful and belligerent that we have to doubt every development, even ones such as this.

Elizondo does have a very impressive career, and has stated he resigned from his government position due to the cover-up of information of his own work. Could be true, could also be a nice cover story to instill trust and confidence in him. He does come across as being very sincere, but admits he has knowledge he cannot share due to his oath of secrecy with the government.

The biggest problem I have with every show with these people and every documentary or show on this subject, is that they are all fear-based. There is constant talk of "violation of American airspace", "Threats to national security" and even the name of the AATIP itself, has 'Threat' right in the middle of its name.

They act as if they have no knowledge of previous history of government interaction with certain Star Nations and continually act mystified over why the government isn't doing anything in response to the perceived threats. I firmly believe the government isn't responding because they are way ahead of this team and have been reverse engineering UFO technology since the 1940s. There are released government documents and eye witness testimony that confirm face-to-face meetings as long ago as the 1940s. There are documents stating that President Dwight Eisenhower held a secret meeting with extraterrestrial visitors during the early hours of February 21, 1954. President Harry Truman set up the Majestic 12 committee to oversee this subject and discredit eye witnesses. It is widely believed that the cabal that runs this planet has been using black budget money to develop technologies that would seem literally "out of this world" to the common man. There have been many reports that we already have hundreds of "UFOs" that have been reverse engineered, that are capable of interstellar space flight.

The point of this is that for a group of the most "qualified" experts in the field, they sure are ignorant of history. Again, have you noticed that every single show on T.V. concerning disclosure has a fear-based agenda? There is always talk of "threats to National Security", so they can brand anyone who mentions this as un-patriotic. That's an old trick.

Let's face it, anyone who can manipulate the laws of physics so far that they can effectively bend space-time and travel to Earth, would have no problem taking over our entire world, *if* that was their intention. Considering they were here long before humans even came along, they also would have done it long before now. The dark forces controlling this planet are already here and have been the entire time. We call them the elite, the International Bankers, the corporate CEOs, and their puppets, the politicians, "royalty", and the filthy rich. It isn't that being rich is inherently evil, it's that being rich too often leads to coveting power. It is them we need to be very concerned with and not the Star Nations who work in the Light, who are visiting us now!

This planet is owned and controlled by Corporations, with the International Bankers at the top of the heap. They own all of the other major corporations such as all major media, big oil and big pharma, etc., and they own the world's governments, politicians and judges. The world's military are their enforcement arm. This does not mean there are not some good people in all of these institutions, it just means good people are not running and controlling any of them. Unfortunately, this is not a conspiracy theory, it is common knowledge. Again, look around you...not one institution on this planet serves the highest good of the people of this planet!

They do not want the masses of humanity to know the truth, because they know they would lose control over the masses! They also have had a not-so-secret, secret agenda in the works for decades, and would like to let it play out if possible. You may have heard of it.

Carol Rosin speaking about her mentor, Dr Wernher Von Braun, the Nazi scientist America brought here after WWII and immediately appointed as head of NASA, had this to say:"I met the late Dr Wernher Von Braun in early '74, at that time Von Braun was dying of cancer, but he assured me that he would live a few more years in order to tell me about the game that was being played, that game being the effort to weaponize space, to control Earth from space and space itself.

"What was most interesting to me was a repetitive sentence that he said to me over and over again… that was, the strategy that was being used to educate the public and decision makers, and the scare tactics, the spin that was being put on (as justification for our advanced) weapons system… (was based upon) how we identify an enemy."The enemy at first, (Von Braun) said, (to justify our) …space-based weapons system… first the Russians are going to be considered the enemy… then terrorists would be identified… then we were going to identify third world crazies… The next enemy was asteroids… [and] against asteroids we're going to build space-based weapons."And the funniest one of all was against what he called aliens, extraterrestrials. That would be the final card. And over, and over, and over during the four years that I knew him and was giving his speeches for him, he would bring up that last card. 'And remember Carol, the last card is the alien card. We're going to have to build space-based weapons against aliens.' And all of it, he said, is a lie."

You must remember, there is absolutely nothing that is beyond these people, concerning the lengths they will go to in order to get or keep, what they want. They have ruined loyal military service men's lives and threatened the lives of many of their families just to keep people from talking about UFOs, that many people have witnessed! This is all documented by the people who were persecuted.

Why all the secrecy to something that the powers that be, claim doesn't even exist?

Profits. Profits mean power, and power gives control and domination.

You really need to ask yourself, why is the government and the military so intent on making people afraid of the craft in our skies? It is obvious that the government does not work for the benefit of the people whatsoever, anymore. Considering the confession of Werner Von Braun mentioned earlier, if any "craft" do turn hostile, you can bet there are Earth humans on board doing it.

The other spin the status quo has put on this situation, is when they try to discredit people who observe UFOs firsthand. The term "credible observer" or "trained observer" will always be used. This is a subtle but useful form of psychological manipulation designed to cause the masses to lose faith in the testimony of anyone except the ones they tell you to believe.

They often point to military personnel, unless that military person said they saw it too! Then they will point to a law enforcement person, again unless they saw it too! Then it's on to the politicians...yeah, right.

I have asked many military persons, on purpose, this question: "Have you ever had any specific and or special training regarding observing or making observations? Have you ever been trained as an observer?" I have never had a single one of them answer in the affirmative! The phrase "Trained Observer" is a con job perpetrated by the government/military to control your thinking.

People who are in the military and the police are just as varied as the population in general. That is, in fact, the proverbial pool from which they come. This means that the population in general is just as reliable, as witnesses, as any one of them. Probably more so, because the population "in general" will not immediately have someone in authority above them, dictating to them what they can and cannot say!

The Star Nations are here. They are here in droves and they have been here a long, long time. Personally, I trust most of them much more than I trust most humans. Look at it this way: They obviously have technology that is so far beyond our standard military weapons, that we cannot "compete" with them. They have been documented for as long as our own written history goes, and our own written history states they were here before we even existed. If they acted like Earth humans and were going to rape, pillage, conquer, control and dominate – why didn't they take us over while we were hunter-gatherers? Why not when we were riding horses and buggies? Why would they wait until we developed higher technologies like jet fighters and nuclear weapons before picking a fight? They must be smart enough to know that conquest is all about plunder, so they would not want to risk the Earth getting irradiated more/again. The fact is, they started showing up in mass quantities as soon as we started setting off nuclear weapons! That's because they understood the spoiled pre-schoolers on the block were playing with nukes and have no idea how dangerous that is and why!

Do they have an agenda? Yes, of course they do. But unlike Earth humans, their agenda is based on love and compassion. We always try to project our violent mentality on everything we fear or are not familiar with. They have no interest in invading us, we are their progeny. Their brothers, sisters, and cousins. They are watching to see if we are going to grow up and save ourselves, or not. They are trying to help us, without violating our free will, so we do not destroy ourselves and our planet. This planet, is not ours to destroy!

Let's go back and review a few things. The most common depiction of what most call "aliens" are that of what have come to be called "the

Greys". These are the beings from Zeta Reticula and are also commonly referred to as "Zeta's". They have a remarkably similar history to us. They too had an advanced civilization that wasn't intelligent enough to not kill off most of the life on their planet. Perhaps it might be more accurate to say that they, like us, lacked the emotional maturity and stability.

In the subsequent millennia since then, they have had to resort to cloning as mentioned earlier. There are a comparatively small group of these greys that have broken off from the main group and have been conducting rogue cloning experiments. These are by far the minority. It is these rogue groups and beings of lower mentality that have formed an alliance with the military/industrial complex, and have traded technology for – what? I'll let you guess at that one.

Meanwhile, back on board the Zeta ships, they have been conducting hybrid experiments to join their DNA with ours. They have advanced to a phenomenal state of mental acuity and we have the emotional genes they so desperately need. They already have two sets of hybrids that are referred to as the Essasani and the Yah-Yel. They are very loving and very intelligent beings that are the best of both worlds. They live onboard vast ships that are orbiting Earth right now. They are waiting and they are watching to see what we will do.

Can we grow up and learn to get along with one another, even while being provoked constantly by our handlers, that are instigating war and hatred? Will we destroy ourselves and most life on this planet too? What is the species that is the greatest hope *and* the biggest concern of the higher realms, going to choose?

No one knows for sure. But there is at least one thing that the most probable timelines have in common. At least some of humanity, as we know it, will survive. Whether that is the majority, or a small minority of the current population is what is not known for sure.

Eventually the Star Nations will make themselves known to all. They will not do so until it is safe for them and for humanity. The intriguing thing is, it is hoped that the hybrid program which they have already started, can evolve into something more and something bigger.

If you have read this far, you understand that humanity is already a hybrid species. What would you think about continuing on with this experiment and perhaps beginning a new phase that involved the Essasani and/or the Yah-Yel? This would leap-frog humanity's evolution tremendously and provide them with the stability of a much larger population to mix with. No one will ever be forced to participate. That is not their way. But the higher consciousness within which they currently exist, could help us fix the damage we have done to ourselves and this beautiful planet. We would have the golden opportunity to clean up our own mess and start acting like adults!

This would also ignite the variety of genetic gifts that have been lying dormant in humanity's DNA that was given to us a few hundred thousand years ago. We could, in one generation, evolve into a civilized civilization that could rightfully take its place at the seats of the Galactic Federation. This would be like lifting the anchor for us and the entire universe as we begin our journey to not just the stars, but the higher dimensions as well!

I highly recommend Steven Greer's approach to establishing contact with the Star Nations. He has created a very common-sense set of instructions that he calls the CE-5 Protocols. You can look them up online. They are a brief list of steps you or your group can take to establish contact and possibly bring about a sighting experience for your group. They are based on creating love or gratitude in your heart and in your mind, so your energies are coherent. When you do this as a group, each person's energy is compounded exponentially. When your group projects this energy to the Star Nations, the Star Nations worth attracting, will sense your energy, and will very often come and check you out.

They want contact with nice, loving, caring humans, not people who want to kill anything they haven't seen before. Kind of makes sense, doesn't it?

It is obvious they have been here for a very long time. It is obvious they are increasing their presence, or at least allowing us to see them more often. They can travel through the stars. They have been clocked at speeds of up to 24,000 mph by the military, and in excess of 70 knots underwater.

They have maintained a constant watch over the world's nuclear power plants and missiles, de-activating them on occasions when it was necessary to avoid major problems. They are present in the skies with our military jets and have been since WW II. They have never instigated any conflict and have only reluctantly defended themselves when absolutely necessary. If they had bad intentions, they would have taken over a long, long time ago.

CHAPTER 17

INDIGENOUS FORMS OF SPIRITUALITY

*"For me there is only the traveling on paths that have heart,
on any path that may have heart.*

*There I travel, and the only worthwhile challenge
is to traverse its full length.*

There I travel – looking…looking breathlessly."

– Don Juan Matus

I am in no way attempting to teach the spirituality of the Native, indigenous peoples. I am not "culturally appropriating" anything. What I am doing is promoting a way of life and mostly a change in consciousness that is in harmony with all life on this planet so that we can survive as a planetary civilization instead of destroying ourselves through our current backwards, unconscious path. I am promoting a way of life that supports Life itself and more closely follows the spiritual intent of "God's" teachings!

I do not attempt to speak for my indigenous brothers and sisters. Nor do I claim to be an expert in their traditions. I only mean to share the beauty and wisdom that I have found that is included in some of their teachings, with the world. I truly honor the Elders who have gone before us, those who are present with us now, and those who council us when we quiet ourselves enough to hear them. I sincerely thank them for the whisperings of wisdom that stir my soul!

Also… while I only cover a small portion of information here, please do your own research and discover the vast and beautiful world of native/ indigenous teachings out there. Every continent is filled with its native peoples and their wisdom. You will probably find their teachings have the beauty and the heart you have been searching for. It is by returning to their understanding of what is divine and how to live in a divine manner that we can save our species and our planet. And yes…the one you know as Jesus approves this message! He told me so. Now then…

There are so many cultures on this planet it would be hard to count them. Every single one of them has had their own unique perspective on life and therefore their own unique relationship with the Divine. There are however, still more things they have in common than there are differences. Each one simply has its own "flavor". Had certain people of the world spent more time talking to others rather than forcing their beliefs on others, this world would have turned out far superior to what it has, because much more wisdom would be common place!

This brings us to a point I want to share. Spirit works with everyone in the manner they best understand. The native, indigenous peoples of the world (from which we **_ALL_** sprang, by the way), have always had and maintained their unity with nature. They never saw themselves as being apart from nature. They knew that the Great Spirit lived within all of creation and that "all" included them!

To a great extent, the "fall" in consciousness that those who followed the organized religions suffered from, did not affect indigenous peoples nearly as much. This is because they never viewed themselves as separate from the Divine in the first place. Yes, consciousness over the entire planet dropped, but an individual's or a cultural belief system had a huge impact on the severity of this drop. The Indigenous peoples honored the Earth as their "Mother", and took care of her and all their brothers and sisters of their tribe, and the Earth!

It was those who got kicked out of the "garden" that came to view themselves as separate from "God" and fell out of unity consciousness. In their sudden emptiness, they tried to fill themselves with material goods, wealth and dominion over their fellow man. That is why when you ask a filthy rich man "When is enough – enough?" His response is typically "A little more!" They cannot be satisfied because they are looking for fulfillment from the world of matter while remaining clueless that the emptiness they feel, is in their souls!

The remainder of this chapter is quotes and writings from Native Elders. The majority is from the book, "Dancing the Dream" by the wonderful Jamie Sams.

Jamie Sams was an inspiration to all who had the privilege to come across her books and teachings! If you do not own Dancing the Dream, I strongly suggest you purchase it soon! (As well as everything else she wrote!)

I present these with all credit going to the original authors, in the hopes that the beauty of their messages, and the wisdom they contain will reach the hearts and touch the souls of more people, so we can all change the world for the better... indeed, for the Highest Good of All Concerned!

The one thing all traditional spiritual traditions have in common is your connection to your own heart's wisdom and your soul's connection to Mother Earth. This is what humanity has lost along the way. It may not be too late to change our ways, if we actually start. NOW.

"If you are alive, you are on a sacred path. In your life you have followed a multitude of paths with different directions, and yet all those paths dovetail, creating the one life Path that represents your unique journey through the physical world. Becoming aware that each of us also travel an intangible or spiritual path is the beginning of the awakening processes found on the seven sacred paths of human initiation and transformation.

"Some people go through life believing that there is no scheme, no rhyme or reason, to the workings of the universe. They see no connection between themselves, other life forms, and the creator – until some life event forces them to go beyond that unconscious condition. How and when life beckons us to change is different for every individual. Many people grow and mature, endure heartache, experience personal breakthroughs, and still do not consciously embrace the paths of transformation.

"The seven sacred paths of transformation are never forced upon us; they present themselves as opportunities. We may feel we are at the mercy of life's events, but even amid tragedy, fears, or loss, we are given choices and the opportunity to wake up. We can deny the existence of these alternate paths of understanding and remain safely unaware of them, or we can risk looking deeper. When the light goes on and we embrace the awakening process, we start to remember the things that our souls have always known. As we become more conscious, we become aware of the divine significance or spiritual purpose that we carry within us. Doors begin to open, and we start to perceive the spirit or life force that animates our universe. Only then do we awaken and realize exactly how our lives are intricately woven within the whole.

"On the first path, the East Direction on the Medicine Wheel, we become illuminated and begin to see clearly that there is a purpose for our lives. We embrace a new form of clarity, which takes us beyond our former "What is life offering me?" perspective. In the Native American traditions, the first path of initiation was originally introduced as a rite of passage into adulthood. Young girls and boys faced various ceremonial tests representing the end of childhood. For females this passage was usually at the time of their first menstrual flow, and for young men it came around their 13th year. Ceremonies varied from tribe to tribe but most involve the test of bravery for the boys and an introduction to the mysteries of Women's Medicine for the girls. After the ceremonies, boys were admitted into the men's counsel and girls into the women's Council in order to listen to their elders and to learn about the adult responsibilities of being of service to the tribe. (Wow! What a concept!)

"The clarity and illumination offered by these rites of passage were found through becoming responsible for the well-being of the tribe as a whole.

Young people learned how to put away negative or childish emotions and to develop the ability to respond – responsibly. The death of childhood and the birth of adulthood marked a new path that signaled the dawning of the process of nurturing and honing the young person's natural gifts into talents that would benefit that person and the whole tribe. This process allowed the individual to find his or her own path, with the best mentors the tribe had to offer providing guidance in the areas of the individuals makeup or personality showing promise. Everyone was served by teaching and through learning, without hidden agendas. The better the student became at his or her chosen role, the more everyone benefited, including the teacher, who would continue to pass hard-earned expertise on to the next generation.

"On the second path, the South Direction on the Medicine Wheel is the place of the return of trust and innocence, the place where our faith is tested or proven, and the place where we have the opportunity to recapture the wonder of being alive that we once held as children.

"For centuries, our people have taught those willing to hear, that human-beings, the two leggeds, are part of the earth. We belong to the Earth Mother whether we think we do or not. On the second path, it becomes evident that we are a part of the earth when we learn to feel the heartbeat of the earth align with our own. For many people, this is a life-changing event. Some feel the heartbeat; others sense it in other ways, such as a sparkling synchronicity when everything they do begins to flow magically in a natural rhythm. When the rhythm of the human heart begins to vibrate at the same resonance as the earth's energy field, synchronicity happens.

"The third path, the West Direction, teaches us how to heal our pasts, our bodies, and our self-esteem. It is a place of introspection and listening. The third path of initiation teaches us about healing and contains many lessons that help us reclaim the fragments of ourselves that may have been wounded or denied at various times throughout our lives. In the west we find ourselves looking at the duality of life: our fears and our loves, our strengths and our weaknesses, our joys and our sorrows. We learn how to respond to our healthy shame when we know we have done something that needs to be corrected, becoming accountable for our actions. We acknowledge our ability to heal when we become willing to correct our behaviors and to make amends if necessary. We learn how to release unhealthy guilt, which comes from accepting the unreasonable expectations of others. We become aware of when we're adopting self-sabotage and shadow-like behavior, and we correct our old ways of being in order to move forward into healing potential.

"On the fourth path, the North Direction, is the place of wisdom. We learn how to share the wisdom we have gained as well as how to live with compassionate, nonjudgmental, open hearts. We learn to incorporate the intellectual knowledge we have by walking it in our lives with impeccability. The north direction offers us the opportunity to review all that we have learned and to learn how and when to share that wisdom with others. The fourth path has been walked by many travelers who have offered new wisdom to humanity as a gift of insight. The vast worlds of consciousness, energy, and spirit in our universe are accessible because some human being had the courage to enter the unknown and to become the adventurous spirit who was willing to find out what unchartered potentials were available to humankind. The unspoken languages of the animals, plants, stones, and the elemental spirits in nature bring us further wisdom about our human roles in the natural world. We discover how to detect the beautiful gifts being offered to us by the life forms on the Earth Mother and how we can apply their lessons to our lives. The realms of angels, spiritual guides, and unseen forces of consciousness offered divine inspiration. In the north direction of the fourth path, we incorporate all the messages we receive from the spiritual consciousness of other life forms into our personal understanding of life on planet Earth. These lessons of wisdom allow us to perceive that all life forms in our universe are more than biological or geological forms; they all contain consciousness or spirit.

"The fifth path is the Above Direction, where we embrace the unseen worlds of spirit, the heavenly realms, the unknown parts of the universe, and the intangible forces in creation. On this level of initiation we encounter all that exists beyond our natural world, as well as the parts of our spiritual natures that contain the urges of the soul. As spiritual warriors on the fifth path, we become fully connected to our own inner guidance and gain an intimate knowledge of our authentic self, the Spiritual Essence. This path offers an overview of how things work in the universe and how our Spiritual Essences are interrelated parts of the Great Mystery. We also learn how all life in our universe is interrelated energetically and spiritually. As we embrace the lessons of the fifth path, all remaining veils of separation are dismantled layer by layer. The destruction of the foundations holding old belief systems in place catapults us into states of new awareness that allow us to see life from to undivided, harmonious sacred points of view simultaneously, one in the Dream Weave, and one in the physical world. This radical departure from our former tunnel vision collapses our preconceptions of time and space, and we must learn how to hold the anchor points of awareness in both worlds.

"The sixth path is the Below Direction, where we learn how to perceive the unseen forces in the natural world and the connections to spirit existing in all living things, and we learn how to bring our own spirits fully into our human bodies. The below direction on the medicine wheel represents our connection to the Earth. Here we learn how to take the proficient knowledge we've gained, including the use of Dream Weave energy, and use that wisdom in daily life. One of the first goals of the below direction is to stay grounded and to function efficiently while our bodies are feeling surges of unexplained energy. The lessons of the sixth path teaches to perceive the nonphysical realities connected to the Dream Weave, discerning the intent and correctly identifying the source before we apply the symbols, metaphors, and other information to our lives.

"The marriage of the tangible and intangible worlds of the fifth path was great! The honeymoon is over. Now, do I sink, swim, or float? It is time to lift the final vestiges of that last veil, to connect with the earth, and to continue to explore the universe's fast realms of consciousness. On the sixth path we learn to discern the differences in the unified energy of all parts of the universe, to embrace the center of Creation, to move through the void, to actualize the neutral viewpoint from the divine, infinite perspective, and master the skills of using universal energy to create healing opportunities in the material world. These challenging tasks can take many years to accomplish. At times we will wonder how we can function with all the various tasks staring us in the face, but in every case, we are required to connect our body to the earth. My one

"On the seventh path, the Within Direction, we learn how to gain access to all life in our universe within our own human body and to walk through life in a state of full spiritual awareness, without any separation or judgment. In the Seneca tradition the seventh direction is called the Within Direction, and the Cherokee call it the Now Direction. Both names are applicable and describe two of the seventh path's characteristic aspects. The Seneca viewpoint is that we must bring all that we have learned into our innermost being and walk the wisdom of all directions in our physical bodies. From the Cherokee viewpoint, the NOW is also bringing wisdom found on all paths into the body and being fully present, walking with that beauty moment by moment. We have the ability to slip into past and future and will the seventh path, and being fully present takes on a whole new level of importance when we embrace the ever-present present of the Now Direction.

"When we are fully present, we become the sum total of all the strengths found in our family trees, and we have surmounted the weaknesses found in the past seven generations. When we are in balance, become the focal point of all that is possible in the future because we are relating to all of that is present in the Now. We open the paths of consciousness for the next seven generations to follow. Time flows through us, but we are not subject to its passing because we have embraced the infinite aspects of humanity and are living extensions of the Eternal Flame of Love. We respect the life force and sparks of awareness found in everything in Creation, allowing ourselves to BE an integral part of the whole.

"The seven paths of human transformation are wheels of experience reflecting the manner in which human beings learn how to use life force. These paths coexist simultaneously. They are not linear, and each individual embraces lessons on several paths at the same time.

"If you choose to pick up the gauntlet of the Seven Paths that have now been placed within your reach, you will be awakened to the fact that human life is the ultimate initiation and that by healing separation, humans discover their places within the infinite wholeness that the Great Mystery embodies in our universe. Embracing the journey of the seven sacred paths is the quest of a courageous spiritual warrior who seeks to understand the mysteries of the unknown, the unspoken languages of the animals, the healing qualities of the plants, the spiritual messages offered in the natural world, the interwoven patterns of the stars, the sweetness of the angelic realms, the aliveness of the universe, the touch of divine intervention, the inner peace of the spirit, and the infinite wholeness that comes from moving beyond the limiting human concepts of separation.

"The Dream Weave is the name used to describe the unseen world of spirit, thought, emotion, and intangible energy that is a part of our physical reality. The common denominator that binds together these two worlds of physicality and intangible energies is a grid of energy lines without visible form. To gain access to the invisible world of the Dream Weave, we must enter the stillness, and go beyond the chatter of the human mind to the infinite, majestic silence. We must still our personal thoughts and feelings so that we can tune into a serene frequency, matching the majestic, universal consciousness of Great Mystery. If you are worried that you will not be able to find the connective tissue of the Dream Weave and gain access to the Universal, relax. Everyone can learn to tap into the Dream Weave. Some people connect through their dreams, some people meditate, others follow a drumbeat and journey out of the body, some fast and pray, and others use ceremonial dancing. Any spiritual discipline, followed faithfully, can allow a person to enter a serene state of stillness, and that practice is the key that opens the door. There is no single correct way to tap the universal consciousness. All paths and methods are valid, taking us to the same place: the serene center of our Spiritual Essence.

"We cannot see the intangible realms that influence our physical reality until we remove the false idea that the energetic world is not a part of the wholeness offered by the Creator to humankind. The valves of separation are created when we are born in human bodies and when we learn to respond to life through our senses, emotions, and thoughts. Our souls or spirits enter our physical bodies, animating the flesh, bone, blood, and organs with divine life force. Prior to her birth our soul or spirit is connected to God, the Creator, the Great Mystery, and as a clear awareness of the oneness of Universal Consciousness and life force. After we are born, every thought and emotion creates an energetic thread that combines with all others, leaving the intangible veils of separation that keep us from remembering authentic oneness, which contains no duality. This is as it should be: duality has a divine purpose and is necessary to the human growth process. The purpose of learning through opposites is one that we begin to see when we embrace the seven sacred paths of human transformation.

"Each of the seven veils has its own qualities. The first veil keeps us from remembering the Oneness of the universe. We forget that everything in Creation exists inside the Great Mystery for God. We forget that everything contains life force and spirit, and is energetically connected. We forget that every atom making up life and form in Creation contains the Eternal Flame of Love, and that everything has a purpose. As we remember these truths, this veil is dissolved or lifted in layers.

"We create the second veil of separation by forgetting our spiritual identity. When we forget our spiritual identities, we also forget why we are here in physical bodies. When we forget why we are here on earth, we also forget original purpose for becoming human. This veil is peeled away in layers every time we encounter another aspect of our spiritual identity, and we remember why we are here and our original purpose with the divine plan.

"The third veil is created through the limitations of our sensory perceptions in developing our human perceptions will begin by discovering life through the physical senses. During early childhood we are open to other perceptions, but those begin to disappear as we are taught not to use any extra senses. We are taught to perceive all of the solid objects that adults considered to be "real", hence we stop using the ability to perceive energy. This veil cannot be lifted if we become addicted to sexual pleasure or other forms of physical sensations. Nor can this veil be lifted if we do not use spiritual disciplines.

"We create the fourth veil when we develop our emotions. An infant is physically helpless but is totally aware of his or her feelings. You can see the emotions that pass through a baby by watching the waves of expressions that cross the child's face in the space of five minutes. As we develop, we learn how to control or even deny our feelings. This veil, created by unexpressed feelings and emotions that have not been healed or released, masks our authentic will.

"Only when this veil is lifted can we gain access to the divine will of the Creator, which exists as a unified part of our Spiritual Essence and our personal free will.

"The fifth veil is composed of our belief systems, our thoughts, mental computations decisions, theories, assumptions, and hypotheses regarding everything we experience in life. During childhood we accept the beliefs that are taught to us by our families. We begin to alter our learned belief systems when we become teenagers, and we adopt new ideas based on our personal experiences, not on what is true for mom and dad. We continue adding thoughts and beliefs that are based upon our judgment what we think is true and false, good or bad, possible or impossible. This type of mental calculation is based upon comparison and duality. Polarized thinking and limited belief systems create a veil of mental separation. This veil begins to be lifted in stages as we remove layer after layer of dualistic beliefs.

"We create the sixth veil of separation when we shut down our perceptions of anything that is not solid. As with the third veil, when we cannot perceive the colors, energy, or spirit connected to matter or solid forms, we perceive life solely from the five physical senses. The sixth veil differs in that it also blocks our access to other worlds, realities, time periods, and dimensions of awareness. Depending on the individual, this veil is created at different times. For some people the veil drops in place at birth, for others the loss of extrasensory perception happens during childhood and for some rare individuals, the sixth veil does not exist. These gifted people who do not have the sixth veil firmly dividing the tangible and intangible parts of life are blessed with extrasensory perceptions, but they can also feel misunderstood because they can easily slip into past or future times perceive things that others cannot. In some people these extrasensory gifts are partially shut down, but can be awakened. The six veil is lifted in increments as we learn to eliminate our judgments during the first five paths of initiation.

"The seventh veil of separation is created by our personal sense of individuality and the rigid concepts that delineate our human identities. We forget the truths that we understood before taking our human bodies, when we were fully aware of being connected to the Great Mystery. We are still connected, but we gain the full awareness of that state of grace in pieces as we remove the veils a thread at a time. We break the threads of separation through our personal growth and revelations, allowing us to perceive the overview of our divine connections. Ultimately we realize that we can walk through life and still maintain full connection to all levels of the Dream Weave." – Jamie Sams

Where are the dances of oneness that I knew before my birth?
Did I surrender my wholeness, in order to walk the earth?
Did I choose forgetting, in order to make life real?
Did I inhabit the human body, so I could learn how to feel?

I am here to dance the dream, in my sacred human form.
To celebrate my uniqueness, and ask no other to conform.
Dancing through life's lessons, I will learn to move with grace.
While I dream of remembering, the potential of the human race.
– Jamie Sams

Native American Prayer

Oh, Great Spirit
Whose voice I hear in the winds,
And whose breath gives life to all the world,
hear me, I am small and weak,
I need your strength and wisdom.
Let me walk in beauty and make my eyes ever behold
the red and purple sunset.
Make my hands respect the things you have
made and my ears sharp to hear your voice.
Make me wise so that I may understand the things
you have taught my people.
Let me learn the lessons you have
hidden in every leaf and rock.

I seek strength, not to be greater than my brother,
but to fight my greatest enemy – myself.
Make me always ready to come to you
with clean hands and straight eyes.
So when life fades, as the fading sunset,
my Spirit may come to you without shame.

(translated by Lakota Sioux Chief Yellow Lark in 1887)
published in Native American Prayers – by the Episcopal Church.

Another prayer that expresses the love and harmony that is inherent in this beautiful way of life:

Walking in Beauty

By Closing Prayer from the Navajo Way Blessing Ceremony
In beauty I walk
With beauty before me I walk

With beauty behind me I walk
With beauty above me I walk
With beauty around me I walk
It has become beauty again
Hózhóogo naasháa doo. Shitsijí' hózhóogo naasháa doo. Shikéédéé hózhóogo naasháa doo.
Shideigi hózhóogo naasháa doo. T'áá altso shinaagóó hózhóogo naasháa doo. Hózhó náhásdlíí'.
Hózhó náhásdlíí'. Hózhó náhásdlíí'. Hózhó náhásdlíí'
Today I will walk out, today everything negative will leave me
I will be as I was before, I will have a cool breeze over my body.
I will have a light body, I will be happy forever, nothing will hinder me.
I walk with beauty before me. I walk with beauty behind me.
I walk with beauty below me. I walk with beauty above me.
I walk with beauty around me. My words will be beautiful.
In beauty all day long may I walk.
Through the returning seasons, may I walk.
On the trail marked with pollen may I walk.
With dew about my feet, may I walk.
With beauty before me may I walk.
With beauty behind me may I walk.
With beauty below me may I walk.
With beauty above me may I walk.
With beauty all around me may I walk.
In old age wandering on a trail of beauty, lively, may I walk.
In old age wandering on a trail of beauty, living again, may I walk.
My words will be beautiful…

White Buffalo Calf Woman
– the Coming of the Sacred Pipe

Before the appearance of White Buffalo Calf Woman, the Native Americans honored the Great Spirit. But among the Sioux, the coming of White Buffalo Calf Woman brought the most important instrument, the pipe, which is now used in all Sioux ceremonies.

Two men of a small band of the Sioux tribe, the Sans Arc, were hunting and saw something approaching in the distance. As the figure drew close, they observed a beautiful maiden, dressed in white buckskin, carrying a bundle wrapped in buffalo hide.

Behold me.
Behold me,
for in a sacred manner
I am walking.

She saying this and repeated the same as she walked slowly toward them.

One of the men had evil thoughts about this maiden and moved toward her. The other hunter tried forcibly to restrain him, but the evil man pushed the good warrior away.

A cloud descended on the evil one, and when it lifted, his body was a skeleton being devoured by worms. This symbolized that one who lives in ignorance and has evil in his heart may be destroyed by his own actions.

The good hunter knelt in fear, trembling as the buckskin-clad woman approached. She spoke to him, telling him not to be afraid, but to return to his people and prepare them for her coming. This was done, and the beautiful maiden appeared in their midst, walking among them in a sunwise, or clockwise, direction. She held forth her bundle and said:

This is a gift, and must always be treated in a holy way.
In this bundle is a sacred pipe which no impure man or woman
should ever see.
With this sacred pipe you will send your voices to Wakan Tanka.
The Great Spirit, the Creator of All, your Father and Grandfather.
With this sacred pipe you will walk upon the earth,
which is your grandmother and mother.
All your steps should be holy.
The bowl of the pipe is red stone which represents the Earth.

A Buffalo calf is carved in the stone facing the center,
and symbolizes the four-legged creatures who live as brothers among you.
The stem is wood and represents all growing things.
12 feathers hanging from where the stem fits the bowl
and are from the spotted Eagle.
These represent all the winged brothers who live among you.
All these things are joined to you
who will smoke the pipe and send voices to Wakan Tanka.

When you use this pipe to pray, you will pray for and with everything.
Sacred pipe binds you to all your relatives;
your grandfather and father, your grandmother and mother.
The Redstone represents the Mother Earth on which you will live.
The earth is red, and the two-legged creatures who live upon it are also red.
Wakan Tanka has given you a red road – a good straight road to travel,
and you must remember that all people who stand on this earth are sacred.
From this day, sacred pipe will stand on the red earth,
and you will send your voices to Wakan Tanka.
There are seven circles on the stone,
which represent the seven rites in which you will use the pipe.

White Buffalo Calf Woman then instructed the people to send runners
to the distant bands of the Sioux nation, to bring in the many leaders,
medicine people, and the holy men and holy women. This they did.
When the people gathered she instructed them in the sacred ceremony
of the first rite, that of the Keeping of the Soul. She told them that the
remaining six rites would be made known to them through visions. As
she started to leave, she said:

Remember how sacred the pipe is,
and treated in a sacred manner,
for it will be with you always.
Remember also that in me are four ages.
I shall leave you now,
but shall look upon you in every age,
and will return in the end.

The Sioux begged the spirit woman to stay with them; they promised to erect a fine lodge and to give her a fine man to provide for her, but she declined their offer.

No, the Creator above, the Great Spirit, is happy with you.
You, the grandchildren, you have listened well to my teachings.
Now I must return to the spirit world.

She walked some distance away from them and sat down. When she rose, she had become a white Buffalo calf. She walked farther, bowed to the four quarters of the universe, and then disappeared into the distance. A sacred bundle was left with the people; and to this day, a traditional Sioux family, the Keepers of the Sacred Pipe, still guards the bundle and its contents on one of the Sioux reservations.

Chief Arvol Looking Horse is the current Keeper of the Sacred Pipe.

(Chief Arvol Looking Horse was born on the Cheyenne River Reservation in South Dakota. At the age of 12, he was given the responsibility of becoming the 19th Generation Keeper of the Sacred White Buffalo Calf Pipe, the youngest ever. He is widely recognized as a chief and the spiritual leader of all three branches of the Sioux tribe.)

"Mitakuye Oyasin" – We are all related.

"I could see that the white man did not care for each other the way our people did.
They would take everything from each other if they could.
Some had more of everything than they could use,
While crowds of people had nothing at all.
This could not be better than the old ways of my people."

– Hehaka Sapa; aka Black Elk

CHAPTER 18

AYURVEDA AND STRESS MANAGEMENT

"If one wishes to attain enlightenment, it is only common sense that they adopt a lifestyle that is conducive to achieving that! It is not a matter of right or wrong, it is a matter of – what is effective and what is not"

– Marty Rawson

Ayurveda is the ancient science of life and longevity from India. It is the oldest natural healing system in the world and is commonly referred to as the "Mother" of all Healing. All of the traditional healing methods originated here. It is not simply a natural healing system however; it is a way of life. It is the lifestyle practiced by the ancient Rishis of India that allowed them to commune with the Divine and attain liberation. It only stands to reason, that if one wishes to achieve enlightenment, one may want to follow in the footsteps of those who have achieved it!

Here is a simple truth: You cannot do spiritual work when you are sick or in pain. Your body simply has more urgent matters to attend to.

Ayurveda understands that each of us are unique individuals and that we react to different substances and stimuli differently. They have differentiated between different body types and call these "doshas".

Ayurveda puts emphasis on keeping your body's unique metabolism, your "prakruti", in a state of balance that is perfect for you. It is not a simplistic, "one size fits all" method. It is a sophisticated science that treats you as the unique individual you are.

It starts by determining the unique balance of what is called "Doshas". This unique balance is called your Prakruti (original creation), meaning how your body was balanced in your original, healthy form. Then, it determines the doshic nature of your ailment. Last, your treatment is determined by which "medicines" (with their opposite doshic nature) will treat your ailment, without aggravating your body's original doshic balance (Prakruti). This way, the only side effect is better health! (The basic concept is literally as simple as using water to put out a fire, instead of using gasoline or wood, but not so much water that you cause a flood.)

I highly recommend that everyone take up the Science of Life that is Ayurveda! It is one of the most important steps you can take with regard to taking charge of your own health! In the west, the definition of health has typically been defined as the "absence of disease". In Ayurveda, it is defined as that state of being where you are *so healthy and happy* that you achieve a state of bliss, thus making the journey to enlightenment, a small step.

Ayurveda is where the original understanding comes from that everything you take in, through all your senses and your thoughts contribute to making you who you are and what your life will be. In modern parlance we have two sayings that kind of sum this up – "You are what you eat" (albeit, through all your senses), and "GIGO: Garbage in, Garbage out."

Ayurveda helps you create the entire lifestyle and home environment that is conducive to your maximum state of health, happiness and yes, even bliss.

I am not in any way saying you should not go to a doctor when a doctor's care is called for! To throw away the advances of western medicine would be absurd. What I am suggesting is that if everyone learned how to keep themselves healthy in the first place, they would not have to visit the doctor nearly as often!

I am saying however, that big pharma has a stranglehold on America in particular, and this is killing us for nothing more than their profit! I am not saying to never take prescriptions, I am saying to only take them when you really have to, for only as long as prescribed and then use Ayurveda to help restore your body to balance after you have completed the prescription. Anytime someone gets to the point that they are taking 5 or more prescriptions; it has been proven they are drastically shortening their lifespan. Many times, there are natural methods of dealing with the same issues that prescriptions deal with. Another aspect of Ayurveda is the concept of using your food as your medicine and your medicine as your food. There is great wisdom in this concept!

The three doshas are Vata, Pitta and Kapha. Everyone has all three "doshas" but it is your unique balance of them that gives your body its unique metabolism. Ayurveda simply helps you to restore your body's systems, organs and tissues to their original balance that you were born with. Ayurveda has a much more thorough understanding of the entire disease process, and can literally help you reverse this process up to the final stages of most disease development. With the skyrocketing price of healthcare nowadays, you cannot afford to *not* try this!

Ayurveda is the sister science to yoga. Yoga is actually meant to be practiced according to Ayurvedic dosha types. It is hoped that as time goes on, more yoga instructors will begin to put increased emphasis on their clients' doshas, here in the west. As for the western approach to yoga, I will simply state that if you are consumed with how your butt or the rest of your body looks, you are not doing yoga. Period. If your instructor is using gimmicks, you are not doing yoga! Yoga is a combination of moving meditation and still meditation where your attention and your awareness is placed inward, all while doing Marma therapy on yourself. Has anyone else not noticed the difference between how the yogis in India do yoga as compared to the marketplace, puppy-mill variety practiced here in the U.S.?

A brief explanation of yoga and why it works is in order here. I have never met a yoga instructor who actually knows why yoga is so effective in helping people physically, mentally, emotionally and spiritually. I am not saying there are none that do, I am saying I have not met them, nor have I heard of them. This is a sad reflection on the teaching of yoga, here in the west.

In order to explain this, we have to bring in another science, called Marma Therapy. It is concerned with the 107 points on the physical body where the Anatomy of the Spirit (the Etheric body; the Soul) meet at the surface of the physical body and can be influenced.

Many, many people try to match the chakras up to the acupuncture points of the TCM system. This is, to be blunt, a rookie mistake.

The acupuncture system works on the nervous system, while the Marma system works on the points where the "Nadis" of the non-physical body reach the surface of the physical body. These "Nadis" originate from the chakras themselves. They are a direct energetic pathway to the chakras as well as everything else that makes you and your soul – you. Both systems are very effective and I have used both for decades. You simply need to understand which system is most effective for the issue you are attempting to work on! They do have, I believe, 37 points in common. While some of these are in fact, points that effect the chakras... if you want to truly understand the science of the chakras and the anatomy of the Spirit, you really do need to familiarize yourself with at least the basics of Marma therapy.

The reason yoga works on everything, even Spiritual issues, is because the various poses provide stimulation to various and specific Marma points of the Spiritual anatomy. This then has a significant effect on your physical body, your emotional body, and your mental body. Everything is inextricably tied together and all systems affect each other. It only stands to reason that if you wish to maintain physical, emotional, and mental health and harmony, you might want to learn how to access and heal the Master controller, which is the etheric, Spiritual body...also known as "your Soul". It is after all, the eternal aspect of, and who you really are. So...when you are doing yoga, you are doing Marma therapy on yourself! That is why it works!

I highly recommend that everyone practice yoga and meditation in a peaceful, relaxing setting that does indeed promote harmony and relaxation. Stress is a formidable issue in these times and I cannot over emphasize its impact on your health and well-being.

Besides yoga, Ayurveda has much to offer. Below is a short set of recommendations with regard to stress management. Stress is one of the most significant factors in health that there is. It is at pandemic levels in our society and greatly adds to the problems people are having with inflammation, nervous system disorders, mental and emotional health and so on! Due to the nature of stress, it is generally treated similarly in most cases. If there are any terms you are unfamiliar with, I suggest looking them up and expanding your knowledge into this wonderful world that is the Science of Life and Longevity.

Doshas and their reactions to stress

Vata – Vata dominant individuals are generally slender of build and possess sharper, more angular facial features than the other two dosha types. Their eyes appear typically as small slits, or barely open. Their mind is quick and very active but can easily become ungrounded and they may seem "airy-Faery" when not grounded well. Their mind chatter can also cause insomnia. They also tend to suffer more from constipation than the other two dosha types.

Vata individuals are likely to develop reactions to stress such as anxiety, fearfulness, phobias or even anxiety neurosis. They are the hardest hit of all the doshic types, when it comes to stress.

Pitta – Pitta dominant individuals are generally of medium build, with eyes that are open to a medium amount. They have a keen mind that is also very active. They tend towards anger, hatred and rage, and will explode like the proverbial volcano when truly out of balance. They have excessive heat throughout their system and tend to have health problems related to their blood. Since the state of the blood is broadcast through the skin, they also tend to be prone to rashes and skin disorders, in general.

Pitta individuals typically react to stress with anger, hatred and rage. They may also however develop hypertension (high blood pressure), peptic ulcer, ulcerative colitis, rashes or other pitta disorders.

Kapha – Kapha dominant individuals are generally of heavier build, with "big bones". They have the large, almond shaped eyes and are the "gentle giants" of the species. They naturally tend towards lethargy but are also naturally strong physically. When out of balance, they tend towards being lethargic and possessive.

Kapha individuals under stress can develop underactive thyroid function, slow metabolism and increased blood sugar, leading to a pre-diabetic condition. They tend to eat compulsively when stressed out.

Everyone is a combination of all three doshas. The question is, what is your unique balance of these three? You will notice most people have a combination of features representing the doshas dominant in them. For instance, I am a Pitta-Vata Combination with Pitta features overall but with Vata tendencies. My lovely wife is a Vata-Pitta Combination, but while Vata is her dominant Dosha, her eyes are typical of a Pitta type person.

So, without further distraction, let's move on to our recommendations for stress management.

Immediate Considerations

Relax and Breath: To prevent the buildup of stress, the first line of defense is to stay calm and cool during potentially stressful circumstances. Take long deep breaths in through your nose and breathe out your stress as you exhale through your mouth. Relax. Breathe in slowly and into your belly, letting your stomach and ribs expand to the side. Allow your breath to pause after the inhale and then slowly breathe out. Visualize all of your stress and concerns being exhaled with each out breath.

Concentrate on being in the moment. Many times, stress is caused by worrying about future events. If you can limit your thoughts to the present moment and realize that right now you are warm, dry, reasonably well fed, and have people in your life who love you, you may be able to realize that your thoughts are making things worse than they really are. Future events are rarely as bad as we imagine they will be.

How you feel, depends on what you think about.

Remember the Mind/Breath Connection: The mind and the breath are intimately linked together. As you control the breath – the mind will follow. *As the breath goes, so goes the mind.*

Analyze your Stress. Separate the things in your life that you find stressful into two categories, things you can do something about and things you can't. If you can do something about it, then do it! If there's nothing you can do, then surrender to it. Accept it. When there's nothing I can do about the situation, I have to surrender to it, and *in accepting what is, there is peace.*

Monitoring your negative thinking. Stress is often the result of fear that is based largely on imagination. Look at your negative thinking, and replace it with positive thinking. Just changing your thinking or your attitude can alleviate much stress. This includes all of the "What if" worries! I have known people who ruined their lives and made themselves miserable worrying about endless "what if" scenarios. *You cannot live your life in fear of something that has not happened yet!*

Examine your role and your goal. Find the right match between your job and your personality. Job stress is a terrible burden on many people when work and personality are not appropriately matched. If you love what you are doing, there is no stress. If you don't love what you are doing and you still have to do it, that is very stressful. So, you have to discover your true role and your goal. If you cannot change jobs at the time, *meditate more and develop more internal peace.*

Daily Routine Considerations: Meditation cannot be overstated as a means for reducing stress. Meditation can take many forms but we will discuss only a few of them here. Meditation is one of the best ways to relax, dissolve stress, and allow the body to heal. By meditating for 10 to 20 minutes twice a day a person's heart may be healed.

Daily practice of Savasana: This is the yoga position meaning corpse pose. While lying quietly flat on your back with your arms by your sides, watch the flow of your breath. Inhale and exhale, inhale and exhale... You'll notice that after exhalation (and before inhalation) there is a brief, natural stop. Similarly there is a natural stop after inhalation and before exhalation. In that stop, stay naturally quiet, silent, for just a few seconds. This practice brings tranquility and rest, which are healing for the heart and the nervous system. Remain in Savasana practicing this quiet breathing for 10 to 15 minutes.

Lotus pose: Sit in the Lotus pose (or an easy pose with legs comfortably crossed), facing east, and meditate as above. Just observe the inflow and outflow of your breath, with pauses, as described above.)

Ujjayi Pranayama: This can be done while lying in Savasana pose, sitting in lotus pose or the easy pose with your legs comfortably crossed. If sitting let your hands rest on your knees palms up. Keep your head, neck, and chest in a straight line. Lower your head into a slight chin lock by moving your head in and down, toward your chest. Bring your awareness to the throat area.

Now comes the slightly tricky part. Without actually swallowing, start the action of swallowing, to raise the trachea upwards. At the same time, while constricting your epiglottis, as in silently saying the letter E, slowly and deeply inhale into the belly.

The inhaled air will create a soft, gentle whispering sound of rushing air as it brushes the throat, trachea, heart and diaphragm. After inhaling, swallow and hold your breath at the belly for a moment, then slowly exhale the air by again constricting the epiglottis – as if humming, but without producing any humming sound.

Ujjayi pranayama brings great joy. It calms the mind, relaxes the intercostal muscles, and really brings a sense of victory. Ujjayi is good for all three doshas and helps to reestablish constitutional balance. It promotes longevity. Do 12 repetitions, if you can.

Walking meditation: The benefits of walking meditation, especially in nature, cannot be overstated. A casual walk in the woods, or by a stream or lake, will have a wonderfully calming effect on the nervous system. It just feels good, and it reminds us that we are a part of nature. If you must think of anything, let it be your casual breath. By relaxing your mind in this type of setting, you may be pleasantly surprised by the amount of revelations that begin to come your way!

A Soothing Bath: a soothing bath at the end of the day is particularly relaxing. A ginger-baking soda bath is even more so. Add 1/3 cup ginger and 1/3 cup baking soda to a hot bath for greater relaxation and healing.

Oils for relaxation: Rub a little Brahmi oil on the soles of your feet and on your scalp at bedtime. The foot massage and scalp massage will help the medicated oil work into your system and enhance your relaxation.

Let Yourself Cry: If you have a lot of grief, anger, frustration or sadness it will help to cry out your stressful feelings. Crying is an excellent release of emotions, and exactly what it is designed for. Tears actually contain hormones like cortisol…it's the body's way of getting them out of your system.

Stress reducing Tea(s): For teas, I recommend reusable, cotton tea bags to contain the herbs.

Brahmi (Gotu Kola or Bacopa) Tea: add a cup of boiling water to a half teaspoon Brahmi.

"Stressed Out" Tea: use equal portions of Brahmi (Gotu Kola or Bacopa), bhringaraj, jatamamsi and shanka pushpi. Add boiling water to ½ tsp and steep for 10 minutes. You can drink this tea two or three times a day for stress management.

Herbs: Ashwagandha is a common Ayurvedic herb. It has many uses and one of those is as a tonic, rejuvenative and a nervine. It is one of the best adaptogenic herbs in the world. Precaution – it will cause severe congestion if taken in excess. So don't use it in excess!

Anxiety: if your stress has developed into full-fledged anxiety, you may need to also use Vamsha Rochana (Bamboo Manna) – 250mg. - 1 gm.

Environmental Concerns: Every aspect of your environment either promotes peace, or stress. Do you have a calming scent in your home, like sandalwood, lavender, vanilla or rose?

Do you have soothing music in your home or room, or are you listening to heavy metal/head banger tunes? I am not insulting heavy metal/head banger music – to each his own as they say, but if your goal is peace and relaxation, it is not going to get you there.

Do you watch an excess amount of violent, dramatic movies or T.V. shows? Horror movies? If you think these don't cause stress, you really don't pay attention to yourself. You are literally watching them to feel the adrenaline your body pumps into your system when you are watching them! Many people are addicted to adrenaline and other bodily stress hormones and don't even know it. Think about it, do you know anyone who cannot go without arguing or having some kind of drama going on?

The problem is, you are not made to handle being in a permanent state of "fight or flight"!

All of our senses bring input from our environment into our being. Your nervous system must digest all of the input that you inflict upon it. When it is overworked, it will let you know by making you feel stressed. Stress is a warning sign that your nervous system is giving you, to let you know that you need to take better care of yourself.

More on Meditation

Meditation means the process and the ability to look within and contact the higher and deeper aspects of our consciousness, where the source of our life and intelligence dwells. Conversely, meditation means the ability to clear out the negative aspects of our consciousness or negative subconscious habits and impulses that cause problems in life.

Meditation involves placing the mind in a calm and concentrated state in which our mental energies can be gathered, renewed and transformed. Such a definition deals with meditation in the broadest sense, of which there are many helpful techniques like mantra, pranayama, and visualization. Yet whatever meditation techniques we employ, they should be used as aids to place our consciousness into its natural peaceful state, at which stage we can set the techniques aside and rest in the harmony of our true nature. This is called abiding in the Self, the Atman or Purusha.

Meditation is an important tool in Ayurveda for healing the mind and consciousness, but its benefits extend to the body as well. It helps remove the psychological root or psychological complications of the disease process. Meditation is generally prescribed along with other Ayurvedic lifestyle regimens for health maintenance and life enhancement. It can be used for treating specific diseases as well, particularly psychological disorders, in which case it can be used in a specialized manner or even as the primary treatment.

Typically, a meditation session will begin by employing meditation techniques like prayer, mantra, pranayama and visualization. Then formless meditation can proceed, like sitting in silence, self-inquiry or devotional meditation. If we encourage people to merely sit silently without giving them any tools to calm the mind first, they may simply get lost in their own thoughts and end up more frustrated, confused and disturbed.

Meditation is a process that requires the proper preparation and should be grounded in a proper lifestyle, a healthy diet, and subjecting oneself to sattvic impressions and sattvic associations. Sattvic is a Sanskrit word meaning "light," "goodness" and/or "purity." The quality of sattva is said to be life-giving to the body, mind and spirit. Foods and herbs that are sattvic in nature help provide clarity for the mind. Without these preparations, people may not be ready for real meditation, even if they want to practice it. In such cases, the background and preliminaries for meditation should be taught along with the practice of meditation.

There are many types of meditation, and not all of them are suited for everyone. Sometimes the meditation practices people follow may not be helping them from an Ayurvedic standpoint. Vata people may not benefit from trying to space out their minds further. Pitta people may get disturbed by a meditation approach that is too focused or critical. Kapha types may have kapha increased by too imaginary or emotional forms of meditation.

Meditation, prayer and mantra

People in the west have typically been more open to prayer than meditation. Luckily, that is changing. Prayer is an active form of meditation by which we project an intention or supplication, calling on God to help us or to improve our condition or that of others. Ayurveda uses prayer along with mantra and meditation. Mantra is a form of energized prayer, often directed by special sound patterns (Seed Syllables) or vibrations of the

Cosmic Word, when done in the traditional methods of India. However, mantras come in a variety of languages, the most effective being those spoken in one of the 5 Sacred languages, but only if you know the meaning of the Mantra, so you can add the coherence of your mind (thought) and heart (emotions) together.

I highly recommend mantra use for the simple reason that while you are reciting mantras, your mind is far less likely to wander off into negative thought patterns! Look them up with translations, and find ones that appeal to you. Meditation is a more silent or contemplative form of communion in which there may not be any movement of thought or intention. Prayer in the true sense is not the property of any particular religion but a way of relating to the divine powers that govern the universe and also look over our health. The closer one's connection to the divine, the more effective the use of prayer or the direction of positive energies and intentions. Prayer is talking to Source; meditation is listening to Source. To be true communication, it must go both ways!

Visualizations

Visualization goes hand-in-hand with prayer and meditation. We can visualize the healed, or improved state that we wish to achieve. For example, someone suffering from chronic congestion, visualizing the lungs as being clear and open, and full of energy. We can direct prana or healing energy to the people or to the parts of the body that need to be healed. Such visualization may employ certain colors and mantras to aid in its process, or may be directed with the breath.

For healing purposes, different visualizations can be employed to the site affected, or to the body as a whole. Directing a dark blue color is good for countering pitta and infectious and inflammatory disorders. Gold color is good for Vata and for chronic, debilitating and wasting diseases and diseases of the nervous system. Orange or red is good for kapha or conditions of stagnation, depression, edema and congestion.

Please note that these suggestions are not meant to replace medical treatment in any way, but are meant to compliment it. The added benefit is that the more you practice using your consciousness to influence energy, the sooner you will realize that *you can do it!* This is very self-empowering!

The So'Ham Meditation – a great place to start:

Sit in a comfortable posture. This can be a specific yogic posture like the Lotus pose, or sitting in a chair with an erect spine. Without a comfortable and relaxed posture, it is very difficult to meditate.

Energize the breath through pranayama. This directs our energy internally and also gives us energy for meditation. This can be done by the So'Ham pranayama, mentally repeating the mantra "So" upon inhalation and "Ham" (pronounced "Hum") upon exhalation. So'Ham is the natural sound of the breath and brings about a natural expansion of prana. No force or manipulation is required, and no effort is made to forcefully prolong the breath; simply let the breath deepen of its own accord.

Doing some sort of visualization to clear the sensory field and focus the mind internally is helpful. Visualization may be a helpful color, a geometrical design like a yantra, an image in the world of nature, or a deity or guru of one's choice.

Repeating a mantra will also assist in calming the subconscious mind. Mantras are considered by many to be the most important foundational aspect for meditation. Mantras are traditionally done at least 108 times. The Seed syllables or 'Bija' mantras, as well as other ancient mantras in the Sanskrit language are particularly effective due to the fact that Sanskrit is one of the five sacred languages.

Again, the key to working with and connecting to the "Universe" is to have coherence between your Mind (thoughts) which are electric in nature, and your Heart (emotions), which are magnetic in nature. Your heart actually has thousands of brain cells (neurons) in it as well.

This allows for a true connection of the two "systems". This brings your electro-magnetic energy of your Soul into a streamlined, coherent focus, not unlike a laser. Then you can send your intent into the Universal field of the higher dimensions and know that it has been heard and felt!

Finally, silently observe the mind and let it empty itself out. One should take the role of a witness and learn to observe the content of their mind just like watching leaves float down a stream, or clouds float across the sky.

Types of meditation

There are many different forms of meditation, and they all have their values and their limitations. While all forms of meditation can be used by any doshic type, each has its doshic applications that should be considered for optimal application.

Taking the attitude of the witness: this is more for Pitta types but also good for Vata types.

Silent meditation: this is better for pitta types who have self-control but can be good for any type, unless the mind is too agitated.

Walking meditation: This is a great way for pitta people to allow their mind to calm down and establish a dialogue with their inner selves, as long as it is not too hot. It is particularly good for kapha types who feel lethargic if they sit too long, or for Vata types who are too restless to sit.

Self inquiry: This is typically more for pitta types, as it helps to balance their critical nature.

Zen meditation: This is mainly for pitta types as it is highly focused. Kapha types are apt to find it dry. Vata types are prone to space out with it, but can find it helpful if they use it to connect with the world of nature. Tibetan Dzogchen (Atiyoga) is similar in its approach.

Mantra meditation: Different mantras are better for different doshas and different circumstances.

TM meditation: This is a mantra meditation whose benefits depend upon the mantras used. Generally it is better for Vata, as Pitta, and Kapha types may find it dry.

Devotional meditation: Generally using the names and forms of God in a devotional manner. All types benefit from devotion, but this generally appeals more to kapha types.

Kundalini meditation: true kundalini meditation requires a person with a very pure nervous system and a strong control of prana. Otherwise, it can aggravate any doshic type, particularly Vata. It requires special knowledge of yogic techniques and subtle energies to be effective and safe. Therefore, I highly recommend doing this under the guidance of a true, qualified yogi.

Kriya yoga meditation: Many different yogic practices are called Kriyas. More specifically Kriya yoga refers to the teachings of Babaji, popularized by several venerated Masters in India and by Paramahamsa Yogananda in the west, during the mid-20th century. It combines powerful yogic techniques along with devotional and knowledge or wisdom (Jnana) approaches.

For further information on all of these methods, I highly recommend you take the new approach to the acquisition of knowledge, and Google it! We may as well use the technology of the Internet for our advantage!

I would suggest that you investigate the many traditions from around the world that deal with prana/chi, such as Qigong and Tai Chi. The breath work from India known as Pranayama is amazing in its affects. I have found wonderful breathing techniques from every culture I have looked into! The more you check out the wonders that the various peoples of this world have to offer, the more fun it is and the sooner you will realize we are all very much alike!

CHAPTER 19

A SPIRIT ALLIANCE

"They can see and do things in the higher realms that we cannot.

We can do things in this world that they cannot.

Together, we are unstoppable!"

– Marty Rawson

The quickest and most effective way for humanity to heal this world is to form an alliance with Spirit!

The Beings of Light in the higher dimensions work in the Christ/Buddha/Krishna-Unity Consciousness that is Love and Light. Beings at this level have a much higher and far reaching "view" than we do while on this planet. They can see the probabilities of the various timelines and guide us towards what is in the highest good of *all* concerned.

As much as some people have always tried to convince others that "God" and "heaven" are on "our side" of "events", they do not take "sides". If you want their assistance, you need to ask for what is in the highest good of all concerned and learn to think that way yourself!

Spirit can see a lot of things we cannot and they can do amazing things. However, there are things they cannot do. They cannot interfere with our free will, and there are things they cannot do in this physical world, or at least not as easily as we "physical beings" can.

They can do things we cannot and we can do things they cannot.

The only logical solution is to form an alliance with Spirit! Team up!

If we start thinking and acting for the highest good of all concerned and raise our own individual vibrational frequencies, we can create our own connection and relationship with the Divine! This helps every individual with their own lives by gaining the assistance of the Angels and Masters in your personal life. If we get more and more people to do this as individuals, Spirit will begin guiding everyone involved, in the highest way, towards what is best for each individual and our society as a whole. They are constantly in Unity consciousness, so there can be no conflict. In fact, it will be easier for Spirit to guide people to one another when those meetings are mutually beneficial, whether it is for personal or professional purposes.

This way, we do not create another "religion" or any type of organization in the formal context. That is the last thing Earth needs right now. Humanity tends to start out with good intentions, but everything turns quickly into a corrupted aberration of its original intent. No, this is millions or hopefully billions of individuals, each with their own personal connection and relationship with the Divine, being guided towards a better world, under the watchful eyes of Beings of Love and Light. With their "over-sight" and our "boots on the ground", there is nothing we cannot accomplish together! In this movement, anyone from any religion or belief system is welcome. Because religion doesn't matter, only your belief in that which is Divine.

Some people have asked, how do you bring the Angels and Masters into your life? We are not taught these things like we should be. I will go over this again here. They are the beings in this universe who have only Love for you and only wish the very best for you. They are truly your best friends who will never betray you and who want nothing more than to help you and be a part of your life – to the extent you allow them to!

Bringing them into your life is very simple. You simply and sincerely invite the "Beings of Light who work within the Christ Consciousness", into your life. You invite them to take an active part in your life! You ask for their participation! You make friends with them. You talk to them. It may only be in your thoughts, especially if others are around, but you talk to them often... and you do this every day.

Then you pay attention. Very. Close. Attention.

Pay very close attention to your thoughts. Those very subtle thoughts that just come to you when you are trying to figure something out, or just going through your day. Those thoughts that are phrased as if someone is speaking to you, because someone is.

Pay attention to the "synchronicities" in your life. Ask them to help with even the little things and watch your life become magical. Make them a part of your life and have fun with it! They are the best friends you have ever had and they love you unconditionally... They have waited since the day you were born for you to acknowledge them and welcome them into your life!

Once you do, and they get done high-fiving each other and dancing for joy, they will jump at the opportunity to assist you. They will not tell you what to do, or intervene in ways that would be inappropriate. They will guide, protect and council you as best they can and as best as you allow, according to Divine Will and your own Life Contract.

Do not be surprised when they lead you to meet wonderful new people and guide you towards situations where you have the opportunity to learn things you never imagined you can do. They will open up your life to wonderful possibilities and opportunities, if you will only pay extremely close attention to their guidance.

You will have to work on your frequency in order to improve your "connection" with them. The Arcturians, as I have said, have the best advice for this and for the ascension process in general, that is: "Be Love". It is not easy, especially here on Earth, now.

Set time aside for yourself each day. Learn to meditate and raise your Light Quotient/vibrational frequency. Here is another wonderful meditation/Breathing/Energy Practice you may want to try:

Breathe in through your nose and out through your mouth. Imagine a tube of Light running through the center of your body. With every breath in, see beautiful crystalline, clear-white Light coming down from Source, through your crown and down into your Heart Chakra. At the same time, bring beautiful green Light up this tube, from the center of the Earth, into your Heart Chakra as well. Qualify this energy blending in your Heart Chakra with Love, and on the exhale – breath this Love out from your Heart Chakra to the entire planet! This tube of Light is part of your Spiritual anatomy and is commonly called the "Pranic tube" in spiritual parlance and the Shushumna Nadi in Ayurvedic terms. After you practice this for long enough, you may experience actually feeling your own Pranic Tube. It is a feeling you won't soon forget!

Before long, you will realize that you are moving and manipulating energy. You are doing it for the highest good of all concerned, including you! You are helping everyone and everything on the planet by sending the energy of Love and Light, and you are raising your own vibrational frequency at the same time. Imagine what will happen when millions of people are doing this regularly? And it is so simple.

You may want to go on and learn more about energy and energy work. Reiki, Pranic Healing, EMF Balancing, and the like are all wonderful, established approaches that do wonderful work. They all work well together since they are all divinely inspired and are working with divine energy. How could there be any conflict between modalities that are of the Light?

You may want to start doing work to clear and cleanse your own home and create a Sacred space.

Here is one method that I like particularly well. It is quite beautiful.

Sacred Space

Close your eyes
Place your awareness on your Heart Center,
and think about things that you are grateful for and people/
animals you love.

Take a slow deep breath through your nose and exhale, another breath...
and a third one.
Now Relax...

We call forth our Angels and our Guides to assist us and support us, to
be with us and to share their energies with us.
We call forth a pillar of Light in the center of this room.
We call forth 4 more Pillars of Light...one for each corner of this room.

We call forth a Platform of light beneath us... and a Canopy of
Light above us.

We now call forth our beloved Archangel Michael to take his place
within the Central Pillar of Light...with his Flaming Blue Sword of
Divine Truth held high.

We now call forth Lord Sananda, Lord Melchizedek and Lord Buddha to
take their place around the Central Pillar of Light.

We call forth Mother Mary, Lady Venus, Kwan Yin and White Buffalo
Calf Woman to take their places at each of the 4 Pillars of Light in the
corners of the room.

We now ask our beloved and honored guests to assist us in creating a truly Divine, Sacred Space...
Perfectly balanced between the Divine Feminine and the Divine Masculine sacred energies.

We now ask Archangel Michael to surround us with his Holy Legions of Light and we invite all our friends and Family in the higher realms to join us and share their Love and support.

Take a few moments to bask in the energy of Love as they come in and fill this space with their Loving energies.
Feel them around you...

You may call in whomever you want at any time, it does not have to be these particular Beings of Light. They are however a great group to start with!

Also, in the above setting, instead of "room" you can state "House" or "Building", whatever is appropriate.

This method creates a beautiful energy and gets you used to working with the Angelic realm and the Masters. You can custom fit who you invite according to any specific purpose you may have.

For healing work, Archangel Raphael, Mother Mary and Sanat Kumara are highly recommended. Archangel Raphael's name literally means "He who Heals". His divine consort is Mother Mary, whom you already have on the guest list, so you are very well prepared for a truly divine healing session. Sanat Kumara is particularly appropriate when energy work is being done and for emotional healing as well.

If you are working on clearing negative energies and entities from your home or anywhere, I might suggest adding Archangel Azrael. Between him and Michael, there is not anything in this Universe they cannot deal with.

If you are working on simply developing a loving, nurturing energy start working with the Feminine Beings listed above and others you may be drawn too. Kwan Yin is the embodiment of Love and compassion, Lady Venus is the embodiment of Divine Love, and Mother Mary is often called the "Queen of Heaven". White Buffalo Calf Woman embodies both the beauty and the authoritative wisdom of the Divine Feminine. As you work with these and other beautiful beings more and more, you will feel their energies and get to know for yourself who to call in, for what.

It is great fun working with them and your life gets better by the day!

The more heart-centered your life becomes, the more interaction you will have. The more split-minded you are, the less you will have. By split-minded, I mean you cannot support things that harm others one second and claim to be working for the highest good of all, the next second.

Raising your vibrational frequency is what you need to do to communicate with Beings of Light in the higher dimensions. But becoming coherent is what you need to do to take charge of yourself (Self-Mastery) and commune with the Universe... God... All That Is. This is how you communicate and manifest.

I will risk being redundant here and explain this yet again in a slightly different way, simply because this is the foundational key to communicating, manifesting and working with Spirit!

Consider this, your thoughts are electrical energy and your heart emits a magnetic field of energy that extends beyond your physical body. You are an Electromagnetic Being of Light, wearing a meat suit that's a couple of sizes too small.

When you bring your thoughts to someone you love and allow yourself to revel in your own appreciation and gratitude for them, you are bringing your mind and your emotions into coherence.

Let's say you have been very negative for a long time over worldly matters and you have put a lot of low frequency, negative emotion into your heart chakra. This causes your immune system to plummet and makes you very susceptible to disease. Not a good thing right now!

When your emotions match your thoughts, you are said to be in coherence. This is true whether those thoughts are positive or negative. Since energy follows thought/intention, (because it is all conscious energy), whatever you focus your attention on will be influenced by this coherent, electromagnetic force.

So, to work on your Heart Chakra, you think of things you are grateful for and that you Love. Allow yourself to truly feel these emotions along with your thoughts. As you do this, bring your awareness to your Heart Chakra. The longer you do this, the better.

You have now manipulated/worked with energy, learned how to bring your mind and emotions into coherence and worked in/with the quantum field! I love teaching this to people who have never done any form of energy work before, because the pure joy on their faces when they realize they have just accomplished all of this, in a very few minutes is amazing! They begin to realize they are more than they have been taught to believe. They realize they too can work with the energies of the Universe/God/Source, because they are a part of it!

Empowering people to remember who they are is what this is about. We come into these lives with our own pre-written script that has a vague outline of the lessons we need to learn for our soul's growth. We get fed the propaganda, opinions and beliefs of our families, friends and the unconscious world, and we become the product of *that*. We then go through our lives with this tainted lens from which to view life and go through the lessons we needed, with this skewed point of view. That's all part of the challenge of this process.

The goal is to learn the lessons from our experiences and **_unlearn_** the propaganda, opinions and beliefs of others so we can return ourselves to the pure state our soul came in with! This is truly "finding yourself". Much easier said than done, by the way.

One of the hardest things for a man to do, is to look back on his life and at himself, and admit that almost everything he was taught by his parents, his family, and his culture, was wrong. This attacks his very sense of well-being and his identity. His ego will throw a bloody fit! If he can admit to himself that most of his general opinions were actually given to him at a young age, and are therefore not really his own, that is the first step. Understanding that many of your views come from the comments of people you trusted as a child is great progress. The problem is, these people grew up in a very un-enlightened society and formed their beliefs the same way, by listening to unenlightened people (albeit with great intentions). It goes on and on backwards through time and generations. Once you realize this, you can thoroughly examine your core beliefs with less emotional attachment, and consider whether they still serve you or not. Are they based in fear or Love? Are they based in a sense of "lack" or abundance? (Most of humanity's issues stem from fear-based beliefs that are rooted in a fear that they do, or will lack something. It could be a lack of control, a lack of "enough" of anything…)

Are your beliefs actually in accord with where you say you want to go, and with who you want to be? If not, discard them.

Self-examination of one's own belief systems is a crucial step in the Spiritual process. Without it, you are condemning yourself to the realm of the indoctrinated, generational herds of the mindless-minions. You will go with the flow of least resistance, conforming to your "handler's" wishes, and this world will be destroyed in a few decades. I am not exaggerating, although I wish I were. If we all don't take this deadly seriously, we will indeed be dead, along with our children and grandchildren − before their time.

So, let's keep working with Spirit. There are many ways you can work with Spirit and energy. Calling on Spirit and talking to them throughout your day is quite important. Ask for their assistance in almost anything you do. Make it real, and it will be. Understand that this third dimension is just as sacred as any other dimension. It is not less so, just because we are here! We do however, have the individual choice to make it heaven, or hell.

Visualization is a powerful tool. It is through what many people call the "imagination" that you begin your journey in working with energy. If you can "see" it in your mind and use your will-power (intention), the energy will follow your conscious guidance, because again, energy is conscious, as well.

This is what the quantum physicists discovered that rocked their world. Consciousness effects matter!

So... How do we use this to our benefit?

Let's say you are moving into a new place and you want to clear the energy, or you have had some negativity in your own house, and you want to clear it. Here is one way to do it. This is not the only way, but it is how I do it. I am repeating these instructions to help aid your memory and help you to locate this information later.

First of all, let's get something out of the way. You may have seen or known people with a little experience working with Spirit that will attempt to clear a house of dark entities by smudging, drumming, using salt, etc. All of this is fine, except none of it will work on any actual. negative spirit with any "power" – whatsoever. They will stand there and then sniff your smudging like the demon in Modern Problems snorting "Demon dust", shouting "I like it" when they are done! People have come to think these things are for clearing energy, when in fact they are what you use to qualify and purify the energy after you have cleared the actual dark entities, or when you want to uplift and cleanse the energies of a relatively 'clear' environment!

In order to do the following, it is recommended that you practice enough that you can understand what it means to "Stand in your own Light".

When you are comfortable with that, no matter who or what is in your presence, you are ready.

I get myself in a good place, then create a Sacred Space as I showed above. I extend the invitation to any Beings of Love and Light that would be willing to help in this clearing.

I will then call forth a White Tornado that I direct throughout the house or area. I see it vacuuming up any and all lower vibrational forms of energy. This also gets the attention of any viable entities present.

I will the explain to these beings, that the reason they have been so uncomfortable lately is because the Earth itself is raising in its vibrational frequency. I explain that there is nowhere on the planet they can go where this is not so. I then inform them that I, along with Spirit, am offering them the greatest gift one being can offer another, the gift of "Going Home". I ask all Beings of Light present to assist in this work.

For more serious clearings, with large amounts of entities, I will then explain to them who I am and by what authority I speak to them. I will also call in Archangel Michael and Azrael, among others.

I let them know that no matter what they have done or what they have believed, they will be welcomed home with loving arms in the higher realms. I tell them that this is exactly what the parable of the Prodigal Son is all about. I let them know that if Spirit can love me unconditionally, they will surely love them too! I tell them that they can go with one of Archangel Michael's angels from his Legion of Light to the higher Realms that is Home/Heaven, or they can choose to be taken to wherever is right and appropriate for them, if they are not willing to accept this gift. But they cannot stay here! It will only become increasingly uncomfortable and irritating to them if they stay.

This is how Spirit taught me to clear entities, whether they are discarnate beings, demonic beings or entities, and I have cleared untold numbers of beings in my time this way. The more work like this we do, the higher the frequency of the planet! You are not infringing on their free will and you are helping many beings through the energy of loving compassion.

After they make their choices and leave, I call on the Platinum Net. This and the White Tornado are tools that are very handy, and teach you how to use etheric energy tools for your benefit. The Platinum Net is a "screen" of the highest Divine Feminine Platinum Energy. You call it forth from above your house, building, or area, and bring it down slowly, through the entire structure. I do it three times just because it feels good! If you use it enough, you can actually feel it descend down through you! I then command a Platinum Net to be anchored in every doorway in the house and every window, so that it cleanses every being who goes through them.

At this point, I thank everyone present for their assistance and ask them to help wrap this up. When it is done, I thank them again and invite as many angels to stay as possible to help make the place "where Angels prefer to dwell."

Now is the time to burn your sage, sweet grass or Palo Santo. Then do your drumming or put on beautiful music. A final touch that is very powerful is this:

Pour half a cup(or however much) of Epsom salts into a fire proof vessel/cup.
Set this on another fireproof tray such as a cookie sheet, with a folded towel beneath it.
Now pour rubbing alcohol into the vessel until it covers the Epsom salts.
Carefully light it and go sit down. If anyone else is present, have them sit still as well.
Now, feel. Just feel the energy in the room.
By the time it is done, you will be amazed at how different and pure the energy of the air itself feels!
Now you can give thanks and know you have done a remarkably thorough clearing!

A word of caution though. There are a lot of people doing "ghost" hunting and the like, who are trying to gather evidence.

There are a couple of points I need to make. First, if you are trying to prove to "others" that they exist, you are wasting your time. Those that already have had their own experiences and believe, *already know*. Those that are not ready to comprehend the non-physical realities; *cannot and will not* believe anything you put in front of them. Period.

Second...If you are not helping these beings go back home, into the Light, you are using them for your own entertainment purposes, and that will eventually cause karma to bite you right on your butt!

They are not there for entertainment purposes! So, if you find them, help them. Help them go Home.

It will do the Earth good, and help humanity by raising the frequency of the planet, and give you a nice, warm, fuzzy feeling, all at the same time.

To re-cap, *if* your goal is to work in the Light and work towards your own ascension: You might want to analyze your own beliefs, while being devastatingly honest with yourself.

You might want to change the thoughts and beliefs that no longer serve you.
You might want to find the lessons that have evaded you and take them to heart, thus changing your past.
You might want to invite Spirit into your life on a daily basis and request their assistance, with gratitude.
You might want to build your own Light quotient and raise your own vibrational frequency, until you can Stand in your own Light, even in the very presence of the dark side.
You might want to clear your environment of low frequency energies and entities and help heal the planet!

We must succeed, for failure is not an option.

So fill yourself with Love and Light and keep a little laughter in your heart as you go forth into this adventurous journey, on this magnificent, beautiful planet.

As we go forward in a true Alliance with Spirit, we are unbeatable! The very Universe is supporting us, because we are truly working for the Highest Good of All Concerned!

One last thought. Everyone talks about self-love. I have always had a problem understanding exactly what that really meant. I have a habit of taking things too literally, and sometimes get a comical vision of someone staring, all dreamy-eyed in the mirror at themselves! My beautiful and intelligent wife helped me to understand this concept better. Between what she explained, and what I had already gotten from Spirit, I would like you to consider the following:

Self-love is knowing yourself.

It is appreciating your better qualities, while at the same time, recognizing those things about yourself that you still need to work on.

It is understanding and accepting that you are a work in process.

It is understanding that you are, in fact, perfection in process; and the only way to proceed is by loving your more unconscious aspects of yourself, until you transmute them into the light.

You do this by having compassion for yourself, just like you would for someone else, when they make a mistake.

When I say you are "perfection" in process, I do not mean you walk on water or any other "miraculous" concept of perfection that most people have. I mean that you are the perfect "*you*" to experience, and learn, the lessons your soul needs for its greatest growth within this opportunity that *is* your life.

The bottom line is, have compassion for yourself as you are learning your lessons while journeying through the wonderous maze of your life.

After all, in the end, these lives are all about having experiences, that you share with "God" in real time, and the soul growth that accompanies your life's lessons.

These, along with the Love you carry in your heart, are after all, the only things you get to take with you, once you depart this human life and go Home.

Humanity has tried worshipping the divine and even groveling at the feet of angry, jealous and vengeful Gods.

Isn't it about time form a true partnership with the Divine, or should I say, form a Spirit Alliance, like mature adults?

After all, as they told me when I was just a child;
"It's not supposed to be like this...
and it doesn't have to be this way!"
May you walk in Peace, Love and Light throughout your journey...
and may you look back on your life with peaceful contentment and satisfaction!
I pray for you all, the blessings of the Creator!

Please join us at the Spirit Alliance Facebook page and our Spirit Alliance Group page!

Our Greatest Fear —Marianne Williamson

It is our light not our darkness that most frightens us
Our deepest fear is not that we are inadequate.
Our deepest fear is that we are powerful beyond measure.
It is our light not our darkness that most frightens us.

We ask ourselves, who am I to be brilliant, gorgeous,
talented and fabulous?

Actually, who are you not to be?
You are a child of God.
Your playing small does not serve the world.
There's nothing enlightened about shrinking so that other
people won't feel insecure around you.

We were born to make manifest the glory of
God that is within us.

It's not just in some of us; it's in everyone.
And as we let our own light shine,
we unconsciously give other people
permission to do the same.

As we are liberated from our own fear,
Our presence automatically liberates others.

—Marianne Williamson

Now, go shine your light for the world to see and play well with
one another,

After all, we truly are just walking each other home.

Made in the USA
Monee, IL
28 May 2023

34234439R00177